A Women's History of Guernsey
1850s–1950s

A Women's History of Guernsey
1850s–1950s

Rose-Marie Crossan

MÒR MEDIA LIMITED

© Rose-Marie Anne Crossan 2018

All rights reserved. Except as permitted under current legislation, no part of this work may be photocopied, stored in a retrieval system, published, performed in public, adapted, broadcast, transmitted, recorded or reproduced in any form or by any means, without the prior permission of the author.

Rose-Marie Anne Crossan has asserted her right to be identified as the author of this work in accordance with sections 77 and 78 of the Copyright, Designs and Patents Act 1988.

First published 2018
Mòr Media Limited, Benderloch, Argyll, Scotland
www.mormedia.co.uk

ISBN 978-0-9954874-8-2

A catalogue record for this book is available from the British Library.

The publisher has no responsibility for the continued existence or accuracy of URLs for external or third-party internet websites referred to in this book, and does not guarantee that any content on such websites is, or will remain, accurate or appropriate.

*For El, Mich, Trees and Ed
my siblings and best friends*

Contents

List of illustrations	ix
Acknowledgements	xi
Abbreviations	xii
Notes on the text	xiii
Introduction	1
1 Governance, Economy and Society	5
2 Education, Work and Health	27
3 Marriage	63
4 Domestic Abuse and Sexual Violence	111
5 Female Criminality and Prostitution	139
6 Public Office, the Vote and States Membership	187
Conclusion	217
Appendices	
Distribution of female occupations, 1851 and 1951	223
Guernsey Women's History Timeline	224
Female States Deputies, February 1924–March 2016	228
Bibliography	231
Index	251

Illustrations

Maps

1.	Channel Islands and adjacent French and English coasts	xiv
2.	Parishes of Guernsey	xv

Plates

1.	States of Guernsey, 1860s	8
2.	Barque Courier, built in 1876 by P. Ogier of St Sampsons	11
3.	La Lande quarry, Vale, early twentieth century	12
4.	Cutting stone, St Sampsons, early twentieth century	13
5.	Growing daffodils under glass, early twentieth century	15
6.	Loading tomatoes for export, St Peter Port, early twentieth century	15
7.	St Peter Port, c.1880	17
8.	Class of girls, Hautes Capelles School, Vale, c.1903	28
9.	Guernsey Ladies' College, 1905	30
10.	Domestic Science Centre, Granville House, 1935	34
11.	Telephonists, Central Exchange, St Peter Port, 1931	39
12.	Women marketing produce, St Peter Port, late nineteenth century	40
13.	Women picking tomatoes, late nineteenth century	41
14.	Women harvesting potatoes, late nineteenth century	42
15.	Women cracking stone, St Sampsons, early twentieth century	43
16.	Tomato packing shed, late 1950s or early 1960s	43
17.	Washerwomen at a St Peter Port lavoir, late nineteenth century	45
18.	World War I Communal Kitchen Committee	48
19.	Women field workers, Pleinheaume, 1917	48

20.	Poor children, St Peters coast road, late nineteenth century	54
21.	Sir Ambrose Sherwill	87
22.	Sir Peter Stafford Carey	124
23.	British soldiers at Fort George, 1904	162
24.	Cornet Street, early twentieth century	163
25.	Laura Ormiston Chant	173
26.	Henry Wilson, MP	175
27.	Josephine Butler	175
28.	Sir Thomas Godfrey Carey	176
29.	Marie Randall	200
30.	Marguerite Ross	206
31.	Kathleen Robilliard	206
32.	Retired and serving female Deputies, 1976	210
33.	Nina Worley	213

Figures

1.	Distribution of convictions by sex, selected decades, 1850s–1950s	142
2.	Distribution of male convictions, 1850s	143
3.	Distribution of male convictions, 1950s	143
4.	Distribution of female convictions, 1850s	144
5.	Distribution of female convictions, 1950s	144
6.	Advertisements for abortifacients, Guernsey newspapers, 1888–1920	156

Table

| 1. | Males per 100 females, Guernsey and England and Wales, 1851–1951 | 21 |

Acknowledgements

First and foremost, I would like to express my gratitude to my niece Emilie Yerby, whose suggestion one December afternoon in 2015 inspired the writing of this book. I would also like to thank Dr Darryl Ogier for his kind interest in, and encouragement of, this project and its predecessors. Further thanks are due to Anna Baghiani, John Kelleher, Roy Le Herissier, Samantha McFadzean and Harry Stirk for generously forwarding information about Jersey, as also to Fiona Russell and David Robilliard for advice on aspects of the law and judiciary in Guernsey. As always, I am most grateful to Nathan Coyde, Vikki Ellis and their colleagues at Guernsey's Island Archives for their very capable professional assistance, as also to the staff, past and present, of the Priaulx Library and Greffe. Particular thanks are due to Lisa Burton, Michèle Bisson, Sue Laker, Alpha Wearing, Rebecca Nel and Mike Deane for their help in sourcing photographs, and to Helen Crossan for her kind assistance in preparing the text for publication. My greatest debt is however to my husband Jonathan for his unstinting patience and support.

Rose-Marie Crossan, MA (Oxon), PhD
Guernsey, July 2018

Abbreviations

Billet	*Billet d'Etat*[1]
GG	Greffe, Guernsey
IA	Island Archives, Guernsey[2]
LSE WL	London School of Economics, Women's Library
O in C	Order in Council[3]
Ord	Ordinance of the Royal Court
PL	Priaulx Library, Guernsey
PP	Parliamentary Papers
NA	National Archives, Kew
TSG	*Transactions of La Société Guernesiaise*

---

[1] *Billets d'Etat*, which contain the agenda and supporting material for States meetings, will be referred to by the date of the meeting for which the *Billet* was compiled, and will be found in the bound volumes held at the Priaulx Library.

[2] Records in the custody of the Island Archives and other record offices will be referred to by their date, followed by the institution's reference code. A detailed description of each record will be found in the Bibliography.

[3] Orders in Council and ordinances issued prior to 1950 will be referred to by their date, and, unless otherwise stated, will be found in the published volumes held at the Priaulx Library. Post-1950 legislation will be found online at www.guernseylegalresources.gg.

Notes on the text

1. Most of Guernsey's pre-twentieth-century records are in French. I have provided translations silently and without reproduction of the original, except in cases of unresolved ambiguity. French words and phrases left untranslated (except the titles of local officials and institutions) are italicised.

2. Guernsey parishes are referred to by the English version of their names, and those prefixed 'St' are rendered with a terminal 's' unpreceded by an apostrophe. While acknowledging that it is normally considered appropriate to insert an apostrophe here (the names St Saviour's, St Peter's, etc., denoting a possessive, as in 'the parish *of* St Saviour', '*of* St Peter');[4] I have chosen to dispense with this punctuation mark in order to reflect modern spoken usage, where the final 's' has in practice become accreted to the names (as in the British towns of St Albans, St Helens, St Andrews, etc.).

3. All sums in pounds and pence relating to local affairs are in Guernsey currency. The Guernsey pound was worth 19s 2½d sterling until 1921, when it was fixed at parity with sterling.

4. Measurements, monetary sums, percentages and ages over twenty will be rendered in figures. In other cases, numbers up to one hundred and round numbers higher than one hundred will be rendered in words. I reserve the right to deviate from these rules wherever consistency within a sentence or paragraph requires it.

5. The names of all individuals suspected or convicted of violent or sexual crimes after 1850 have been changed or withheld, as have the names of their victims and of individuals figuring in judicial separation records held at Guernsey's Greffe.

---

[4] St Peters is also known as St-Peter-in-the-Wood (in French, Saint-Pierre-du-Bois).

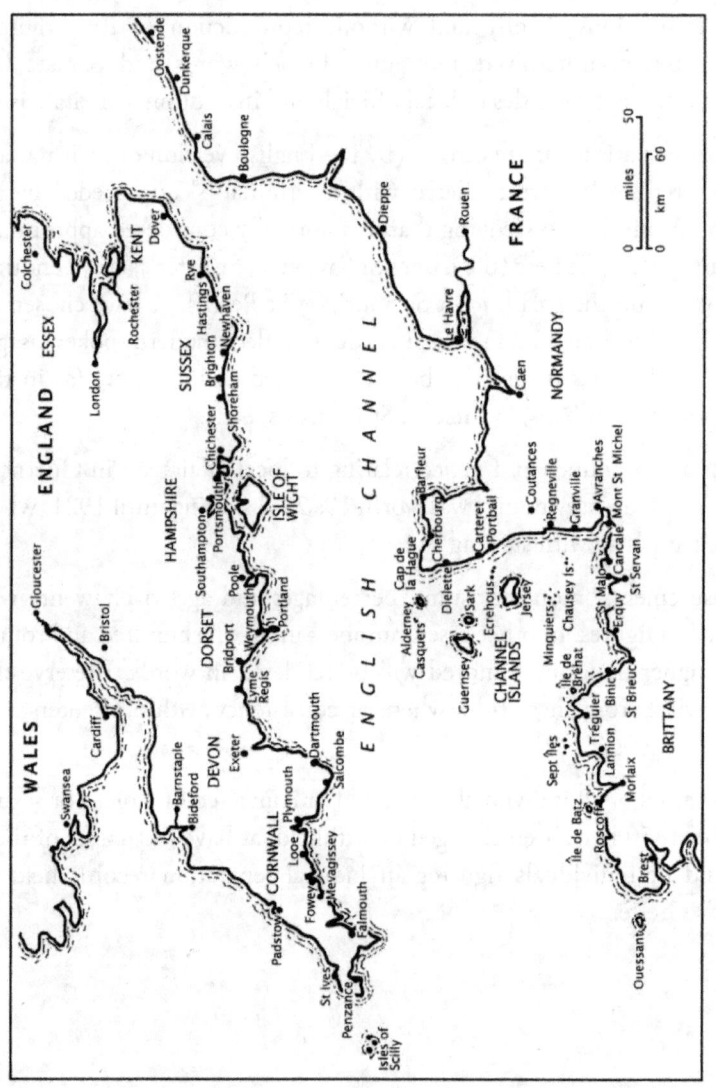

Map 1. *Channel Islands and adjacent French and English coasts*

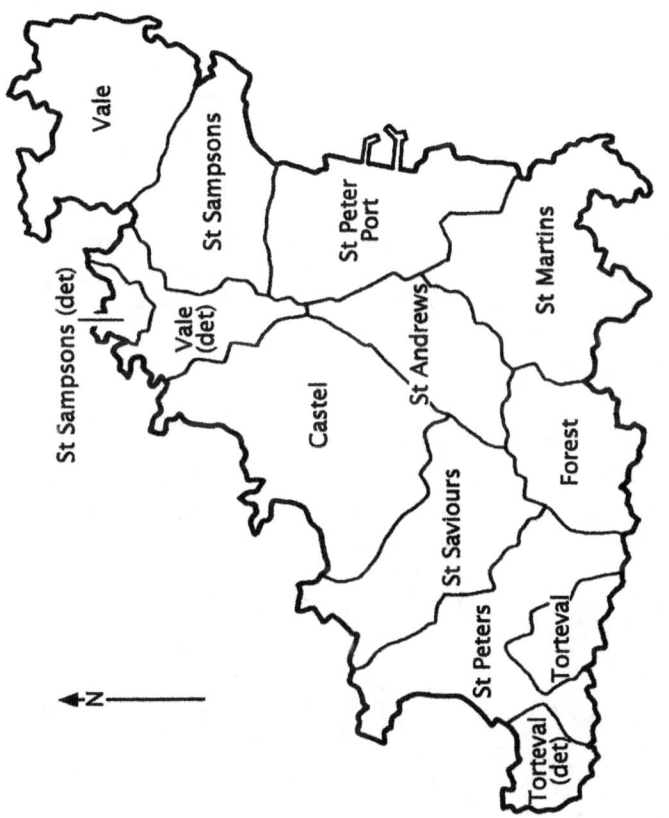

Map 2. Parishes of Guernsey

Introduction

Guernsey is an island of 24½ square miles situated in the Gulf of St Malo. To the east lies the Normandy coast, some 30 miles distant; to the south lies the Breton coast, 65 miles distant; to the north the English coast, 80 miles distant; and to the west lies the open sweep of the Atlantic. The island is the second largest of the Channel Islands archipelago. Together with Alderney, Sark, Herm and Jethou, it forms the Bailiwick of Guernsey.[1] Since Alderney and Sark have enjoyed a measure of independence within the Bailiwick which makes their history different from that of Guernsey, this book will deal with the island of Guernsey only.[2]

Until the thirteenth century, the Channel Islands shared a common history with north-west France. It is thought that they became part of the Roman Empire at the same time as Gaul, and were inhabited after the fall of the Empire by a Gallo-Roman population under the Frankish monarchy.[3] In the 900s, the Islands and adjacent Cotentin peninsula were absorbed into the territory of the Dukes of Normandy. Duke William's conquest of England in 1066 brought no change to the Islands, which continued to be governed from Normandy as before. In 1204, however, the Islands were politically severed from the Norman mainland when John, king of England and duke of Normandy, lost the continental portion of his duchy to the French king. The Islands gained strategic value as stepping-stones between England and John's remaining continental possessions, and he and his successors contrived by various means to secure their allegiance.[4] An important way in which

---

[1] The largest of the Channel Islands is Jersey (46 square miles), which, together with the outlying reefs of Les Minquiers and Les Ecrehous, forms the Bailiwick of Jersey. The two Bailiwicks have been politically and administratively separate since at least the fifteenth century.
[2] Herm and Jethou, smaller and closer to Guernsey than the other islands, are to a large extent administered by Guernsey, and will be considered as subsumed within it for the purposes of this book.
[3] H. Sebire, *The Archaeology and Early History of the Channel Islands* (Stroud, 2005), p. 109.
[4] J.A. Everard and J.C. Holt, *Jersey 1204: The Forging of an Island Community* (London, 2004), p. 115.

insular sympathy was won lay in the decision of post-1204 monarchs to respect the Islands' existing law and institutions, as also to allow them substantial autonomy over their internal affairs.[5]

In the 1250s, Henry III granted the Islands to his heir, the future Edward I, 'in such manner that the said lands ... may never be separated from the Crown'.[6] This meant that whoever henceforth was king of England was by that fact also lawful sovereign of the Channel Islands. However, the Islands were never subsumed into the realm of England, nor, later into the United Kingdom. Consequently, they were never represented at Westminster, and for several centuries after becoming Crown possessions, they continued to be regulated by ancient laws and customs directly traceable to pre-medieval Normandy. These laws and customs exerted an influence well into the twentieth century, and, as will be shown, their persistence had a significant bearing on the condition of insular women.

The late twentieth and early twenty-first centuries have seen the publication of several full-length academic studies on Guernsey's social history.[7] While women feature tangentially in all of these studies, none has addressed the roles and experiences of women directly. Indeed, the only modern treatment of what might be considered a women's topic is an essay by Dr Darryl Ogier on neonaticide during the Reformation, which was published in an edited volume in 2005.[8] Given that Britain, Europe and North America have seen a burgeoning of women's history since second-wave feminism took hold in the 1970s, this is a deficit which needs to be remedied.[9]

---

[5] Everard and Holt, *Jersey 1204*, pp. 155–65, 187–8.
[6] J. Loveridge, *The Constitution and Law of Guernsey* (1975; Guernsey, 1997 edn), p. 1.
[7] D.M. Ogier, *Reformation and Society in Guernsey* (Woodbridge, 1996); G. Stevens Cox, *St Peter Port, 1680–1830: The History of an International Entrepôt* (Woodbridge, 1999); R.-M. Crossan, *Guernsey, 1814–1914: Migration and Modernisation* (Woodbridge, 2007); R.-M. Crossan, *Poverty and Welfare in Guernsey, 1560–2015* (Woodbridge, 2015); R. Hocart, *The Country People of Guernsey and their Agriculture, 1640–1840* (Guernsey, 2016).
[8] D.M. Ogier, 'New-born child murder in Reformation Guernsey', in G. Dawes (ed.), *Commise 1204: Studies in the History and Law of Continental and Insular Normandy* (Guernsey, 2005).
[9] The term 'second-wave feminism' is used to distinguish the Women's Liberation movement which began in the late 1960s from an earlier phase of feminism which was at its height between the 1850s and World War I.

This study begins in 1850. At this period, male dominance was deeply embedded in all of Guernsey's cultural, economic, social, legal and political institutions. Female disadvantage began in childhood, when inferior school provision limited girls' educational opportunities. It continued in the workplace, when custom compounded educational disadvantage to preclude women from earning as much as men. It continued in marriage, when the law placed wives under the tutelage and control of their husbands. It affected succession matters, when sisters were prevented from inheriting as much as their brothers; and it affected political matters, when women were debarred from participation in government. A twentieth-century scholar has defined patriarchy as

> a familial-social, ideological, political system in which men—by force, direct pressure, or through ritual, tradition, law and language, customs, etiquette, education, and the division of labour—determine what part women shall or shall not play, and in which the female is everywhere subsumed under the male.[10]

In all of these senses, 1850s Guernsey was undoubtedly a patriarchy. Nevertheless, this decade has been identified as an appropriate point of departure because, as well as marking the patriarchal high tide, it also saw the first intimations of a weakening in male dominance—not primarily in Guernsey but in other parts of Europe, notably Great Britain.

Following a thematic framework now well-established in women's history, this book will chart the major milestones in Guernseywomen's progress towards equal citizenship from the 1850s onwards. After an initial chapter setting out the context for the study, chapter 2 will examine the areas which formed the background to Guernseywomen's daily lives: education, work and health. Chapter 3 will then address the subjects of marriage, separation and divorce. Chapter 4 will develop this theme by tackling the related issues of domestic violence and sexual abuse, and, in a reversal of focus, chapter 5 will look at crimes committed by women themselves. Finally, chapter 6 will trace the protracted process by which Guernseywomen gained a vote and a seat in insular government.

Among the most important sources drawn on for this study are the published volumes of local legislation and the *Billets d'Etat*. The former

---

[10] J. Bennett, 'Feminism and history', *Gender and History*, 3 (1989), p. 260.

embody a vivid chronological record of legal developments and the latter provide the background to these in the form of supporting material for States debates. A further major source are Guernsey's police and judicial records, which not only yield information on the nature of crimes involving women, but illuminate broader social attitudes by revealing the ways these crimes were treated. The third and last major source are contemporary local newspapers, which are invaluable for filling gaps left by other sources and for recovering long vanished social values.

Throughout this study, an effort is made to compare and contrast developments in Guernsey with those taking place in the United Kingdom, Jersey and France. This approach enables the experience of Guernseywomen to be placed on a comparative scale which takes account of culture and *mentalités* as well as political allegiance. It also facilitates a concluding assessment of how far Guernseywomen contributed towards their own emancipation, and how much of it was achieved on the shoulders of pioneers elsewhere.

1

Governance, Economy and Society

Governance

In the period with which this book is concerned, Guernsey had considerable autonomy in all matters aside from defence and foreign affairs, for which the British government was responsible. The island was also largely financially independent. Westminster's only monetary contribution was towards the garrison, whose expenses it paid; the militia, which it partially funded; and the construction and upkeep of some (though not all) insular fortifications.

The Crown was represented locally by a resident Lieutenant-Governor. Besides acting as intermediary between British and insular authorities, his responsibilities were chiefly military. He was in overall command of the garrison and local militia until the former was withdrawn and the latter disbanded just prior to World War II. He had a right to address the States but no vote in that assembly. The influence exercised by the Lieutenant-Governor on insular affairs progressively declined over the late nineteenth and early twentieth centuries, and in the post-World War II period, his role became primarily ceremonial.

Guernsey, and the Channel Islands in general, had no representation in the Westminster parliament. Prior to the period with which we are dealing, the British government had, on a small number of occasions, sought to impose Acts of Parliament on the Islands against their will. Insular authorities disputed their ability to do this. The position was never explicitly resolved, but by the beginning of our period, the constitutional convention had become established that—given the Islands' lack of representation—legislation should not be extended to them without serious cause, and, even then, not without their prior consultation and consent.

Guernsey's government and administration fell into three tiers. Much basic work was done at parish level. The island was divided into ten parishes which exercised both civil and ecclesiastical functions. Parishes were responsible for the upkeep of the parochial church and graveyard, as well as local infrastructure such as roads, watch-houses and sea walls. In addition, Guernsey's parishes bore all the costs of poor relief until 1925, and, until 1935, a substantial proportion of the costs of the parochial schools, of which there was one in each parish.

Guernsey's ten parishes each possessed a body elected by its Chefs de Famille (adult male ratepayers) which was known as the Douzaine. This body was composed of Douzeniers, who were twelve in number in all parishes aside from the Vale, which had sixteen, and St Peter Port, which had twenty.[1] The most important function of the Douzaine was to assess and levy parochial rates and apportion parochial expenditure. At the apex of parish structure were the two Constables, who were also elected by the Chefs de Famille. As well as being responsible for public order, the Constables acted as parish treasurers and executive officers of their Douzaines.

At island-wide level, much administrative, legislative as well as judicial work was performed by the Royal Court. The Court was composed of the Bailiff (chief magistrate), who was appointed by the Crown, and twelve Jurats (ancillary magistrates), elected for life by an electoral college.[2] The Court had wide-ranging ordinance-making powers on matters of internal domestic regulation which it could (and, until the mid-1800s, frequently did) exercise without reference to higher authority. The Court also had jurisdiction over civil and criminal law within Guernsey. It could sit either as the Full Court, for which the Bailiff (or his Lieutenant) and at least seven Jurats were required, or as the Ordinary Court, requiring the Bailiff (or his Lieutenant) and at least two Jurats. The Full Court heard serious criminal trials and appeals. The Ordinary Court dealt with all other business, sitting, for instance, as *la Cour d'Héritage* when it dealt with the attachment of realty, as *la Cour de Meubles* when it dealt with chattels, debts and transgressions, and

---

[1] Between 1844 and 1948, St Peter Port also had an additional forty-eight 'cantonal' Douzeniers, serving on four subsidiary Douzaines.
[2] The office of Jurat was prestigious and usually reserved for men of the highest social class. The body which elected Jurats was known as the States of Election and comprised all the members of the States (see over), plus the Constables and Douzaines of each parish.

as *la Cour de Police Correctionnelle* when it dealt with minor criminal offences.[3] Jurats were not normally legally trained, and neither, until the late nineteenth century, were Bailiffs, thus many trials were heard by a completely lay Court.[4] Until 1964, the Jurats were sole judges of law as well as of fact. There were no juries in Guernsey.

The top tier of local government was the States. This was essentially an expanded version of the Royal Court, to whose members were added representatives of the parishes. In 1850, the States were composed of thirty-seven voting members: the Bailiff (president and speaker of the assembly), HM Procureur,[5] the twelve Jurats, eight parochial rectors,[6] six St Peter Port Douzaine deputies and one Douzaine deputy from each of the other nine parishes.[7] None of these States members were directly elected. In 1899, 1920 and 1948 the States underwent a series of reforms which introduced and then extended democratic representation.[8] Plate 1 (overleaf) shows the States as constituted at the beginning of our period. The Bailiff, Sir Peter Stafford Carey, is seated centrally. To his immediate right is the Lieutenant-Governor, and further to his right are the Jurats. The rectors are seated to his left. The Douzaine delegates are not shown.

---

[3] For details of the Royal Court and its various divisions at the beginning of our period, see J. Duncan, *The History of Guernsey* (London, 1841), pp. 477-97. See also D.M. Ogier, *The Government and Law of Guernsey* (Guernsey, 2005), pp. 48-58.

[4] Guernsey's last non-legally qualified Bailiff was Sir Edgar MacCulloch, who retired in 1895.

[5] HM Procureur was a Crown-appointed Law Officer, roughly equivalent to the English Attorney-General. Guernsey had two Law Officers; the other, who had a seat but no vote in the States, was HM Comptroller, roughly equivalent to the English Solicitor-General.

[6] There were only eight rectors, because until 1859 and 1867 respectively, St Sampsons/the Vale, and Torteval/the Forest each formed one living. Thereafter the eight seats remained and were filled by the ten rectors in rotation until the number of sitting rectors was increased to ten in 1899.

[7] The Douzaine deputies were parochial Douzeniers delegated to attend States meetings with voting instructions from their Douzaine.

[8] These reforms will be discussed in chapter 6.

Plate 1. States of Guernsey, 1860s
© The Priaulx Library, Guernsey

The primary function of the States was to legislate on matters deemed beyond the domestic scope of the Royal Court. By our period the States had two methods of legislating. In minor matters of regulation they often legislated by ordinance (although such ordinances had to be passed by Royal Court on the States' behalf, since the States had no formal ordinance-making powers). In more important matters, the States followed a legislative process which resulted in Orders in Council. Indeed, this was the only way they were able to institute new taxes, alter superior legislation or introduce major new legislation, since these required the approval of the monarch in Council and could not be effected by ordinance. By the mid-nineteenth century, the States' legislative procedure in such matters was as follows: proposals for new laws were submitted by the Bailiff and debated by the States.[9] If approved in general terms, they were then passed to the Law Officers for drafting in the form of a *projet de loi*. Such *projets* were re-submitted to the States for approval in their final form, and then forwarded to the Privy Council for ratification. When the Council gave their sanction (sometimes not without negotiation), these *projets de loi* acquired the status of Orders in Council and were registered as insular laws by the Royal Court.

---

[9] Bailiffs could submit proposals on their own initiative, or on the petition of any ten States members.

Orders in Council originating from the States had been rare prior to the nineteenth century but became increasingly common after c.1840 owing to the growing complexity of insular life. Although the Royal Court continued to issue ordinances both on its own and the States' behalf throughout the nineteenth and early twentieth centuries, one consequence of the growing prevalence of Orders in Council was to reduce the Court's power and influence. In 1948, when the Royal Court's ordinance-making powers were finally transferred to the States, the States achieved a monopoly of legislative power.

Population and economy

At the start of the 1850s, Guernsey had 29,757 inhabitants. With an area of only 24½ square miles, this made for a population density of 1,215 persons per square mile. In comparison with other British islands, this was a very high density. In 1851, the Isles of Man and Wight had population densities of only 237 and 343 persons per square mile respectively. At 1,236 persons per square mile in 1851, Jersey was the only other British island which could compare with Guernsey.[10] This was in part because both islands, though small in area, had relatively large towns. In 1851—and for most of the nineteenth century—the town of St Peter Port accommodated over half of Guernsey's population.[11]

St Peter Port had prospered and grown in the eighteenth century as a result of its role as an *entrepôt* in the Atlantic economy.[12] Many of its leading citizens had become merchants and shipowners specialising in the import of

---

[10] Guernsey and Jersey data from *Census of Great Britain, 1851: Population Tables, Scotland and Islands in the British Seas* (London, 1852). Data for the Isle of Wight from http://www.visionofbritain.org.uk, and for the Isle of Man from http://www.isle-of-man.com/manxnotebook/history/pop.htm.
[11] Note that St Peter Port, which had a small rural fringe to the north, west and south of its built-up area, was always administered as a parish rather than a town.
[12] G. Stevens Cox, *St Peter Port, 1680–1830: The History of an International Entrepôt* (Woodbridge, 1999).

luxury goods such as wines, spirits, tobacco, tea and textiles.[13] Extensive warehousing was built to store these goods, as well as facilities where wine and spirits could be decanted into smaller containers, and dry goods such as tobacco could be processed and repackaged. The town acted as a depository and bulk-breaker for dutiable goods destined for legal entry into Britain before the introduction of the bonding system, as also a supply base from which such goods could be sourced by English smugglers. The latter of these roles appears to have been more important to the town's economy than the former, since St Peter Port's career as an *entrepôt* effectively came to an end when the British government passed two anti-smuggling Acts encompassing the Channel Islands in 1805 and 1807. The demise of the *entrepôt* was compounded by a reduction in the size of the garrison following Waterloo, and for a while St Peter Port's economy floundered. It was, however, slowly revived by half-pay military and naval officers arriving to settle, who, in combination with the retired *entrepôt* merchants, generated a considerable demand for goods and services. Moreover, a decade or two after the imposition of the anti-smuggling Acts, Guernsey's shipping industry re-invented itself. The rump of shipowners who did not retire in the immediate aftermath of the Acts turned their sights south and built up a successful carrying trade between Europe and South America. Although this trade physically bypassed St Peter Port, it nevertheless employed large numbers of local seafarers. At its peak in the 1860s, Guernsey's shipping fleet directly employed around 1,200 seamen.[14] The carrying trade also stimulated a shipbuilding industry, which itself employed large numbers of locals.[15] By the 1890s, however, both the shipping and shipbuilding industries had all but disappeared. Insular shipowners had lacked the capital to invest in modern steam technology and iron ship construction, with the result that, during the 1870s and 1880s, their wooden sailing ships were displaced from the worldwide market. Guernsey's shipbuilders, who had virtually no external clientele, went out of business as local shipowners ceased placing orders. The island's ageing fleet continued to operate in inshore waters for a few years

---

[13] They also engaged in privateering as opportunity arose during the many eighteenth-century Anglo-French wars.

[14] 26.1.1865, IA, AQ 44/05.

[15] Between 1815 and 1880 nearly three hundred ships were built in yards along the island's east coast, most of them ocean-going vessels for Guernsey's carrying trade (E.W. Sharp, 'The shipbuilders of Guernsey', *TSG*, 27 (1970), p. 492).

more, but by the turn of the twentieth century neither seafaring nor shipbuilding were any longer significant employers.

Plate 2. Barque Courier, built in 1876 by P. Ogier of St Sampsons
Guernsey Museums & Galleries (States of Guernsey) 2018

Of the 43 per cent of islanders living in parishes outside St Peter Port in 1851, nearly a third were concentrated in the two northern parishes of the Vale and St Sampsons. These two parishes were dotted with quarries producing hard-wearing granite for road-building. In 1847, a statistical return to the Home Office identified 434 men at work in the eighty-four quarries situated in these two parishes.[16] The number of quarrymen increased as the industry expanded in the second half of the century, and they were joined by a large casual force of stone-crackers when a change in the law on the other side of the Channel allowed stone for macadamising English roads to be broken in Guernsey.[17] Many of the quarries were owned or leased by

---

[16] NA, HO 98/88.
[17] R.-M. Crossan, *Guernsey, 1814–1914: Migration and Modernisation* (Woodbridge, 2007), p. 25.

English firms.[18] They produced stone almost exclusively for the English market and exported it from St Sampsons harbour, around which a semi-urban area developed. The quarrying industry remained vibrant throughout the second half of the nineteenth century and peaked just before World War I. By the 1920s, however, stone had been largely superseded by asphalt as a road-making material and the quarrying industry declined, never to regain its former importance.

Plate 3. La Lande quarry, Vale, early twentieth century
Guernsey Museums & Galleries (States of Guernsey) 2018

---

[18] John Mowlem & Co. were among the first English firms to operate in Guernsey. They were later joined by other players such as A. & F. Manuelle, Wm Griffiths, Nowell & Robson, E. & H. Beevers, and Fry Bros Ltd.

Plate 4. Cutting stone, St Sampsons, early twentieth century
© Mike Deane, www.deanephotos.com

In Guernsey's seven other parishes—St Martins, the Castel, St Andrews, St Saviours, St Peters, Torteval and the Forest—agriculture was the principal occupation. Together these seven parishes accommodated about 30 per cent of the insular population in the early 1850s.[19] They contained a mass of tiny farms.[20] In the 1851 census, 821 Bailiwick farmers gave details of their holdings, of which at least 750 were located in Guernsey.[21] Over 91 per cent of these farms were under 25 acres in size; 38 per cent were under 10 acres, and 8 per cent were under 5 acres. Most were owner-occupied and family-worked. The larger holdings enabled their owners to live self-sufficiently, with the addition of a reasonable marketable surplus. The smaller ones usually functioned as an adjunct to another occupation, providing food for the household and/or cash-earning crops, while their owners worked primarily as carpenters, painters, stonemasons, etc. Even the

---

[19] Unless otherwise stated, all census data in the remainder of this chapter are taken from the printed reports held at the Priaulx Library and/or from census analysis published in Parliamentary Papers (for references, see under Primary Sources in Bibliography). These data are also available online at www.histpop.org.
[20] There were also many small farms in the northern parishes and St Peter Port's rural fringe.
[21] We cannot be sure of the precise number, because the census report did not disaggregate Guernsey farms from those elsewhere in the Bailiwick.

poorest rural parishioners usually had some scrap of land, be it only a small field or a garden. These were always intensively cultivated, and provided their owners with a back-up to cash earnings from labouring or fishing.

Before the mid-nineteenth century, most of the local agricultural surplus was disposed of in St Peter Port. Small amounts of produce were from time to time exported to England, but these exports were not on a scale to impact greatly on the island's overall economy.[22] This was to change in the late 1860s, when the construction of new steamer berths in St Peter Port coincided with the opening of rail links allowing rapid transit from the south coast of England to the wholesale market in Covent Garden. These developments stimulated local farmers to experiment more extensively with commercial crops, particularly those whose early production was facilitated by Guernsey's mild climate. One such crop was hot-house grapes, which had been grown in Guernsey and exported in small quantities since the eighteenth century. From the early 1870s, many of Guernsey's small farmers began to build their own hot-houses. As well as grapes, they used them to grow other crops such as beans, melons, flowers and tomatoes. Exports of these crops proved generally remunerative, which encouraged islanders from all walks of life and all parts of Guernsey to buy up small rural plots and erect greenhouses on them. By 1887, an English observer was able to note that the 11,773 acres under cultivation in Guernsey were divided into 2,506 holdings, of which the average measured just over 4⅔ acres and contained at least one greenhouse.[23] Small producers were later joined by ambitious horticultural entrepreneurs, some of them non-local, who established industrial-scale enterprises employing large teams of workers. From the 1890s onwards, tomatoes superseded other crops as the island's main horticultural export, and horticulture superseded other industries as the mainstay of Guernsey's economy.[24]

---

[22] Produce exported included cider, cattle, potatoes, cauliflower and hot-house grapes. For more detail, see R. Hocart, *The Country People of Guernsey and their Agriculture, 1640–1840* (Guernsey, 2016), pp. 177, 184, 192, 239–40.

[23] W.E. Bear, 'Glimpses of farming in the Channel Islands', *Journal of the Royal Agricultural Society of England*, 24 (1888), pp. 387–9.

[24] For more on the development of horticulture, see E.A. Wheadon, 'The history of the tomato in Guernsey', *TSG*, 12 (1935), pp. 338–50; P.J. Girard, 'Development of the bulb and flower industry in Guernsey', *TSG*, 13 (1939), pp. 284–98; P.J. Girard, 'The Guernsey grape industry', *TSG*, 15 (1951), pp. 126–44.

Plate 5. Growing daffodils under glass, early twentieth century
© Mike Deane, www.deanephotos.com

Plate 6. Loading tomatoes for export, St Peter Port, early twentieth century
Guernsey Museums & Galleries (States of Guernsey) 2018

Horticulture was to remain central to Guernsey's economy throughout the period covered by this study. In 1951, it occupied over a third of all working males over school-leaving age, more than a quarter of them on their own account. By this time also, tourism had become an important part of the economy. It had begun in the 1820s with the introduction of regular steamer services to and from England, but for a long time it had remained the preserve of a small number of specialised travellers. With the onset of mass tourism in the 1920s and 1930s, the island started to attract a larger volume of holiday-makers and, after the hiatus of World War II, numbers expanded significantly. By the last decade with which we are concerned—the 1950s— the tourist industry was of more economic importance to the island than ever before, and supported a seasonal workforce in excess of 1,500.[25]

Throughout our period, the main contribution made by St Peter Port to Guernsey's economy was as the island's administrative, retail and service centre. As well as the Royal Court and the States, the town housed the island's most important churches, hospitals, schools, assembly halls and libraries. It accommodated most of Guernsey's doctors, dentists, opticians and professionals of all kinds. It hosted the main post office and the local headquarters of insurance companies, shipping agents, law firms and banks. It accommodated the principal markets for fish, meat, fruit and vegetables, as well as large numbers of shops selling everything from baby linen to ironmongery. In addition to all of this, St Peter Port was also a manufacturing centre for most of the nineteenth century. Its workshops, yards, plants and foundries accommodated artisans and craftsmen of all stripes, from coachbuilders and cabinetmakers to tinsmiths and saddlers, all of them catering largely for the home market.

---

[25] This is an estimate based on a total of more than 1,000 hospitality workers enumerated in the 1951 census, which was taken just after Easter.

Plate 7. St Peter Port, c.1880
© Mike Deane, www.deanephotos.com

It was on account of such activities that the town parish continued for so long to house more of Guernsey's inhabitants than all the other parishes combined. Its numerical preponderance over other parishes, however, came to an end in 1891. At this point, horticulture-driven growth in the country parishes outstripped the increase in town (whose manufacturing sector had shrunk due to imports of ready-made goods from England), and St Peter Port's share of population dropped to 48 per cent of the insular total. St Peter Port ceased growing altogether in 1901, when its population peaked at 18,264. Between 1911 and 1921, through the effects of war and emigration, the town parish went on to lose a tenth of its inhabitants. Its recovery from these losses was slow, and its population in 1951 stood at just 16,849.[26]

The country parishes, too, sustained population losses between 1911 and 1921, and, in the course of this decade, Guernsey's total population fell from 41,823 to 38,283. This represented an overall drop of 9 per cent, and an abrupt check to the rising trend which had been maintained since the eighteenth century. For all that, the downturn proved to be merely a temporary blip. The fundamentally healthy state of horticulture and tourism discouraged emigration and encouraged immigration, and the population

---

[26] St Peter Port's population has only recently regained its 1901 level, reaching 18,207 in 2014 and 18,599 in 2015 (States Annual Electronic Census Reports, 2014 and 2015, accessed at www.gov.gg).

began growing again in the late 1920s.[27] This upward trend continued until 1940, when some 17,000 people were evacuated to the United Kingdom in anticipation of the arrival of German troops. After the war, however, most of these evacuees returned, and, joined by further incomers, produced a population total of 43,554 in the census of 1951. This represented a population nearly half as large again as in 1851, and larger than it had been at any time since figures were recorded.

Language, ethnicity and social structure

Prior to the nineteenth century, Guernsey's population had been of largely Norman extraction. Norman surnames predominated, and islanders spoke a variant of Norman French. Aside from a small influx of English *entrepôt* workers in the eighteenth century, the population had to date remained ethnically fairly stable. The nineteenth and early twentieth centuries were, by contrast, marked by major waves of immigration. Between Waterloo and the 1850s, large numbers of immigrants from south-west England entered the island in the wake of England's post-Napoleonic agricultural depression. They were at their most numerous in the census of 1851, when they were joined by refugees from Ireland's Great Famine. At this point, migrants from England and Ireland comprised more than a fifth of the island's total population. Some 80 per cent of these migrants were based in St Peter Port, and the remainder mainly in the northern quarrying parishes.[28] In the last third of the nineteenth century, immigration from England and Ireland declined, but immigration from France increased as Breton peasants fled their own agricultural slump. By 1901, French-born immigrants accounted for just less than a tenth of Guernsey's population.[29] In contrast to their English and Irish predecessors, a majority of late nineteenth-century French immigrants settled not in town but in parishes outside St Peter Port, where they found work in the stone trade, farming and horticulture.[30]

---

[27] A.C. Robin, 'The population of the Bailiwick of Guernsey', *TSG*, 16 (1955), pp. 51–69.
[28] Crossan, *Guernsey, 1814–1914*, pp. 93, 107.
[29] Crossan, *Guernsey, 1814–1914*, p. 124.
[30] Crossan, *Guernsey, 1814–1914*, pp. 55–7, 125.

French immigration to Guernsey came to an end with World War I. Thereafter, immigration slowed and reverted to its predominantly British origin. By 1951, 80 per cent of the Bailiwick's non-native contingent were of United Kingdom origin, 13 per cent from other countries, and 7 per cent from Jersey. At 24 per cent of the Bailiwick population, however, non-natives now accounted for a smaller proportion of total inhabitants than in either 1851 or 1901.

During the nineteenth century, English and Irish immigrants to Guernsey did not mix readily with islanders. They stayed within their established communities in St Peter Port and the northern parishes, and they usually married among themselves.[31] French immigrants appear to have mixed more easily with their rural neighbours, with whom, to some extent, they shared a language and a culture.[32] Still, the real fusion of local with migrant stock took place in the twentieth century. The process began with the improvement of public transport after World War I and reached its zenith after World War II, when a liberalisation of social mores and better job opportunities for both sexes mingled young people from all parishes and all backgrounds in workplaces, dance-halls, clubs and cinemas. This ensured a thorough blending of native and non-native stock, such that today there can be very few Guernseymen with a claim to 'pure Norman blood'.

As well as new genes, immigration (and external influences generally) brought important social changes to Guernsey. One of the first of these changes affected the island's religious complexion. In the sixteenth century, Guernsey had been converted to the Reformed faith via France, and for a century after the Reformation, it was Calvinistic in belief and Presbyterian in organisation. This came to an end in 1662 when Charles II extended the provisions of the Act of Uniformity to the island and made Anglicanism the established religion. Thereafter Guernsey remained exclusively Anglican until the late eighteenth century, when Nonconformity, in the form of Quakerism and Methodism, was introduced to the island by English migrants and missionaries. Methodism took hold particularly strongly, and was joined in the next few decades by other Nonconformist denominations such as Brethren, Baptists and Congregationalists. Roman Catholicism was

---

[31] Crossan, *Guernsey, 1814–1914*, pp. 220-9.
[32] Crossan, *Guernsey, 1814–1914*, pp. 219-20, 227.

re-introduced in the 1790s by *émigrés* from the French Revolution and bolstered by Irish immigration in the 1850s. By 1893, when a local census of church attendance was held, Nonconformist attendances accounted for 57 per cent of all church attendances, with 34 per cent accruing to Anglicans and 9 per cent to Roman Catholics.[33] A stern current of Biblical literalism, particularly among rural Nonconformists, will be seen to have impacted on attitudes to women.

Immigrants also brought changes to Guernsey's linguistic make-up. For centuries, islanders had spoken their own variant of Norman French, and used standard French as its written form. The presence of large numbers of English and Irish migrants in nineteenth-century St Peter Port—nearly 39 per cent of the town's civilian population in 1851—effectively anglicised the town, to the extent that the St Peter Port variant of Norman French became extinct by 1900.[34] The anglicisation of the country parishes took longer, not least because there was little settlement by English-speakers until the twentieth century. In 1951, although a majority of country parishioners spoke English as their first language, these parishes still accommodated significant numbers of native Norman French speakers.

The outward emigration of islanders did not take place on any scale until the early nineteenth century, when Westminster's imposition of anti-smuggling Acts in 1805 and 1807 provoked an initial exodus to North America. After this time, long-distance emigration became an entrenched part of insular life. Censuses between 1841 and 1911 show that, at the same time as large numbers were entering the island, almost equally large numbers were leaving it, attracted by the same opportunities in the New World that were drawing their contemporaries from all over Europe. Decades particularly marked by emigration were the 1850s, 1870s and 1900s. Australia was the destination of choice in the 1850s and North America thereafter.[35] A large contingent of emigrants from Guernsey were male, attracted by the chance to own land overseas. Conversely, a majority of immigrants into Guernsey were female, many of them young unmarried domestic servants.[36] These two circumstances, combined with the fact that seafaring detained many men at

---

[33] *Comet*, 15.7.1893.
[34] E. Martel, 'Philological report', *TSG*, 17 (1965), p. 709.
[35] Crossan, *Guernsey, 1814–1914*, pp. 55-7.
[36] Crossan, *Guernsey, 1814–1914*, pp. 58-9.

sea, produced highly unbalanced sex ratios for most of the nineteenth century. Since this phenomenon had a direct bearing on the subject of this study, we will pause at this point to examine sex ratios in detail.

Table 1 compares Guernsey's sex ratios with those of England and Wales at each census between 1851 and 1951.[37] Alongside the all-island ratio, separate figures are given for St Peter Port (SPP), the two northern quarrying parishes (V and SS), and the seven other parishes.

Table 1. Males per 100 females, Guernsey and England and Wales, 1851–1951

	E & W	GSY	SPP	V & SS	Other parishes
1851	96	84	77	95	91
1861	95	84	74	113	90
1871	95	81	71	106	90
1881	95	89	82	109	92
1891	94	92	84	115	94
1901	94	95	88	110	97
1911	94	95	90	108	98
1921	91	91	85	108	94
1931	92	94	86	101	100
1951	93	94	89	95	98

The first two columns of this table show that, in England and Wales as well as in Guernsey, there were consistently fewer males than females in all censuses between 1851 and 1951. At first glance, this seems odd, given that nature is known to produce on average about 105 male babies for every 100 female ones.[38] However, the imbalance in both jurisdictions was caused by two main factors. The first was men's greater historical propensity to emigrate. The second—and the more significant—was men's greater propensity to die early due to illness, accident and warfare.[39] That said,

---

[37] For sources of Guernsey data, see n. 19, above. Data for England and Wales were obtained from the Max Planck Human Mortality Database accessed at www.mortality.org.
[38] R. Woods, *The Demography of Victorian England and Wales* (Cambridge, 2000), p. 51.
[39] Note the drop in sex ratios in both England and Guernsey in 1921. This was caused primarily by excess male deaths in World War I, which continued to exert a depressive effect on sex ratios in the censuses of 1931 and 1951.

Guernsey's imbalance was noticeably more pronounced than that of its northern neighbour until the end of the nineteenth century. As noted above, this was principally due to the combined impact of seafaring, male-dominated emigration and female-dominated immigration. After 1900, sex ratios in the two jurisdictions drew closer as the influence of these factors abated and male life expectancy increased in both.[40]

The table also shows that, throughout the period between 1851 and 1951, St Peter Port had a much larger gender imbalance than the rest of the island. This was especially marked during the nineteenth century when it was due to the localised double effect of a strong deficit of males and an equally strong surplus of females. Deficit and surplus alike were caused by the concentration in town of housing at the two extremes of the cost spectrum. Cheap lodgings attracted not only seafaring households whose menfolk might spend long periods at sea, but also households of impoverished lone spinsters and widows. High-class housing, by contrast, created a demand for female servants, who were more numerous in St Peter Port than elsewhere in Guernsey.[41] St Peter Port's sex imbalance continued at a relatively high level until the 1950s (and beyond). The persistence of this phenomenon in the twentieth century was caused less by a deficit of males than a surplus of females. This is likely to have been primarily due to the relative abundance of female jobs in urban shops, banks and offices, and the continued availability of cheap lodgings.

In stark contrast with St Peter Port, and indeed the rest of the island, the Vale and St Sampsons had a surplus not of females but of males at every census from 1861 to 1931 (even in 1921, despite World War I losses). This was a common feature of areas with extractive industries. With work in quarries and stone-yards always available, these quarrying parishes not only retained their male inhabitants but drew in men from outside.

The seven more agricultural parishes had sex ratios below the average seen in England and Wales until the late nineteenth century. This was principally due to the emigration of men born on the land. The rural parishes' small

---

[40] By 2016 there were 99.5 males for every 100 females in Guernsey, and 97 males for every 100 females in the United Kingdom (https://www.gov.gg/population; http://countrymeters.info).

[41] Crossan, *Guernsey, 1814–1914*, pp. 208–9.

farms could not sustain everyone born on them, and many younger sons precluded by Guernsey's inheritance system from inheriting sustainable holdings were driven to leave their home parishes.[42] However, as horticulture began to flourish from the 1890s, the male population of the country parishes increased and sex ratios crept steadily upwards. After a short-lived drop due to war losses in 1921, sex ratios in the seven rural parishes were higher than the all-island average in both 1931 and 1951.

For much of the period under consideration, St Peter Port and the country parishes had differing social and political complexions. In the countryside, widespread property ownership and the absence of large landed estates obviated what contemporaries called 'extremes' of wealth and poverty.[43] Nevertheless, social gradations did exist, and country-dwellers were strongly aware of them, observing what one writer has described as a 'caste system' which kept the larger farmers, who comprised at most a third of the rural population, 'quite distinct' from less well-off parishioners.[44] It was from these more substantial farmers that rural ratepayers, Constables and Douzeniers were largely drawn, since payment of rates was based on the value of a parishioner's property, and thresholds were relatively high. The two-thirds of rural parishioners with more modest holdings did not normally pay rates and were thus excluded from voting at parish meetings and holding parochial office. This ensured that the country parishes remained in the hands of hereditary oligarchies until well into the twentieth century.[45] Since the primary goal of these oligarchies was to maintain the *status quo*, rural politics retained a distinct conservative cast until at least World War II.

In St Peter Port, social and material gulfs were more pronounced. Collectively, town parishioners were wealthier than the residents of all the other parishes combined, but the town's wealth was concentrated in very few hands. Less than a quarter of St Peter Port's adult parishioners owned any real estate at all in 1851, and life could be hard for the other three-quarters

---

[42] Guernsey's system of modified partible inheritance will be examined in detail in chapter 3.
[43] P. Jeremie, *On Parochial and States Taxation in Guernsey* (Guernsey, 1856), pp. 83–4.
[44] P.J. Girard, 'Country life and some insular enterprises of the late 19th century', *TSG*, 19 (1972), p. 89.
[45] T.F. Priaulx, 'Secular parish administration in Guernsey', *The Quarterly Review of the Guernsey Society*, 21-4 (1965–8), pp. 50–1.

who spent their lives in rented lodgings.[46] The Town Hospital, St Peter Port's parochial workhouse, accommodated an average of two hundred to two hundred and fifty inmates in Victorian times, and a further two hundred or so paupers were relieved in their homes. By contrast, the Country Hospital, a workhouse run collectively by the other nine parishes, housed on average only about one hundred and fifty inmates, besides which perhaps another fifty received domiciliary relief.[47]

The fact that parochial affairs were the prerogative of the propertied also meant that an even smaller proportion of urban than rural residents qualified to vote at parish meetings and hold parochial office. In 1854, the parish electorate comprised just 15 per cent of St Peter Port's adult male population.[48] During the period covered by this book, St Peter Port's parochial administration was largely in the hands of substantial businessmen, with a leavening of *rentiers*. This gave them a very different outlook from their rural counterparts, in comparison with whom they viewed themselves as modern and forward-looking. While St Peter Port's representatives in the States attempted on several occasions in the nineteenth century to promote what they saw as progressive policies, they were repeatedly stymied by the rural interest. From 1845 to the end of the century, the country parishes sent a total of nine Douzaine delegates to the States, whereas St Peter Port sent only six. This numerical advantage, combined with the fact that country Jurats and rectors were also largely conservative in outlook, did much to delay political change.

With the twentieth century came a gradual flattening of the social structure in both town and country as St Peter Port's *rentier* contingent faded away and horticulture spread its material benefits over the countryside. Analysis of Guernsey's 1951 census returns is illuminating. A table in the printed report compared the distribution of social classes in the Bailiwick with that in England and Wales.[49] Males over school age were divided into five classes according to their occupation, and the proportion per thousand

---

[46] R.-M. Crossan, *Poverty and Welfare in Guernsey, 1560–2015* (Woodbridge, 2015), pp. 21, 70–1.
[47] Crossan, *Poverty and Welfare*, pp. 72–7, 83, 126.
[48] 8.3.1854, IA, AQ 0966/01; 1851 St Peter Port census enumerators' books (microfilm, PL).
[49] *Census 1951: Report on Jersey, Guernsey and Adjacent Islands* (London, 1956), p. xl.

inhabitants in each class was stated in separate columns.[50] The Bailiwick contained a markedly smaller proportion in the highest class than did England and Wales (nineteen per thousand as opposed to thirty-three per thousand). Proportions in the second and third highest classes were also smaller than in England and Wales, and the proportion in the lowest class was smaller still (eighty-six per thousand as opposed to 131 per thousand). Where the Bailiwick proportion was distinctly higher that of its northern neighbour was in class 4: 252 per thousand as opposed to the 161 per thousand recorded in England and Wales. This was essentially because this class encompassed most of those who worked in horticulture, waged workers and self-employed alike.[51] The mid-twentieth-century Bailiwick population was thus strongly clustered towards the middle-to-lower end of the social spectrum, and, in terms of material resources, perhaps more homogeneous than it had been at any other time in our period.

The clustering of Guernseymen in class 4 however made for an uninspiring general standard of living. The 1951 census showed that more than two-thirds of Bailiwick households lacked exclusive access to one or more of five key domestic amenities, as compared with under half of households in England and Wales.[52] Some 46 per cent of Bailiwick households did not have exclusive use of a kitchen, and 61 per cent of households in St Peters, and 42 per cent in town, had no fixed bath.[53]

These were the conditions under which Guernsey people lived and laboured in 1951. A lack of cookers, sinks and piped water would of course have borne more harshly on women than on men, since household responsibilities rested squarely on women's shoulders. It is on these women and their female forebears that the remaining chapters of this book will now concentrate. The next chapter will look in detail at three factors central to all women's lives: education, work and health.

---

[50] Class 1 contained professionals such as doctors, lawyers, architects and accountants; class 2 contained managers and academically qualified workers such as schoolteachers; class 3 contained white-collar workers such as bank clerks and insurance salesmen; class 4 contained skilled and semi-skilled blue-collar workers; and class 5 contained unskilled workers.
[51] In lifestyle terms, there was little to distinguish a man who worked his own three or four greenhouses from his neighbour who was employed in a vinery.
[52] The five amenities were a piped water supply, kitchen sink, cooker, toilet and fixed bath.
[53] *Census, 1951*, pp. xxii–xxiv.

2

Education, Work and Health

Education

The historian Merry Wiesner-Hanks has noted that, in the eighteenth and nineteenth centuries, much greater numbers of boys' schools than girls' schools were established in both urban and rural districts Europe-wide.[1] The same was largely true for Guernsey. Although all ten of Guernsey's parishes had their own schools by the early nineteenth century, not all of these schools accommodated girls. A return to the Parliamentary Select Committee on the Education of the Poor in 1818 showed that St Peters' parish school taught only boys in a single-sex schoolroom, and St Andrews' school, though it did teach girls, had not in the past taught enough of them to warrant a separate girls' schoolroom.[2] Statistics for 1824 published by John Jacob showed that the ten parish schools, together with St Peter Port's National School and the Town Hospital school, taught 827 boys and 603 girls, i.e., 27 per cent fewer girls than boys.[3]

Guernsey's States first began to involve themselves in education in the mid-1820s when they rebuilt the ancient grammar school known as Elizabeth College with public funds. Some of these funds were also used to assist the parochial authorities in extending their schools and supplementing teachers'

---

[1] M.E. Wiesner-Hanks, *Gender in History: Global Perspectives* (2001; Oxford, 2011 edn), p. 181.
[2] PP 1819 IX.
[3] J. Jacob, *Annals of Some of the British Norman Isles Constituting the Bailiwick of Guernsey* (Paris, 1830), p. 403.

salaries.⁴ While ensuring that all parish schools would now have a separate girls' schoolroom and schoolmistress, the States and their parochial partners followed prevailing wisdom in building all of the girls' schoolrooms smaller than those of the boys.⁵ The main reason for this was that education was seen as less of a priority for girls than for boys, since the former were destined to live out their lives as wives and mothers in the home, while the latter needed to forge their way in the wider world as breadwinners and providers.

Plate 8. Class of girls, Hautes Capelles School, Vale, c.1903
© Mike Deane, www.deanephotos.com

Guernsey's parish schools were elementary schools.⁶ In the nineteenth century, these schools were attended by children between the ages of about five and ten, who were taught a very basic curriculum, consisting mostly of the three Rs. All girls were in addition taught sewing and knitting. Any family who wished their children to acquire more than these rudiments was obliged to turn to private provision. Some better-off families sent their daughters to boarding schools in England or France. Many, however, sent them to one of

---

⁴ R.-M. Crossan, 'The retreat of French from Guernsey's public primary schools, 1800–1939', *TSG*, 25 (2005), pp. 858-9; R.-M. Crossan, *The States and Secondary Education, 1560-1970* (Guernsey, 2016), pp. 9-15.
⁵ *Billet*, 19.3.1866.
⁶ By the mid-1800s St Peter Port also had two National Schools and a British and Foreign School. In 1872 all three were taken over by the States and re-designated parish schools.

the private girls' schools in St Peter Port.[7] To basic literacy and numeracy, most of these schools added instruction in embroidery, painting and drawing, as well as training in social accomplishments such as singing, dancing and piano-playing.

For a century and more this had been the standard educational fare of middle-class girls all over western Europe. At around the beginning of our period, however, middle-class female education in England was on the cusp of an important change. Here, the recently-founded feminist movement had identified the improvement of girls' schooling as vital to progress, and wished to give middle-class girls access to the same academic curriculum studied by their brothers. Frances Buss and Dorothea Beale, principals of the North London Collegiate School for Girls and Cheltenham Ladies' College respectively, fully subscribed to these feminist goals, and during the course of the 1850s, they sought to redefine middle-class girls' education by modelling their own establishments on boys' public schools.[8] Over the next few years, the ideas of Buss and Beale gained traction, and by the 1870s, a significant proportion of British middle-class families were beginning to consider a sound academic education as essential for their daughters.[9] In many British towns and cities, girls' educational associations were set up to provide courses of instruction and lecture series for females. These were followed by the founding in June 1872 of the Girls' Public Day School Company, a development which accelerated the establishment of girls' high schools all over the country by setting a precedent for the use of the joint-stock model. The Company itself founded thirty-eight girls' schools in this way between 1872 and 1897, and in so doing stimulated many other bodies to follow their lead.[10]

---

[7] In 1847, there were fifty-nine small private schools in St Peter Port, seventeen of which were for girls (NA, HO 98/88).
[8] M.E. Bryant, *The Unexpected Revolution: A Study of the Education of Women and Girls in the Nineteenth Century* (London, 1979), pp. 64, 69, 72, 93–4.
[9] This period also saw the beginnings of a change in attitudes to female education in France, where in 1867 the country's education minister created secondary courses for middle-class girls in a number of major towns (F.K. Ringer, *Education and Society in Modern Europe* (Bloomington, 1979), p. 120).
[10] J. Kamm, *Indicative Past: A Hundred Years of the Girls' Public Day School Trust* (1971; Abingdon, 2007 edn), p. 1 (the organisation changed its name to the Girls' Public Day School Trust in 1906).

Guernsey's middle-class residents were not oblivious to these developments, and January 1871 saw a group of leading islanders (all male) establish what they called the Guernsey Ladies' Educational Association to provide girls and young women with 'good solid food for the mind'.[11] A year later, in the autumn of 1872, the same group of people went a step further and founded their own girls' high school. Like those of the Girls' Public Day School Company, the school was set up on the joint-stock model. In imitation of Cheltenham Ladies' College (from which the school's first principal was sourced), it was named the Guernsey Ladies' College.[12] In their first prospectus, the school's founders announced that their establishment was to offer 'educational advantages for Girls equal to those which Elizabeth College affords to Boys'.[13] This did not however preclude the school from also offering 'feminine' subjects such as needlework, domestic science and music, all of which it taught from its beginning.[14]

Plate 9. Guernsey Ladies' College, 1905
Island Archives Service, Guernsey

Elizabeth College, which recruited boys from Guernsey's top social stratum, had been subsidised by the States since its rebuilding in the 1820s. Ever since that time, Guernsey's shopkeepers and small farmers had been lobbying the States for a secondary school suitable to their own offspring.[15]

---

[11] *Star*, 19.1.1871.
[12] Crossan, *States and Secondary Education*, p. 23.
[13] 26.8.1872, IA, AQ 1044/01.
[14] J.E. Buckfield, *The History of the Guernsey Ladies' College, 1872–1963* (Guernsey, 1965), p. 7.
[15] Crossan, *States and Secondary Education*, pp. 24–6.

In 1883, their persistence paid off when the States opened what they called the 'Intermediate School for Boys'.[16] This fee-paying school, catering for boys up to their mid-teens, was to be administered by the States, and any shortfall in fee income was to be made good from States' general revenue. At the time the States were formulating plans for the Boys' Intermediate, they had promised to look into establishing a similar school for girls. While a further twelve years elapsed before one was set up, an 'Intermediate School for Girls' was eventually opened in 1895. Targeting the same age range as its male counterpart, it taught English, French, mathematics, book-keeping, history, geography, drawing, domestic science and needlework.[17] For many years, however, the Girls' Intermediate School was smaller, less well-staffed and less well-funded than the Boys'.[18]

Throughout this period, the girls in the parish schools had continued to follow much the same curriculum as the boys, aside from sewing and knitting.[19] Traditionally, however, they had not been expected to perform so well as their brothers in scholastic pursuits. It therefore came as something of a surprise that, when annual examinations were introduced in the 1850s, female pupils regularly did better than males.[20] The highest-achieving girls were henceforth encouraged to stay on at school as pupil-teachers.[21] High-achieving boys were also offered this opportunity, but the scheme proved less popular with them. By the later nineteenth century, this had tilted the sex balance in the parish schools slightly in girls' favour, with some 1,094

---

[16] 24.1.1883, IA, AS/MB 104-01.
[17] Anon., *Ecole Intermédiaire, 1895–1955: Souvenir* (Guernsey, 1955), pp. 9–13.
[18] These disparities are evident from the reports on the Intermediates published in States' *Billets* from the 1890s onwards. To give just one example: in 1909 the Boys' School was granted a States' subsidy of £444, while the Girls' received just £327 (*Billet*, 13.1.1909).
[19] In this they were better off than their contemporaries in the Town Hospital school: here girl inmates of the Victorian era had a solid diet of sewing and knitting punctuated by only one hour's daily instruction in the three Rs, while boy inmates received 25 hours' instruction a week in reading, writing, arithmetic and other subjects such as geography (6.3.1876, IA, DC/HX 136-09).
[20] See for instance the 1854 examiner's report in *Billet*, 2.5.1855.
[21] This was an apprenticeship scheme for producing home-grown teachers, whereby recruits taught younger pupils during the school day and received supplementary instruction from the master or mistress after hours. Introduced in the 1850s, it was modelled on a similar scheme instituted in England in 1846 (Crossan, *States and Secondary Education*, p. 19).

boys and 1,161 girls on their combined rolls in 1880.[22] It also led to the gradual feminisation of the parochial teaching-force, such that, by 1908, of sixty-six assistant teachers in the parish schools, some sixty-one were women.[23]

Aside from the pupil-teacher scheme, there was little scope to extend or develop either male or female talent at Guernsey's Victorian elementary schools. From the late nineteenth century, the States sought to ameliorate this situation by offering a number of competitive scholarships to promising pupils of both sexes who wished to pursue their studies at the Intermediate Schools. However, just as the Boys' Intermediate received more States' funding, so it was also awarded a greater number of States' scholarships. In 1911, the States were funding twenty-five scholarships at the Boys' School but just sixteen at the Girls' (they were also funding six at Elizabeth College and two at the Ladies' College).[24] This led to a degree of unfairness in the scholarship examination, as girls tended on average to attain higher scores than boys. In 1916, for example, the top eight girls each scored an average of thirty-eight marks more than the top eight boys. These sixteen children all gained scholarships, but six of the successful boys scored marks below those of any of the successful girls, and there were a number of girls with scores equalling those of the successful boys who failed to gain scholarships at all.[25] This *prima facie* injustice to high-scoring girls was a phenomenon also observed in scholarship examinations in the United Kingdom.[26]

In 1900, *la Loi relative à l'Education Primaire Obligatoire* made schooling compulsory for all Guernsey children between the ages of five and twelve, with the leaving age set at a child's thirteenth birthday.[27] In 1923, the leaving age was raised to a child's fourteenth birthday.[28] Most children spent their entire school careers in the parish schools. When discussing how the extra school year should be used in the summer of 1923, the States' Education

---

[22] *Billet*, 3.6.1881.
[23] *Billet*, 5.6.1908.
[24] *Billet*, 6.3.1912.
[25] 31.7.1916, IA, AS/MB 103-09.
[26] D. Thom, 'Better a teacher than a hairdresser?', in F. Hunt (ed.), *Lessons for Life: The Schooling of Girls and Women, 1850–1950* (Oxford, 1987), pp. 134, 141.
[27] O in C, 17.9.1900.
[28] O in C, 17.4.1923.

Council decided that boys in their final year should have an extra four hours of mathematics a week, plus two hours of woodwork; girls, on the other hand, were to have two extra hours of needlework, two hours of domestic economy, and one hour of 'household arithmetic'.[29] Since 1921 the States had run a Domestic Science Centre in St Peter Port for female pupils from town schools. This was at first based at Eldad schoolroom and subsequently moved to Granville House (shown in plate 10, overleaf). Male town pupils had their own Handicrafts Centre at Brock Road. A few years later, the States provided for girls from the country parishes by building a Domestic Science Centre at Delancey in St Sampsons, while boys from the country parishes were provided for by a Handicrafts Centre in the same location.[30] By the late 1930s, all girls in their last year at the parish schools spent one full day a week at a Domestic Science Centre, learning cookery, laundry work and housecraft, while their male contemporaries studied woodwork and metalwork in their own Centres.[31] A majority of parents probably welcomed this, as perhaps did the children themselves. It suited the needs of a community where, in 1930, 36 per cent of male elementary school-leavers went into greenhouse work, and 69 per cent of female leavers entered domestic occupations.[32] It also guaranteed that very few school-leavers were equipped to do anything else.

---

[29] 16.7.1923, IA, AS/MB 105-02. Since the 1820s, the States had progressively wrested control of the elementary schools from the parishes. A law of 1916 had set up the States' Education Council, which ran both the elementary and Intermediate schools and had oversight of education in Guernsey generally (Crossan, *States and Secondary Education*, pp. 34-5).
[30] E.J. Bowes and H.V. Gregg, *A Short Survey of the Development of the Education System in the Island of Guernsey* (unpub. monograph, 1968, PL), p. 17.
[31] *Billet*, 29.4.1938.
[32] 25.2.1931, IA, AS/MB 104-09.

Plate 10. Domestic Science Centre, Granville House, 1935
© The Priaulx Library, Guernsey

After the Second World War, Guernsey's education system underwent a number of changes. All but a handful of the island's private schools disappeared, and the States' schools were formally divided into a primary and secondary tier, with the transition to secondary level at eleven. A selective system was introduced, whereby children successful in the scholarship examination would attend the Intermediates or Colleges, and those who were not would attend secondary modern schools adapted from some of the pre-war elementaries.[33] These schools continued to be organised along traditional gender lines, and while boys at Guernsey's post-war secondary moderns studied woodwork, metalwork and technical drawing, girls were steered towards cookery, needlework and childcare.[34]

Soon after World War II, the number of scholarships available to boys and girls was increased and equalised, and the size and funding of the two

---

[33] It was 1959 before the first purpose-built secondary modern (Les Beaucamps) was opened (Crossan, *States and Secondary Education*, pp. 52–3, 78).
[34] Crossan, *States and Secondary Education*, pp. 82–3.

Intermediates became more comparable.[35] The school-leaving age nevertheless remained frozen at fourteen until 1963,[36] and although the States' Education Council attempted to enforce a leaving age of sixteen for scholarship-holders, they were not always successful in persuading parents and children to comply. Numbers staying on in education past the age of fourteen were low to the end of our period, and the number of girls staying on notably lower than boys. The 1951 census showed that only 12.6 per cent of Bailiwick girls aged fifteen to nineteen were in full-time education as compared with 14.6 per cent of boys in the same age group.[37]

Despite the post-war improvement in girls' access to academic education, female horizons at both the Girls' Intermediate and Ladies' College remained relatively low. Notwithstanding that the States had since 1946 made means-tested grants available to school-leavers of both sexes wishing to study at university or college, few girls took them up over the decade and a half to the end of our period.[38] In July 1959, some forty-one girls left what was now the Girls' Grammar School to start their lives in the wider world.[39] Of these, nearly a quarter had not yet reached the age of sixteen. Not one of these leavers went to university, but three went into nurse training and three into teacher training. Nine others became clerks, and the other twenty-six went into reception work, retail or hairdressing.[40] The situation at the Ladies' College was not dissimilar: of thirty-eight leavers in the summer of 1960, just two went to university, four to teacher training college, and the remaining thirty-two found jobs in local offices and banks.[41]

The problem now was not so much a dearth of educational opportunities, but that extraneous factors were preventing girls from taking these

---

[35] In 1947, seventy-eight States' scholarships were awarded to boys and seventy-six to girls (*Billet*, 30.6.1948). In a later terminological change, the scholarship examination became known as the 'eleven-plus' and scholarships 'special places'.
[36] Crossan, *States and Secondary Education*, p. 57.
[37] In England and Wales, where the leaving age had been raised to fifteen by the 1944 Education Act, the figure for girls was 14.8 per cent, and for boys 15 per cent (*Census 1951: Report on Jersey, Guernsey and Adjacent Islands* (London, 1956), p. xxxiv).
[38] 16.9.1946, IA, AS/MB 105-04.
[39] The Intermediates were officially re-designated Grammar Schools in 1955 (O in C, 30.6.1955).
[40] IA, EC 062-10.
[41] IA, EC 077-10.

opportunities up. Almost everyone, including the girls themselves, still saw their ultimate destiny as marriage and motherhood. In waiting for 'Mr Right' to come along, there were many low-level jobs girls could do in Guernsey's flourishing 1950s economy. For most of these jobs, an advanced education was not necessary. Indeed, an advanced education often yielded qualifications unusable in Guernsey. Many parents resented their daughters remaining at school when they could be earning money, and girls themselves often champed at the bit. 'I find it a hard struggle keeping [my fourteen-year-old] at school,' wrote the mother of a Ladies' College scholarship-holder in 1958. '[She] wants to be a dressmaker, I see no advantage in her remaining at school a further two years, in fact she is at a disadvantage as she will be losing two years as an apprentice.'[42]

By 1967, when this fourteen-year-old might still have been at university had she not been diverted by dressmaking, there were 38,109 full-time female undergraduates studying at universities in England and Wales.[43] Major expansion in the sector following the Robbins Report four years earlier had tripled female student numbers since the 1950s. Over the remaining decades of the twentieth century, the number of girls taking up university places rose steadily, such that by the early twenty-first century female students comprised over half of the British student body.[44] This in due course led to an increase in the number of women taking up professional careers and in female earning-power generally. Ultimately, Guernseywomen also participated in these benefits, but their resort to higher education in large numbers took place beyond our period and is hence the subject of a different book.

Work

Throughout the period between the 1850s and 1950s, women's main sphere of activity was the home. Running households was seen as the primary duty of all females, married or not. In the twenty-first century, when modern conveniences have eliminated much domestic drudgery, it is difficult to

---

[42] 15.4.1958, IA EC 145-05.
[43] D. Wardle, *English Popular Education, 1780–1975* (Cambridge, 1976), p. 148.
[44] M.E. David, 'Women and gender equality in higher education?', *Educational Sciences*, 5 (2015), p. 14.

conceive how labour-intensive the running of a nineteenth- or early twentieth-century home could be. Housework involved much vigorous scrubbing, mopping and sweeping. Cooking often necessitated drawing water from a pump and making up a fire before preparing ingredients from scratch, often for many mouths. The weekly wash involved soaking, boiling, rubbing and starching, not to mention drying and ironing, and it often stretched out over two or three days. In the evenings, there were always clothes and linen to make and mend. Looking after a household was arduous, repetitive, dawn-till-dusk work. Girls were expected to assist their mothers from an early age, but sons were generally spared—which helped perpetuate the notion that domestic work was not for men.

With all this work to do in their homes, it seems impossible that women could have had time for anything else, yet evidence shows that many women, married as well as single, also participated in the work economy. This evidence is to be found in two main sources: census reports, which contain quantitative data on women's occupations, and literary sources such as contemporary writings and memoirs. We will look first at censuses, since these provide an outline of the chief sectors in which women worked.[45] Before we do so, however, we must enter the caveat that the picture they present is far from complete. In censuses between 1851 and 1951 no more than one-quarter to one-third of working-age Guernseywomen ever specified any occupation at all. One reason for this was that wider society defined men as breadwinners and women as dependants, so that any work the latter might do was regarded as merely incidental. Thus many women who were casually or intermittently employed, or who worked in family enterprises such as farms and shops, did not consider it worth declaring their activities.[46]

Such as they are, census data show that, in the nineteenth century, about a third of females who declared an occupation were in domestic service,

---

[45] Unless otherwise stated, all census data in this section are synthesised from the printed reports held at the Priaulx Library and/or from census analysis published in Parliamentary Papers (for references, see under Primary Sources in Bibliography). These data are also available online at www.histpop.org. Statistics are for the entire Bailiwick.

[46] On these matters as they affected occupational data in British censuses generally, see E. Higgs, 'Occupations and work in the nineteenth-century censuses', *History Workshop Journal*, 23 (1987), pp. 59–80, and T.J. Hatton and R.E. Bailey, 'Women's work in census and survey, 1911–1931', *The Economic History Review*, 54 (2001), pp. 87–107.

making this sector the largest employer of women.[47] Needlework trades generally formed the next largest sector, with retailing also near the top, followed closely by unskilled occupations such as charring and laundry work. At the bottom of the nineteenth-century female occupational hierarchy were hospitality (occupying about 4 per cent); teaching (also 4 per cent); nursing (2 per cent); and clerical work (0.1 per cent).[48]

These proportions gradually changed in the first half of the twentieth century. The clerical sector, from being one of the smallest sectors, was the one which grew most substantially. By 1931, it employed 7 per cent of the female workforce, and by 1951 it employed 13 per cent.[49] The hospitality sector also grew significantly, roughly equalling the clerical sector as an employer of females by 1951. The third sector which registered growth was retail, but here the increase was only slight: from 19 per cent of females stating an occupation in 1851 to 25 per cent in 1951. The sector which declined most between 1851 and 1951 was that comprised by needlework trades, where the proportion of females employed dropped from 19 per cent in 1851 to 3 per cent in 1951. Domestic service also declined, but—interestingly—not as much as might be expected: in 1851, it had accounted for 32 per cent of females stating an occupation, and in 1951, 18 per cent. That this sector still employed so many females in the mid-twentieth century is perhaps indicative of the relatively unsophisticated state of Guernsey's economy at that time. Interestingly, too, the proportion of women in teaching and nursing remained unaltered between 1851 and 1951. Although absolute numbers in these sectors increased in line with rising population, the proportion of the female workforce they represented—around 4 per cent—was much the same in 1951 as it had been a century earlier.

---

[47] Occupational census data for 1851 and 1951 are represented graphically in Appendix 1.
[48] For the purposes of this analysis, the hospitality sector includes waitresses, barmaids and those who ran and staffed inns, beershops, hotels and lodging-houses; the teaching sector includes schoolmistresses, governesses and those who ran and worked in dame schools and other private schools; the nursing sector includes general nurses and midwives; the clerical sector includes clerks, book-keepers, telegraphists and telephonists.
[49] A fair proportion of these were telephone operators. In 1931, for instance, fifty of the 306 women working in the clerical sector were employed as telephonists.

Plate 11. Telephonists, Central Exchange, St Peter Port, 1931
Guernsey Museums & Galleries (States of Guernsey) 2018

As noted above, the picture of women's work presented by census data is far from complete. For the finer detail, we will now turn to literary sources, beginning with those dealing with female occupations in Guernsey's country parishes. Here, as well as performing their domestic chores, most women appear to have played some part in their household's cash-earning efforts. The majority of Guernsey's farms were small enough to allow owners to work them themselves, and female as well as male family members were required to contribute. There was, however, an established gender order, where men performed the more physically demanding tasks such as ploughing, scything and threshing, and female family members did lighter work in the dairy, calf sheds, pigsties, poultry yard and kitchen garden.[50] It was also women's duty to market the farm's produce. Frank Dally wrote in 1860 of farmers' wives and daughters bringing cartloads of 'vegetables, poultry, eggs and butter, twice in every week' to sell in town.[51] Nevertheless, farmers' wives and daughters could do field work too, especially at times of peak demand. Peter Girard has described it as the task of his female forebears to tie the corn

---

[50] D.O. Heaume, *Life in Guernsey, 1904–1914* (Guernsey, 1967), pp. 5-7.
[51] F.F. Dally, *An Essay on the Agriculture of the Channel Islands* (Guernsey, 1860), p. 30.

sheaves after harvest, even in the late nineteenth century.[52] After the horticultural industry had become established, a large number of growers' wives also played a part in the routine tasks of tomato and flower production: disbudding, trimming, picking, bunching and packing.

Plate 12. *Women marketing produce, St Peter Port, late nineteenth century*
© The Priaulx Library, Guernsey

---

[52] P.J. Girard, 'Country life and some insular enterprises of the late 19th century', *TSG*, 19 (1972), p. 95.

Plate 13. Women picking tomatoes, late nineteenth century
Guernsey Museums & Galleries (States of Guernsey) 2018

Earlier in the nineteenth century, the wives of smallholding tradesmen or fishermen often worked family plots while their husbands were occupied at their trades.[53] They would then hawk their produce, or their husbands' fish, around the local neighbourhood. In 1834, Henry Inglis mentioned

---

[53] J. Jeremie, *An Historical Account of Guernsey* (Guernsey, 1821), pp. 162-3.

fishermen's wives hawking their husband's catches.⁵⁴ Doris Heaume evoked the image of the Edwardian fisherman's wife 'in her black scoop, fishy apron and two wicker baskets calling at the back door with mackerel or whiting freshly caught along the west coast.'⁵⁵

Even the wives of the poorest labourers occupied niches in the rural economy. They might gather crabs and shellfish from the foreshore for sale to their neighbours.⁵⁶ They might collect and burn seaweed, selling the ashes on as fertiliser.⁵⁷ Alternatively, like their husbands, they might hire themselves out for taskwork of various kinds. Ansted and Latham described women weeding crops in rural fields.⁵⁸ Nineteenth-century newspapers described women cracking granite in northern stone-yards.⁵⁹ In the twentieth century, many rural (as well as urban) housewives maintained regular seasonal jobs in greenhouses and packing sheds.

Plate 14. Women harvesting potatoes, late nineteenth century
© The Priaulx Library, Guernsey

---

⁵⁴ H.D. Inglis, *The Channel Islands*, 2 vols (London, 1834), 1, pp. 49–50.
⁵⁵ Heaume, *Life in Guernsey*, p. 7. 'Scoop' was the term for the local style of peaked bonnet.
⁵⁶ F.F. Dally, *A Guide to Jersey, Guernsey, Sark, Herm, Jethou, Alderney, etc.*, (London, 1858), p. 238.
⁵⁷ Jacob, *Annals*, p. 190.
⁵⁸ D.T. Ansted and M.A. Latham, *The Channel Islands* (London, 1862), p. 478.
⁵⁹ *Comet*, 30.9.1861, 25.4.1891.

Plate 15. Women cracking stone, St Sampsons, early twentieth century
Guernsey Museums & Galleries (States of Guernsey) 2018

Plate 16. Tomato packing shed, late 1950s or early 1960s
Courtesy of Blue Diamond Group

Most rural women from lower social strata also worked at some point in their lives as domestic servants. Given the shortage of other outlets for full-time work, domestic service was almost a rite of passage for country girls. Doris Heaume reported that country parents 'were anxious to get their daughters into service as soon as they left school.'[60] Some of these girls became daily servants in the households of their better-off neighbours. Their many duties ranged from cleaning and cooking to minding children and looking after the elderly—in addition to which, girls in service on farms generally also participated in outdoor work.[61]

Country girls also found work as servants in St Peter Port, where they were more likely to live in. Rural households keeping live-in servants never exceeded a tenth of all country households in the nineteenth and early twentieth centuries, whereas the proportion in St Peter Port was nearly double. In 1851, 21 per cent of St Peter Port's female servants were born in the country parishes; in 1901, 27 per cent.

What other employment opportunities did St Peter Port offer women? As noted in the previous chapter, the town housed most of the island's businesses. Among these were hotels, lodging-houses, beershops, inns and eating-houses, which were all important employers of female labour. Opportunities for casual charring and laundry work were also plentiful in town, as they were for putting-out work such as shirt-making and shoe-binding. Between 1857 and 1879, Keillers of Dundee also operated two confectionery and marmalade factories in St Peter Port which at their height employed more than one hundred hands, many of them female.[62] All these openings represented valuable income sources for unsupported spinsters and widows, as well as for wives whose husbands were at sea.

---

[60] Heaume, *Life in Guernsey*, p. 5.
[61] Hocart, *Country People of Guernsey*, pp. 50–1.
[62] W.M. Mathew, *The Secret History of Guernsey Marmalade: James Keiller & Son Offshore, 1857–1879* (Guernsey, 1998), p 6.

Plate 17. Washerwomen at a St Peter Port 'lavoir', late nineteenth century
Guernsey Museums & Galleries (States of Guernsey) 2018

As well as female employees, St Peter Port also had its female business-owners. In his memoirs, G.W.J.L. Hugo, born in 1862, listed all the major shopkeepers operating in St Peter Port in the last third of the nineteenth century.[63] Perhaps a quarter of these were women running businesses on their own account. In Smith Street alone, there were Mrs Durant who kept a toyshop; Mrs Le Lacheur who had a baby linen business; Mrs Brennan, a grocer; Miss Duplain, an umbrella retailer; and Mrs Angel, a bookseller. In the town's fish, meat and vegetable markets, Mesdames Collivet, Abraham, De La Cour, Le Duc, Dumont, Sebire, Irish, Green and Nicolle all kept stalls of various kinds. There were in addition a considerable number of female publicans and lodging-house keepers, as also of female private school proprietors and, to a lesser extent, female commercial photographers.[64] More surprisingly perhaps, Victorian St Peter Port also hosted two female newspaper proprietors: Ellen Le Lievre and

---

[63] G.W.J.L. Hugo, *Guernsey as it Used to Be; Some Aspects of the Island in my Boyhood, Youth, and Early Manhood, with Allusions to Well-known Persons* (Guernsey, 1933), pp. 12-15, 27, 30.

[64] At least five female commercial photographers have been identified in Victorian St Peter Port (N. Wilkinson, 'Photographers working in St Peter Port, 1843-1910', *Société Guernesiaise Family History Section Journal*, 10 (1997), pp. 18-19).

Elizabeth Maillard, who had continued to run the *Star* and the *Comet*, respectively, after their husbands' deaths.[65]

Outlets for middle-class ladies such as Mesdames Le Lievre and Maillard were, however, relatively few. As an alternative to paid work, many ladies from St Peter Port's *rentier* sector occupied themselves with charity work. For some of these, philanthropy became almost a full-time job, which they approached as professionals. This was a phenomenon common to leisured women all over nineteenth- and early twentieth-century Britain.[66] Many middle- and upper-class Guernsey ladies did valuable work in St Peter Port and other parishes, running Dorcas Circles, Lying-in Charities, and a plethora of Visiting Societies, Provident Societies, Rescue Societies and Temperance Societies, most of them associated with religious denominations.[67]

Female professionals who worked for a living were, however, extremely rare in nineteenth-century Guernsey. One pioneer was Mrs William Sharshaw, a qualified pharmacist, who, according to her obituary in 1889, had practised in St Peter Port for decades, in partnership with her husband and brother.[68] The first female doctor licensed to practise in Guernsey was Mary Sinclair, wife of Medical Officer of Health Henry Bishop. Dr Sinclair was licensed by the Royal Court in February 1900, followed by Helen Greene in September 1900 and Mina Dobbie in July 1901.[69] Although women doctors continued to be licensed in Guernsey at the rate of one or two a decade until the 1950s, it is unclear how many of them actually practised, since the only census between 1901 and 1951 in which a woman returned herself as a working doctor was that of 1931, when two women did so.

For all that, women doctors appear to have been in the vanguard as far as local female professionals were concerned. It was not until seventy years after Mary Sinclair had been licensed that Guernsey's Bar admitted a female

---

[65] A. Bennett, 'A history of the French newspapers and nineteenth-century English newspapers of Guernsey' (unpub. MA dissertation, Loughborough University, 1995), pp. 59–60.
[66] F.K. Prochaska, *Women and Philanthropy in Nineteenth-Century England* (Oxford, 1980).
[67] R.-M. Crossan, *Poverty and Welfare in Guernsey, 1560–2015* (Woodbridge, 2015), pp. 105–6.
[68] *The Monthly Illustrated Journal*, February 1889.
[69] 3.2.1900, 15.9.1900, 13.7.1901, GG, *Ordonnances*, 1899–1902.

advocate. In the United Kingdom, women began to be appointed as lawyers after the passage of the 1919 Sex Disqualification Removal Act. France had admitted women as advocates since 1900.[70] Guernsey did not admit a female advocate until 1973.[71]

The passage of the Sex Disqualification Removal Act had in part been stimulated by British women's increased activity in the workplace during World War I, which also marked something of a watershed in Guernseywomen's employment. On the eve of the armistice, a local journalist, E.V. Davis, compiled a chronicle of the war as it had affected Guernsey. He had much to say on women's contribution, recounting how upper- and middle-class women had stepped in to run wartime charities such as the Guernsey War Relief Fund, the Communal Kitchen, Boot Clubs and the Schoolchildren's Dinner Fund. He also noted the service overseas of younger, mostly middle-class women in Voluntary Aid Detachments, the Women's Auxiliary Corps, the Land Army, and munitions factories. More significantly for our purposes, Davis documented the many local jobs taken over by women to fill the gaps left by men. Among other things, he recorded women working as law clerks and bank clerks, insurance agents and business canvassers, greenhouse workers and farmhands, post office messengers, tram drivers and conductors—even as 'lady reporters' for the local press.[72] Initially, some employers resisted engaging women in these roles, but, for the women themselves, it was often a case of necessity. The Separation Allowances and Widows' Pensions given by the War Office to women whose husbands were fighting or killed did not fully make up for lost breadwinner income, and, amid high wartime inflation, many women were forced to work in order to survive, especially if they had families.[73] Thus, while some women found these increased employment opportunities liberating, others were no doubt glad when returning husbands relieved them of their burdens.

---

[70] S.K. Foley, *Women in France since 1789* (Basingstoke, 2004), p. 147.
[71] The advocate in question was Rosalyn Brelsford (*Guernsey Evening Press*, 5.7.1973).
[72] E.V. Davis, *Sarnia's Record in the Great War* (Guernsey, 1919), pp. 16, 23.
[73] Some mothers were forced to have children admitted to poor law institutions so as to be able to work full-time (see 5.1.1918, 3.3.1918, GG, Royal Court Letter Book No. 23).

Left to right: Mrs. W. J. Le Page, Mrs. J. Vessey, Mrs. W. R. French, Mrs. E. V. Gibson, Mrs. J. Vivian Thomas, Mrs. E. C. Ozanne (President), Miss Violet Carey, Mrs. S. Cooper, Miss Clothier, Miss Christine Ozanne.

Plate 18. World War I Communal Kitchen Committee
Guernsey Museums & Galleries (States of Guernsey) 2018

Plate 19. Women field workers, Pleinheaume, 1917
Guernsey Museums & Galleries (States of Guernsey) 2018

In the post-war period, there was a backlash against women's employment all over Europe as governments sought to free up jobs for demobilised soldiers. In one country after another, women were excluded from the workforce by 'protective' legislation which limited their hours and enhanced their safety but also kept them out of the higher-paid jobs which might involve non-standard hours or conditions. The drive to 'protect' working women was embodied in a Convention of the League of Nations' International Labour Organisation. The United Kingdom was a party to this Convention and asked Guernsey to draw up compliant legislation. Thus in 1926 the island passed its own restrictive law, which limited women's ability to be employed on night-shifts and in certain industries.[74]

It is thought by some historians that the post-war backlash against women workers inaugurated a 'golden age' of domesticity for married women; one has asserted that, during the inter-war period, the 'vast majority' of British wives did not work outside the home.[75] Given the shortcomings of the census, we are never likely to know whether this was entirely true, particularly in Guernsey where so much women's work was seasonal, part-time or in family enterprises. It is interesting to note however that, whereas a quarter of Bailiwick women aged 45–64 had returned themselves as working in 1901, the figure for 1931 was only 17 per cent.

One feature of women's work which did remain constant throughout our period was poor pay. Prior to the late twentieth century, women in western Europe had generally been paid about one-half to two-thirds less than men for the same or similar tasks.[76] The main reason for this was society's traditional view of men as breadwinners. A man's pay was conceptualised as a 'family wage', whereas a woman's pay was seen just as 'pin money'. This failed to take account of the fact that many spinsters and widows had nothing but their own earnings to live on, and that some also had children to support. In 1851, in the midst of Guernsey's Victorian seafaring heyday, over half of St Peter Port's adult women were spinsters or widows, and almost a quarter of the town's households consisted either of a lone mother with children, or a single woman living alone. The lack of male breadwinners in these households prompted the founding of a local 'Working Society' which tried to provide income by farming out sewing on a piece-work basis. One of the

---

[74] *Loi ayant rapport à l'Emploi de Femmes, de Jeunes Personnes et d'Enfants* (O in C, 5.11.1926). This was modelled on the United Kingdom's Employment of Women, Young Persons and Children Act 1920. Jersey passed its own *Loi sur l'Emploi de Femmes, de Jeunes Personnes et d'Enfants* in 1930.
[75] S.K. Kent, *Gender and Power in Britain, 1640–1900* (London, 1999), pp. 298–9.
[76] Wiesner-Hanks, *Gender in History*, p. 68.

Society's organisers observed in 1875 that many lone women could only 'with difficulty obtain, by unremitting toil, sufficient to keep themselves from starvation.'[77]

A few figures will illustrate the extent of the pay gap across all sectors from the beginning to the end of our period. In 1847, masters at Guernsey's parish schools earned on average £41 per year, but mistresses only £25;[78] in 1951, the head of the Boys' Intermediate School earned £929, but that of the Girls' £832.[79] In 1854, the Town Hospital Master received £80 a year, but the Mistress received just £30;[80] in 1930, the maximum salary for the Hospital Master was £190, but for the Mistress it was £80.[81] In 1888, male greenhouse workers were paid 4s a day, but female workers 2s 6d;[82] in 1958, the adult male greenhouse wage was £7 10s per week, but that of females £5 8s.[83] As late as 1960, the salary ceiling for a female clerical officer in Guernsey's civil service was £665 per annum, whereas a male clerical officer could earn up to £775.[84]

In 1955, the concept of equal pay for equal work made an important advance in the United Kingdom when the government announced that salaries of women working in the civil service, local government and education would be equalised with those of their male counterparts through a series of increments over the next six years.[85] This was noted in Guernsey, but the only sector in which the States chose to institute a similar scheme was teaching.[86] The main reason for this was the Education Council's reliance on teachers recruited from the United Kingdom. In 1961, female teachers employed by the States became the first women in Guernsey to be paid the same rates as men.

---

[77] *Star*, 2.12.1875.
[78] NA, HO 98/88.
[79] 16.3.1951, IA, AS/MB 104-09.
[80] 6.2.1854, IA, DC/HX 054-05.
[81] IA, DC/HX 272-10.
[82] W.E. Bear, 'Glimpses of farming in the Channel Islands', *Journal of the Royal Agricultural Society of England*, 24 (1888), p. 393.
[83] *Star*, 27.3.1958.
[84] *Billet*, 16.11.1960.
[85] P. Thane, 'Women since 1945', in P. Johnson (ed.), *Twentieth-Century Britain: Economic, Social and Cultural Change* (Harlow, 1994), p. 398.
[86] *Billet*, 18.4.1956.

The United Kingdom went on to make further strides towards equality with the passage in 1957 of the Sex Discrimination Act and the creation of the Equal Opportunities Commission. This was followed in 1970 with the Equal Pay Act, which established the principle of equal pay for equal work, or work of equal value.[87] In Guernsey, there was no sex discrimination law until 2004,[88] and, at the time of writing, there is still no equal pay law.

Another obstacle to sexual equality in the workplace came in the form of the marriage bar. In many of Guernsey's public sector occupations, this operated informally, since it was taken for granted that female workers would resign upon marriage. In teaching, a *de facto* marriage bar had pertained (though not without exceptions) since before the start of States' involvement in education. It was officially lifted in 1946, when the Education Council decreed that no woman would henceforth 'be disqualified from employment as a teacher ... or be dismissed from such employment by reason only of marriage.'[89] Guernsey's female post office clerks were relieved of a similar bar a few years later.

In 1957, a local newspaper reported that nearly three thousand married women were now paying their insurance stamp.[90] Six years previously, the census had enumerated 8,909 married female under-60s in Guernsey. If we add to the women who paid their stamp all the growers' wives who worked informally, we might speculate that about half the married women in Guernsey were now working for some part of the year. The Insurance Authority explained that this was 'due to a desire on the part of these women to maintain and improve their standard of living and so offset the continual rise in prices.'[91] Prices continued to rise over ensuing decades, and wives were increasingly compelled to work. For this reason, paid work progressively became the norm for most Guernseywomen at most stages in their lives.

---

[87] Thane, 'Women since 1945', pp. 406-7.
[88] The Prevention of Discrimination (Enabling Provisions) (Bailiwick of Guernsey) Law 2004; Sex Discrimination (Employment) (Guernsey) Ordinance 2005.
[89] 8.4.1946, IA, AS/MB 106-03.
[90] *Star*, 18.1.1957.
[91] *Star*, 18.1.1957.

Health

Information on the general health of Guernsey's female population in the nineteenth and early twentieth centuries is sparse, so this section will focus primarily on women's reproductive health, this being an area to which Guernsey's Medical Officers of Health devoted regular attention in their annual reports.[92] To set the context, we must begin with birth statistics.[93] From about 800 per year in the 1850s, numbers of births rose slowly to exceed a thousand a year in the 1890s and early 1900s. This upward trend was halted by World War I, when annual numbers dropped below 700 for a few years, and then recovered somewhat in the 1920s to average around 800 in the rest of the inter-war period. In World War II, numbers fell again, this time to an average of just 350 a year. They then bounced back sharply with the return of evacuees, reaching a mid-twentieth-century peak of 900 in 1947. This peak proved relatively short-lived, and numbers eased off to an annual average of about 700 during the 1950s.[94]

It is interesting to note that, during the second half of the nineteenth century, Guernsey's birth rates were consistently lower than those of England and Wales (though both were declining relative to increasing population).[95] The most likely reason for Guernsey's lower rates was the male deficit due to seafaring and sex-specific emigration, as described in chapter 1. What is also interesting is that the position reversed after World War I, and Guernsey's birth rates were invariably higher than those of England and Wales from the

---

[92] Medical Officers of Health were first appointed in Guernsey in 1899, and their reports are preserved in States' *Billets d'Etat*.

[93] Pre-twentieth-century statistics are derived from civil and church registers (microfilm, PL; see also R.-M. Crossan, *Guernsey, 1814–1914: Migration and Modernisation* (Woodbridge, 2007), p. 50). Twentieth-century statistics are from civil registers and Medical Officer of Health's annual reports.

[94] The so-called post-war 'baby boom' was relatively short-lived, and was chiefly a 'boom' in comparison with subsequent, rather than previous, trends (especially when these trends are considered long-term).

[95] In 1851, Guernsey's birth rate was 27.1 per thousand inhabitants, compared with 34.3 in England and Wales. In 1901 it was 26.9 compared with 28.5 in England and Wales (Crossan, *Guernsey, 1814–1914*, p. 50; B.R. Mitchell, *European Historical Statistics, 1750–1975* (1975; London, 1981 edn), pp. 125–34).

1920s until the end of our period.[96] This is consistent with the finding of the 1951 census that Bailiwick women who had been married for at least twenty-five years had produced on average 3.4 children, while the figure for England and Wales was just 3.[97] The reason for this disparity may perhaps lie in differential birth control practices. Inhabitants of the United Kingdom are thought actively to have practised some form of family limitation from the late nineteenth century onwards.[98] In Guernsey, the diffusion of birth control knowledge and practice would appear to have occurred later.[99]

Another factor we should take into account before turning to women proper is infant mortality.[100] Guernsey's infant mortality rate was a major source of concern to the island's early Medical Officers of Health, since for the first three decades of the twentieth century, it was on average higher than that of England and Wales. In the 1920s, for instance, there were 77 infant deaths per thousand live births in Guernsey, while the figure for England and Wales was 74.[101] A majority of Guernsey's infant deaths were caused by diarrhoea followed by dehydration and convulsions. As we saw in the last chapter, insular standards of living even in the 1950s were comparatively low. In the early twentieth century, large parts of the island had no public water supply or drainage system, and housing conditions for many families were very basic. Medical Officers of Health repeatedly drew attention to the local habit of siting 'cesspools, accumulations of household refuse, manure heaps and pits, pig sties and latrines' in close proximity to wells and housing.[102] In this kind of environment, water quality was often suspect, and the contamination of food by flies was commonplace. The parish of St Peters, deemed by the Medical Officer of Health to be 'the poorest parish in the

---

[96] In the 1920s, Guernsey's average birth rate was 20.5 per thousand inhabitants, compared with 19.3 in England and Wales. In the 1950s it was 16.7, compared with 15.7 in England and Wales (*Billets*, 27.10.1926, 28.10.1931, 11.7.1951, 14.12.1960; Mitchell, *European Historical Statistics*, pp. 125-34).
[97] *Census, 1951*, pp. l-li.
[98] R. Woods, *The Demography of Victorian England and Wales* (Cambridge, 2000), pp. 149-50.
[99] For more on the subject of birth control, see chapter 5.
[100] Infant mortality is defined as death in the first year of life.
[101] *Billets*, 29.11.1922, 5.12.1923, 29.10.1924, 27.10.1926, 24.10.1928; Mitchell, *European Historical Statistics*, pp. 138-42.
[102] *Billet*, 23.3.1899.

island, the worst housed and least advanced in modern ways and thought', consistently had the worst infant mortality rate.[103] In 1915, ten of the forty-four children born in this parish died before their first birthday, which gave it an infant mortality rate of 227 per thousand live births.[104] Medical Officers of Health speculated that Guernsey's high rates were caused by 'parental ignorance', 'the absence of breast feeding', and the large number of mothers 'who leave their homes to work'.[105]

Plate 20. *Poor children, St Peters coast road, late nineteenth century*
© The Priaulx Library, Guernsey

Guernsey's stillbirth rates were also a cause for concern. The first figures we have for these relate to 1913, a year for which there were no official statistics for England and Wales.[106] The rate reported by the Medical Officer of Health was very high: 67.7 stillbirths for every thousand live births.[107]

---

[103] *Billet*, 8.9.1915.
[104] *Billet*, 20.9.1916.
[105] *Billets*, 26.11.1902, 30.9.1914, 31.10.1917.
[106] Compulsory registration of stillbirths came into force in Guernsey in 1907 and in England and Wales in 1927.
[107] *Billet*, 30.9.1914.

In 1918, the rate was 53.1.[108] The figure for England and Wales when registration began in the late 1920s was just over 40.[109] The factors responsible for Guernsey's high stillbirth rate are likely to have been (as elsewhere) a combination of poor maternal nutrition, insufficiently spaced pregnancies, poor general health, poor living conditions and, possibly, overwork. Although Guernsey's Lying-in charity made some attempt to boost maternal health by providing pre-parturient 'poor and respectable married women' with free groceries, this would have done little to reverse the effects of years of under-nutrition.[110]

A third area of concern to early twentieth-century Medical Officers of Health was maternal mortality. The first time statistics appeared in annual reports was 1922, when it was observed that, between 1917 and 1921, twenty-one Guernsey mothers had died in childbirth. This yielded a rate of 5.7 maternal deaths per thousand live births.[111] The rate in England and Wales over the same period was 4.1, and other countries such as Denmark had a rate just over 2.[112] The Guernsey mothers' deaths were due to three main causes: puerperal fever, haemorrhage and eclampsia, as was also the case Europe-wide. A historian of maternal mortality has estimated that puerperal fever, caused by bacterial infection, alone accounted for as much as 40 per cent of European maternal deaths in the early twentieth century.[113] Once the anti-bacterial drugs known as sulphonamides were introduced in the mid-1930s, maternal mortality dropped sharply across the western world.[114]

Midwives were crucial to the safety of parturient mothers, since they, and not doctors, were responsible for a majority of deliveries, which took place in the home. Some of the census reports between 1851 and 1911 detailed the

---

[108] *Billet*, 3.11.1919.
[109] H.C. Chase and E.W. Curran (eds), *Infant and Perinatal Mortality in England and Wales* (Washington, 1968), p. 51.
[110] *Star*, 18.2.1908.
[111] *Billet*, 29.11.1922.
[112] I. Loudon, *Death in Childbirth: An International Study of Maternal Care and Maternal Mortality, 1800-1950* (Oxford, 1992), pp. 153, 543.
[113] I. Loudon, 'Puerperal fever, the streptococcus, and the sulphonamides, 1911-1945', *British Medical Journal*, 295 (1987), p. 485. The bacterium involved was streptococcus pyogenes, present in people with sore throats, colds and skin conditions, and carried asymptomatically by 7 per cent of the population.
[114] Loudon, 'Puerperal fever, the streptococcus, and the sulphonamides', pp. 485-90.

number of midwives in the Bailiwick.[115] On average, about seven women stated their occupation as midwives in each of these censuses. It seems inconceivable that such a small number could have served the Bailiwick's needs, when in Guernsey alone the annual number of births sometimes exceeded one thousand. It is therefore likely that these seven or so women were complemented by a larger number of informal practitioners who, as well as attending births, probably also undertook other tasks such as sick-nursing and laying-out. Doris Heaume mentions one woman living at la Rocque Poisson in St Peters in the early 1900s who may well have been a 'midwife' of this sort.[116] In 1921, Guernsey's Medical Officer of Health reported that 'many country labours' were attended by 'ignorant women without any training'.[117]

From the mid-nineteenth century, St Peter Port's parochial authorities employed two parish midwives, who, in addition to their private work, attended poor law cases in return for a fee of £5 a year.[118] Most of the country parishes also engaged poor law midwives later in the century.[119] There is no evidence that parish midwives were any better trained than other birth attendants. No formal qualifications were available to midwives until the late nineteenth century, and most midwives, even in the United Kingdom, learned their craft on the job.[120] Evidence shows that birth attendants of this sort were often unable to deal with complications and lacked the skills to repair birth injuries, frequently leaving their patients with permanent problems.[121] It is difficult for historians to uncover direct evidence of these private matters, but one case from Victorian St Peter Port may give us cause for reflection. In 1856, a post-mortem was carried out on the body of Ann Ellis who had given birth four months previously and was known to have sustained birth injuries. The cause of her death was unconnected with childbirth, and doctors' findings in this respect merely incidental. However, the post mortem recorded that 'on removing a cloth between the thighs, a

---

[115] 1851, 1861, 1871, 1881, 1901 and 1911. In 1891 and later censuses, occupational figures conflated midwives with nurses.
[116] Heaume, *Life in Guernsey*, p. 5.
[117] 25.3.1921, Medical Officer of Health to Board of Health President, IA, LO 027-22.
[118] Crossan, *Poverty and Welfare*, p. 91.
[119] Those which did not were compelled to do so by O in C, 24.9.1917.
[120] F.B. Smith, *The People's Health, 1830-1910* (1979; London, 1990 edn), p. 45.
[121] Loudon, *Death in Childbirth*, p. 180.

large cork fell out [and] the lower parts of the body were [found to be] much diseased.'[122] We can only speculate what had caused Ann Ellis's problems, and, indeed, how many other post-parturient women were left to cope in this condition.

More plentiful in the public record are cases where a maternal death resulted directly in an inquest and/or trial. The early twentieth-century inquest on Melina Le Marchant and subsequent trial of Martha McPherson is one example which will stand for others. Mrs Le Marchant (33) of Park Street, St Peter Port died on 12 May 1900 from acute septic peritonitis caused by the rupture of her uterus during childbirth three days earlier.[123] She had been attended by Mrs McPherson who had served as St Peter Port parish midwife for the past sixteen years. The baby had been lying transversely and Mrs McPherson had attempted to deliver it by pulling on its arm. Mrs Le Marchant's sister, also present at the birth, testified that, although it was clear that there was something wrong with the delivery, Mrs MacPherson had refused to call a doctor and went on pulling at the baby's arm, causing the mother great suffering. Eventually, Mrs Le Marchant's husband took it upon himself to call Dr Gibson, who arrived to find the mother in a state of exhaustion 'with the child's right arm hanging by only a thread from the vagina'. Dr Gibson went on to deliver the baby himself, but it was dead on delivery. On questioning Mrs MacPherson, the doctor had found her 'rather muddled'. The court judged Mrs McPherson to have been negligent in failing to summon medical assistance. She was convicted of manslaughter and sentenced to three years' imprisonment.[124]

In England and Wales, untrained midwives like Mrs McPherson became much thinner on the ground after the passage of the 1902 Midwives Act.[125] This statute created a national roll of midwives and decreed that no-one whose name was not on the roll could legally practise after 1903. The roll contained three categories: midwives who had obtained certificates prior to 1902; uncertificated midwives whose *bona fides* were established by their practice record;[126] and new recruits who had passed the examination of the

---

[122] *Comet*, 17.11.1856.
[123] 15.5.1900, IA, AQ 0994/03.
[124] *Star*, 19.6.1900.
[125] A similar Act was passed in Scotland in 1915.
[126] These were permitted to practise only until 1910.

Central Midwives Board (CMB). The CMB was a new body created by the 1902 statute in order to supervise and examine midwives. A second Midwives Act in 1918 required local authorities to pay the fees of doctors summoned in an emergency by midwives, and another in 1936 compelled local authorities to provide a salaried midwifery service adequate to the needs of their area.[127]

In 1922, Jersey passed its own version of the Midwives Act which incorporated many of the same provisions.[128] This provoked an immediate request from Guernsey's Medical Officer of Health for similar action locally. Guernsey's authorities did not however consider the matter a priority, and nothing was done. In the event, work on legislation only began in the mid-1930s. This was prompted by the personal intervention of the Bailiff after nine women had died in childbirth in the course of 1933.[129] The result was the Midwives Ordinance of 1936.[130] This ordinance was based on the English Midwives Acts of 1902 and 1918. It introduced registration for midwives and prohibited the unregistered from practising. Midwives could only be included on Guernsey's new register if they possessed an appropriate professional qualification or had practised in the island for at least five years and been approved as competent by an examining panel. Importantly, the ordinance also placed an onus on midwives to call for the assistance of a doctor 'in the case of any sudden or urgent necessity', in which case the States' Board of Health would pay the doctor's fee (up to a maximum of one and a half guineas). This fee was to be recoverable from the patient if her circumstances permitted.[131] During 1937, emergency medical aid was summoned by midwives in 114 cases. This cost the States £182, of which £42 was recovered from patients.[132]

The 1936 Midwives Ordinance was the States' first major venture into the field of maternal and infant health. By this time, however, the United Kingdom had made much greater strides. Most notably, the Maternity and

---

[127] Loudon, *Death in Childbirth*, pp. 207–9.
[128] *Loi (1922) sur la Santé Publique (Sages-Femmes)*.
[129] 5.10.1933, IA, LO 027-22; *Billet*, 28.12.1934.
[130] Ord, 1.2.1936.
[131] These provisions were refined but not substantially changed by a second Midwives Ordinance in 1950.
[132] *Billet*, 13.7.1938.

Child Welfare Act of 1918 had empowered local authorities to fund the provision of midwives, health visitors, infant welfare centres and day nurseries for mothers who needed them.[133] Guernsey's States saw no call to replicate this legislation, and all these areas remained the preserve of the island's voluntary sector throughout the inter-war period.

The most important contribution to maternal and child health in inter-war Guernsey was made by the island's District Nursing Associations, which supported themselves by means of subscriptions, fees, donations, legacies, bazaars and flag-days. Guernsey had three such Associations: the Vale and St Sampsons Association, founded in 1902; the St Peter Port Association, founded in 1913; and the Country Parishes Association, founded in 1932.[134] All of these Associations provided Queen's Institute-trained midwives at a reasonable cost.[135] The surviving casebook of Myra Pipe, a St Peter Port Association midwife, shows that, under the guidance of doctors, local District Nursing Association midwives were by the 1930s providing efficient and up-to-date care: in 1937, just two years after sulphonamides had become available, Nurse Pipe was routinely administering them to her patients.[136] All three District Nursing Associations also ran Mother and Baby Centres, which provided advice (though not care) to expectant and post-parturient mothers. In addition to the District Nursing Associations, a number of Guernsey's parishes were served by Infant Health Associations which concentrated primarily on the provision of milk and food supplements.[137]

The island's first dedicated Maternity Home was opened under the auspices of the St Peter Port District Nursing Association in 1922. Named

---

[133] A. Hardy, *Health and Medicine in Britain since 1860* (Basingstoke, 2001), p. 87.
[134] *Star*, 18.7.1958.
[135] The Queen's Nursing Institute was established in 1887 to train nurses for the British District Nursing Service. All District Nursing Associations were locally funded and organised but were usually affiliated to the Queen's Institute.
[136] IA, AQ 0819/72. Myra Pipe worked for the St Peter Port District Nursing Association between 1934 and 1954.
[137] The records of the Infant Health Associations have not survived, but references to these bodies may be found in newspapers and *Billets* (for instance, *Billet*, 31.10.1917 and *Star*, 18.7.1958).

the Lady Ozanne Maternity Home after one of its patrons,[138] the Home had five wards, including a labour ward and a ward for unmarried mothers. This institution was intended to accommodate less well-off mothers who required or desired residential care, and charged fees according to its patients' means.[139] In 1924, some seventy-six babies were delivered at the Lady Ozanne Home, together with a further nineteen in the island's commercial nursing home.[140] The remaining 658 babies born in Guernsey that year were delivered at their parents' residence.[141]

The overwhelming majority of Guernsey's babies continued to be born at home until 1940, when the situation was abruptly reversed in the space of a few months. In 1939, the British government had established what it called the 'Emergency Maternity Service', which aimed to shield parturient women from the danger of air-raids by concentrating them in residential maternity units.[142] This was a logical development of the trend towards the hospitalisation of childbirth already noticeable in inter-war Britain.[143] At the beginning of the Occupation, the States' Health Officer, Dr Angelo Symons, issued an instruction that all births were henceforth to take place at the States' Emergency Hospital, adding that anyone opting for a home birth did so at their own risk, since curfews, blackouts and petrol shortages meant that medical attention could not be guaranteed.[144] Childbirth was hospitalised almost overnight, and the States also acquired a monopoly in the provision of maternity facilities which they never subsequently relinquished. The Lady Ozanne Maternity Home closed during the Occupation and never reopened. It was formally dissolved and its assets distributed among the three District Nursing Associations in 1954. When the Emergency Hospital itself closed in the late 1940s, the States opened their own dedicated Maternity Hospital,

---

[138] Frances Ozanne, *née* Boyd, the Irish-born wife of Sir Edward Chepmell Ozanne, Bailiff between 1915 and 1922.
[139] *Star*, 26.10.1922.
[140] The Alexandra Nursing Home at Les Frieteaux, St Martins.
[141] *Star*, 22.3.1926.
[142] Loudon, *Death in Childbirth*, pp. 263-4.
[143] Hardy, *Health and Medicine*, p. 105.
[144] *Star*, 16.7.1940.

and, for the next quarter-century, the vast majority of insular births took place there.[145]

Between 1945 and the end of our period, only one further important development took place in the area of maternal and child health. This was the introduction of Health Visitors. Thirty years after the Medical Officer of Health had first called for them, two States' Health Visitors were appointed in 1949.[146] This was too little too late: births were by this time at around their post-war peak, and the volume of work was too great for the two women appointed. They reported the following year that they were unable to visit all newborns in their homes, let alone pay them the quarterly post-natal visits which were also part of their duty.[147] Mindful as ever of costs, the States increased numbers only slowly, so that by 1956 there were three Health Visitors, and by 1963 there were four.[148]

One innovation notable for *not* having been introduced during our period was States' maternity benefit. The state had been providing this benefit to working women in Britain since 1909, and in France since 1913.[149] In Guernsey, States' maternity benefit was not introduced until 1971.[150]

For all the States' tardiness in these matters, we should not lose sight of the huge advances in the field of maternal and infant health achieved in Guernsey between 1900 and the 1950s. A comparison of the indicators used by successive Medical Officers of Health will summarise these advances. In the period 1900-4, nearly 25 per cent of all Guernsey's deaths each year were of infants aged under 12 months.[151] By 1959, this proportion had dropped

---

[145] The States replaced the Emergency Hospital with a new general hospital in 1949. It was to this facility that births were ultimately transferred when the Maternity Hospital was closed down in 1973 on the grounds that it no longer met modern safety standards. In 1977, the States took over the District Nursing Associations, transforming them into the Community Nursing Service.
[146] *Billets*, 3.11.1919, 19.7.1950.
[147] *Billet*, 19.7.1950.
[148] *Billets*, 27.6.1956, 29.9.1965.
[149] L. Abrams, *The Making of Modern Woman: Europe, 1789-1918* (Harlow, 2002), p. 123.
[150] Social Insurance (Overlapping Benefits) (Amendment) (Guernsey) Regulations 1971; Social Insurance (Maternity Benefit) (Guernsey) Regulations 1971.
[151] *Billet*, 31.10.1917.

to just over 2 per cent.[152] In roughly the same space of time, the stillbirth rate had fallen from 67.7 per thousand live births to 19.7.[153] Maternal mortality had also sharply declined. In the early twentieth century, almost every year saw the death of one or two women in childbirth. During the whole decade of the 1950s, there was only one such death, after which there were no more until 1964.[154]

This concludes our exploration of the background to nineteenth- and early twentieth-century Guernseywomen's lives. In the next chapter we shall turn our attention to an area which was very much at the forefront of their experience. This chapter will explore the subject of marriage. Opening with a general discussion of the origins and function of marriage, the chapter will go on to consider the evolution of local laws governing this institution. It will then broaden the analysis to include a variety of related topics which range from separation and divorce, to property-ownership and inheritance.

---

[152] *Billet*, 14.12.1960.
[153] *Billets*, 30.9.1914, 14.12.1960.
[154] *Billets*, 27.6.1956, 29.9.1965.

3

Marriage

General

Marriage, throughout the world and throughout history, has been a near-universal institution.[1] It probably originated as an informal way of organising sexual companionship, child-rearing and the daily tasks of life. With the passage of time it became more elaborately regulated, gradually accreting around itself a whole body of conventions, practices and laws, which varied in detail from culture to culture, but, because human imperatives were everywhere similar, resembled each other in fundamentals. For centuries, marriage did much of the work which governments do today. It organised the production and distribution of goods and people; it co-ordinated the division of labour by gender and age; it orchestrated people's personal rights and obligations in everything from sexual relations to the inheritance of property. For the aristocracy and gentry, marriage was primarily about perpetuating the dynastic line and conserving wealth within it. For the middling classes, it was often about maintaining a household enterprise—a farm or a business—that could not be maintained by one person alone. For the working classes, it was about mutual support in making a living and bringing up children.

In western Europe, marriage came under the jurisdiction of the church in the twelfth century, from which point it was subject to Canon law and the

---

[1] A good general introduction to marriage may be found in S.J. Coontz, *Marriage, A History* (New York, 2005). This paragraph draws in particular on the Introduction and chapter 3.

ecclesiastical courts.² Drawing on scriptural pronouncements concerning marriage, church leaders came to consider it as a sacrament—'Holy Matrimony'. As a result, the institution came to be regarded as a divinely ordained state governed by Biblical injunction, and acquired a semi-mystical overlay while retaining its practical attributes.

In the mid-to-late eighteenth century, marriage in western Europe acquired a further accretion with the introduction of romantic love as a central ingredient. In previous centuries, practicality had dominated, and mutual affection between spouses, where it existed, was seen merely as a bonus.³ This changed in what historians call the 'Romantic' period, which saw the birth of the idea that love was not only desirable in marriage, but an essential prerequisite. This idea rapidly gained currency, to the extent that, by the twentieth century, it had come to predominate over all other notions of marriage.⁴

If we cut through these religious and romantic overlays, however, marriage in times past can be understood essentially as a contract. Mona Caird, a Victorian feminist, lucidly defined this contract as one by which a woman surrendered her person, property and freedom to a man in return for the right to be maintained.⁵ Society as then constituted allowed women so few options for self-sufficiency that most were obliged to marry in order to survive, and this dependence meant that marriage came upon men's terms. It was these terms which were embodied in the various rules and regulations surrounding marriage. The rest of this chapter will seek to demonstrate how these rules applied to Guernsey.

---

[2] M.E. Wiesner-Hanks, *Gender in History: Global Perspectives* (2001; Oxford, 2011 edn), p. 37.
[3] Coontz, *Marriage*, p. 5.
[4] The precise nature of 'love' in this context has always been nebulous, and to an extent it was a cultural construct: a fusion of sexual attraction or infatuation with mystical notions of transcendence and permanence. Notwithstanding that experience has repeatedly put the latter in doubt, the idea has enduring purchase.
[5] M. Caird, *The Morality of Marriage and Other Essays on the Status and Destiny of Woman* (London, 1897).

Marriage in Guernsey—facts and figures

We will begin by examining the statistics of marriage in Guernsey. In the first decade covered by this book, 1850-9, around 250 marriages were solemnised in Guernsey each year. This slowly increased in tandem with population growth to reach 300 by 1890-1910. After a slight drop in the First World War decade, numbers rose again to about 320 a year in the 1920s, broadly plateauing here until 1939. In this year—prompted by anticipations of conflict—the number of marriages climbed to an unprecedented peak of 450. Numbers fell back sharply during the Occupation, only to soar again with the return of evacuees, reaching a second twentieth-century peak of 439 in 1949. Thereafter and until the end of the 1950s, the number of marriages solemnised in Guernsey settled at about 330 per year.[6]

Translated into rates per head of population, there were about seven or eight new marriages per year for every thousand Guernsey residents between 1850 and 1900. This was broadly similar to the rate at which marriages took place in England and Wales, save that Guernsey's rates were slightly lower during the period up to 1880, when unbalanced sex ratios impacted most significantly on women's marriage opportunities.[7] During the 1920s, 1930s and late 1940s, Guernsey's marriage rates were marginally higher than those of England and Wales, but the rate in both jurisdictions harmonised at about 7.5 per thousand in the 1950s. Historically, this was not a particularly high rate, but it was higher than rates seen in the previous two decades, as also in the remainder of the twentieth century.

---

[6] Nineteenth-century figures are from church and civil marriage registers (microfilm, PL), twentieth-century figures from *Billets*, 20.9.1916, 31.10.1917, 29.11.1922, 5.12.1923, 27.10.1926, 24.10.1928, 29.10.1930, 29.2.1933, 27.12.1946, 11.7.1951, 18.5.1955, 14.12.1960. See also *Star*, 7.3.1950 and R.-M. Crossan, *Guernsey, 1814-1914: Migration and Modernisation* (Woodbridge, 2007), pp. 222-5.

[7] Precise rates were as follows: 1850s - Guernsey, 8.2; England and Wales, 8.5; 1860s - Guernsey, 7.7; England and Wales, 8.4; 1870s - Guernsey, 7.9; England and Wales, 8.2; 1880s - Guernsey, 8.4; England and Wales, 7.5; 1890s - Guernsey, 8.2; England and Wales, 7.8; 1900-9 - Guernsey, 7.5; England and Wales, 7.8. For the sources from which Guernsey's marriage rates were calculated, see previous note. English and Welsh rates from ONS (series FM2 No. 16), *Marriage and Divorce Statistics: Historical Series on Marriage and Divorce in England and Wales, 1837-1983* (London, 1990).

In 1851, according to census data, 56 per cent of adults in the Bailiwick of Guernsey were married; 12 per cent were widowed; and 32 per cent were single and had never been married.[8] The proportion of adults who were married increased steadily over ensuing decades to reach 70 per cent in 1951. This increase was not caused by any decline in widowhood, since the widowed proportion remained stable at around one-tenth of the adult population. It was caused instead by a decline in the proportion of the never-married, which had fallen from 32 per cent in 1851 to 19 per cent in 1951. This decline was partly attributable to the improvement in sex ratios, which allowed more women to find partners. However, a substantial fall in the age of marriage also played a part. A fall in Guernsey's marriage age first became noticeable at around the turn of the twentieth century, but early marriage was at its most popular in the 1950s. In 1851, only about a fifth of 20-to-24-year-olds returned themselves as married, but a third of them did so in 1951.[9] The post-war enthusiasm for marriage was replicated all over the western world, and the 1950s have widely been characterised as 'marriage's golden age'.[10]

Another salient feature of the Bailiwick marriage pattern was that, at all times between 1851 and 1951, adult men, though fewer in number than women, were more likely to be married than their female contemporaries. As a proportion of their numbers, 10 per cent more men than women returned themselves as currently married in 1851, and 6 per cent more in 1951. This was partly because fewer women than men ever married in the first place: in 1851, 16 percent of women had reached the age of 65 without ever having been married, while the figure for men was 10 per cent (15 per cent and 8 per cent respectively in 1951). It was also in no small part due to men's greater propensity to remarry when widowed (even at relatively advanced ages). In 1851, 57 per cent of female over-65s returned themselves as widowed, but

---

[8] Adulthood began at 20 in Guernsey, this being the age of majority in Norman customary law. Census data in this section are synthesised from published census reports and tables in Parliamentary Papers (for references, see Bibliography). These data are also available at www.histpop.org.

[9] Note, however, that the move to early marriage affected women more than men. In 1851, 26 per cent of women aged 20-24 were married, compared with 17 per cent of men in this age group. By 1951, some 51 per cent of women aged 20-24 were married, but the figure for men was only 26 per cent.

[10] Coontz, *Marriage*, p. 225.

only 33 per cent of male over-65s (49 per cent and 25 per cent in 1951). Women tended to marry just once and spend a significant part of their lives in widowhood. Men married not just once, but twice and even three times: not only did working widowers need help with their homes and children, they were also financially better placed to attract a mate.[11]

Having considered statistics, we will now look briefly at attitudes to marriage which were particularly characteristic of Guernsey. We will begin with one attitude which is notoriously difficult to assess, namely that of contemporaries to informal cohabitation. Guernsey's church registers and censuses are necessarily silent on such unions, but other sources suggest that they were by no means unheard of. Marie De Garis has mentioned that 'alliances of an irregular character' were a not uncommon feature of the countryside.[12] In St Peter Port, too, a perusal of police, court or poor law records shows that a fair number of such unions existed at all times during our period. They were certainly not encouraged by religious and civil authorities, but Guernsey law recognised their existence and made allowances for them. Unlike the law of England and Wales, the island's customary law had always permitted the legitimisation of children born out of wedlock on their parents' eventual marriage.[13]

Perhaps the main characteristic of insular marriage during the nineteenth and early twentieth centuries was, however, endogamy—the tendency for like to pair with like. The strongest manifestation of this tendency lay in the fact that native islanders from nearly all social strata were more inclined to marry other islanders than pair with incomers, and *vice versa*.[14] Among natives themselves, endogamy also had a class dimension. In the countryside, land-owning farmers whose aim it was to preserve and augment property in the family name, preferred their offspring to choose spouses who could bring

---

[11] For more on this phenomenon, common throughout Britain, see P. Thane, *Happy Families? History and Family Policy* (London, 2010), pp. 46-7.
[12] M. De Garis, *Folklore of Guernsey* (Guernsey, 1975), p. 25.
[13] T. Le Marchant, *Remarques et Animadversions sur l'Approbation des Lois et Coustumier de Normandie usités ès Jurisdictions de Guernezé*, 2 vols (c.1660; Guernsey, 1826), 1, p. 44. This was also the case under Scottish law, but it was not possible in England and Wales until the passage of the Legitimacy Act of 1926.
[14] For a detailed study of nineteenth-century endogamy, see Crossan, *Guernsey, 1814-1914*, pp. 220-7.

property to the union.[15] Peter Girard has observed that a farmer's daughter marrying 'below her class' into a family without land and property would often be ostracised by her relatives.[16] In a small community, this made cousin marriages fairly common. Although precise numbers of such marriages are unknowable (church registers did not record degrees of kinship between spouses), Marie De Garis has observed that they were sufficiently prevalent to result 'in definable facial characteristics which could immediately identify a person with [a] locality'.[17]

St Peter Port was equally class-conscious in marriage matters. Victorian travel writers often mocked the town for its snobbery, basing themselves on the notorious divide between the mercantile elite of the former *entrepôt* and the stratum immediately beneath them.[18] These groups had historically married among themselves, and those who broke ranks often suffered social consequences. When the successful merchant (and future Bailiff) Daniel De Lisle Brock made an 'imprudent marriage with a woman in a very inferior situation', he found himself obliged to ensure that his wife, Esther Tourtel, was out of view whenever he entertained company.[19] Although the original Sixties and Forties families had largely disappeared from St Peter Port by the end of the century, members of the equivalent groups which replaced them continued to practise class endogamy until at least the Second World War. It should be noted, however, that, when members of the urban middle and upper classes could not find local partners of commensurate status, both were more amenable to geographically exogenous unions than their counterparts in the country or lower down the social scale.[20]

---

[15] R. Hocart, *The Country People of Guernsey and their Agriculture, 1640–1840* (Guernsey, 2016), pp. 220, 225.
[16] P.J. Girard, 'Country life and some insular enterprises of the late 19th century', *TSG*, 19 (1972), p. 89.
[17] De Garis, *Folklore*, pp. 17, 24.
[18] The latter were famously known as 'Forties' and the former as 'Sixties'—labels which dated from the opening of St Peter Port's Assembly Rooms and stemmed from the number of families assigned to each group. The 'Sixties', who had founded the Rooms, barred the 'Forties' from admission (H. Boland, *Les Iles de la Manche* (Paris, 1904), pp. 133-4).
[19] W.G. Walmesley (ed. K.C. Renault), *A Pedestrian Tour through the Islands of Guernsey and Jersey* (1821; Chichester, 1992 edn), p. 41.
[20] Crossan, *Guernsey, 1814–1914*, pp. 185-7.

Families who enforced class endogamy in both town and country prized their respectability, which was vital to their social status. In order to preserve this respectability, society insisted on the strict observance of accepted formalities in all things marital. It is with these formalities that the rest of this chapter will be concerned. To begin with, we will consider the legal framework surrounding the institution of marriage in Guernsey.

Marriage in Guernsey—the law

Sources of Guernsey law

Guernsey law rested on the foundation of Norman customary law—*la Coutume normande*.[21] Customary law has been described as a body of legal practices which have evolved spontaneously within a specific region and are applicable to that region only.[22] In the medieval period, most French provinces had their own *Coutumes*. Norman law, which began to evolve long before the creation of the Duchy of Normandy, was one of the first French regional *Coutumes* to be written down. The oldest written version, *le Très Ancien Coutumier*, appeared between 1200 and 1220, and has been described as 'a historical monument to an older society' on the very day of its appearance.[23] An expanded version, *le Grand Coutumier*, appeared between

---

[21] This was also to some extent true of post-Conquest England and Wales, pre-Free State Ireland, and Scotland. For this reason, there were important similarities in marriage law over all the British Isles. We shall return to this theme later. For a summary of the sources of Guernsey law, see G. Dawes, 'A brief history of Guernsey law', *The Jersey Law Review* (February 2006).
[22] J. Musset, *Le Régime des Biens entre Epoux en Droit Normand du XVIe Siècle à la Révolution Française* (Caen, 1997), p. 7.
[23] Z.A. Schneider, *The King's Bench: Bailiwick Magistrates and Local Governance in Normandy, 1670–1740* (Woodbridge, 2008), p. 114.

1235 and 1258.²⁴ It was this version which became the main reference point for Guernsey customary law over the following centuries.²⁵

From time to time, local jurists seeking clarification on points of detail also referred to published commentaries on Norman law, which added explanatory glosses and elucidations to the *Coutumier*. One such commentary—Guillaume Terrien's *Commentaires du Droict Civil tant Public que Privé Observé au Pays et Duché de Normandie*—was published in 1574. This publication took on a particular significance for Guernsey, when, during the early 1580s, Crown officials requested the Royal Court to set out Guernsey's laws in writing. Guillaume Terrien's commentary being the latest available, the Royal Court's statement of laws took the form of a review of his text with notes on what accorded with, or varied from, local law and usage. The statement was ratified by Order in Council and, as *L'Approbation des Lois*, assumed authoritative status.²⁶

Two further works of importance for Guernsey followed in the seventeenth and eighteenth centuries: Thomas Le Marchant's *Remarques et Animadversions* of c.1660 and Laurent Carey's *Essai sur les Institutions* of c.1750.²⁷ These commentaries, both by local writers, further clarified aspects of Guernsey's customary law and were frequently referred to by local jurists.

---

²⁴ Musset, *Régime des Biens entre Epoux*, p. 12. The most accessible versions of *le Grand Coutumier* available today are W.L. De Gruchy (ed.), *L'Ancienne Coutume de Normandie* (Jersey, 1881) and J.A. Everard (ed.), *Le Grand Coutumier de Normandie* (Jersey, 2009).
²⁵ In Normandy, *le Grand Coutumier* was superseded in 1583 by an official revised version compiled by command of the French king. Its full title was *Coustumes du Pays de Normandie, Anciens Ressorts et Enclaves d'Iceluy*, but it was more commonly known as *la Coutume Réformée*. This *Coutume* formed the basis of mainland Norman law until its abolition by Napoleon who instituted a uniform legal system over the whole of France through the introduction of his *Code Civil* in 1804 and *Code Pénal* in 1810 (Musset, *Régime des Biens entre Epoux*, pp. 18-19).
²⁶ O in C, 27.10.1583; see also *Approbation des Lois, Coutumes, et Usages de l'Ile de Guernesey ratifiée au Conseil Privé le 27 Octobre 1583* (Guernsey, 1822). On this episode, see D.M. Ogier, *The Government and Law of Guernsey* (Guernsey, 2005), p. 84.
²⁷ T. Le Marchant, *Remarques et Animadversions sur l'Approbation des Lois et Coustumier de Normandie usités ès Jurisdictions de Guernezé*, 2 vols (c.1660; Guernsey, 1826); L. Carey, *Essai sur les Institutions, Lois et Coutumes de l'Ile de Guernesey* (c.1750; Guernsey, 1889).

The position of women under Norman customary law

Scholars generally agree that the Norman *Coutume* embodied 'the most severe situation of inferiority for women' of all the French regional customs.[28] Usually, this severity is attributed to the sheer age of the *Coutume* and the fact that it carried the imprint of Frankish and Norse culture, which was warlike, patriarchal and feudal.[29] In a feudal society, ownership of property brought with it a duty to perform military service, which was the monopoly of men. From this sprang the *Coutume*'s emphasis on male ownership and male succession, which relegated wives to little more than instruments for perpetuating the male line.[30] Reflecting this status, *le Grand Coutumier* gave husbands complete ownership and control of the persons and property of their wives, stating explicitly that a husband was entitled to do as he wished with both his wife and her possessions,[31] and that all she owned belonged to him.[32] Effectively, a wife's legal personality was subsumed into that of her husband. These principles were re-stated in Terrien's commentary and *L'Approbation des Lois*, and they were later repeated by Le Marchant and Carey.[33] This view had repercussions not only for wives but also for daughters. Since daughters were destined to perpetuate not their own but a stranger lineage, the *Coutume* deprived them of any right to inherit family property unless the family had no sons.[34]

---

[28] Schneider, *King's Bench*, p. 118.

[29] Musset, *Régime des Biens entre Epoux*, p. 203.

[30] That women remained 'blood strangers' to their husbands' line was expressed in the fact that they retained their maiden surnames after marriage, a practice followed for centuries in Guernsey (S. Poirey, 'The role of lineage in matrimonial union in Normandy', in G. Dawes (ed.), *Commise 1204: Studies in the History and Law of Continental and Insular Normandy* (Guernsey, 2005), pp. 73, 84).

[31] '*Il peut faire à sa volonté de elle, et de ses choses, et de son héritaige*', (De Gruchy (ed.), *Coutume de Normandie*, p. 241).

[32] '*Elles ne peuvent rien avoir pour elles que tout ne soit à leurs maris*', (De Gruchy (ed.), *Coutume de Normandie*, p. 45).

[33] G. Terrien, *Commentaires du Droict Civil tant Public que Privé Observé au Pays et Duché de Normandie* (1574; Rouen, 1654 edn), p. 16; *Approbation des Lois*, p. 1; Le Marchant, *Remarques et Animadversions*, 1, p. 252; Carey, *Essai sur les Institutions*, pp. 119, 122-3.

[34] De Gruchy (ed.), *Coutume de Normandie*, p. 79. See also S. Poirey, 'The status of women in Norman law before the Revolution', *Guernsey Law Journal*, 27 (1999), p. 137.

Following the Norman Conquest, many of these notions were transplanted to Britain. In England and Wales, they crystallised over time into the legal doctrine of 'coverture', whereby, as the eminent jurist Sir William Blackstone put it,

> [husband and wife] are one person in law: that is, the very being or legal existence of the woman is suspended during the marriage, or at least is incorporated and consolidated into that of the husband; under whose wing, protection and cover she performs everything.[35]

In Scotland, there was no formal doctrine of coverture, but, in practical terms, the situation of wives was substantially the same.[36] In France, notwithstanding the abolition of regional *Coutumes* in 1804, the situation was also similar, since the *Code Civil* which replaced the *Coutumes* enshrined married women's status as minors under spousal tutelage, and subjected them to many of the same disabilities as affected British women.[37]

Evolution of Guernsey marriage law

By twelfth-century papal decree, all that was necessary for a binding marriage was the verbal exchange of vows, expressed in the present tense and witnessed by two persons.[38] This came to an end during the Reformation, when both Protestant and Catholic churches decreed that no marriage would henceforth be valid without a witnessed public ceremony, accompanied by a written entry in a parish register.[39] In England, officially prescribed forms for the solemnisation of marriage were definitively set out in the Anglican Canons

---

[35] Sir W. Blackstone, *Commentaries on the Laws of England*, 4 vols (Oxford, 1765-9), 1, p. 430.
[36] K. Barclay, *Love, Intimacy and Power: Marriage and Patriarchy in Scotland, 1650-1850* (Manchester, 2011), pp. 48-51.
[37] J.F. McMillan, *France and Women, 1789-1914* (London, 2000), pp. 38-40.
[38] Coontz, *Marriage*, p. 106.
[39] L. Stone, *The Road to Divorce: England, 1530-1987* (1990; Oxford, 1995 edn), pp. 26, 52, 55. Note, however, that, in Scotland, a witnessed verbal contract in the present tense not only remained binding in ecclesiastical law but carried with it full civil property rights until the passage of 1939 Marriage (Scotland) Act.

approved by the Crown in 1604.[40] These procedures were broadly followed in Guernsey after the imposition of Anglicanism in 1663.[41]

Procedures for the solemnisation of marriage in England were ultimately made a matter of civil rather than ecclesiastical law in 1753, when Lord Hardwicke's Act for the Better Preventing of Clandestine Marriages set out a modified version of the Canon law forms and laid down that any celebrant purporting to solemnise a marriage without observing them would henceforth be liable to fourteen years' transportation.[42] Hardwicke's Act applied only to England and Wales. Guernsey, for its part, continued broadly to observe old Canon law. This rendered the island attractive to those who, for one reason or another, wished to circumvent the provisions of the 1753 Act. The *Gentleman's Magazine* reported in 1760 that there were always vessels ready at Southampton 'for carrying on the trade of smuggling weddings to Guernsey'.[43] Most of these marriages seem to have been performed in St Peter Port. The registers of the Town Church show that the average annual number of marriages almost doubled from 117 in 1740-9 to

---

[40] Articles 62-3 and 99-104 of the Canons related to marriage. Technical details are as follows: marriages were only to take place in Anglican churches and chapels, only during canonical hours, and only after banns had been called on three Sundays in the spouses' home parishes, or after the issue of a licence. In the case of banns, if the parties were minors, a parent or guardian had to give his consent personally or 'by sufficient testimony'. In the case of a licence, the parties had to swear that they were of age or had parental consent, and were required to give security in support of such statements. No residence requirements were specified for either banns or licences.

[41] It should however be noted that Guernsey never formally adopted the 1604 Canons, nor any other (N.M. Ozanne, 'La Cour Ecclésiastique', *The Review of the Guernsey Society*, 48 (1993), p. 107; Ogier, *Government and Law*, p.18).

[42] Under the terms of Hardwicke's Act, the solemnisation of marriage continued to be restricted to Anglican clergymen in Church of England premises. Provisions regarding banns and licences remained essentially the same, with the important exception of a new requirement, in the case of banns, for the parties to give notice to the clergyman at least seven days before these were to be called, and in the case of licences, for at least one party to have resided for four weeks in the parish where the marriage was to be performed. Where one or both parties were minors, the Act additionally stipulated that the requirement for parental consent was to be strictly enforced. For more on Hardwicke's Act, see J.R. Gillis, *For Better for Worse: British Marriages, 1600 to the Present* (Oxford, 1985), pp. 140-1.

[43] *Gentleman's Magazine*, 30 (1760), pp. 30-1. See also J. Jeaffreson, *Brides and Bridals* (London, 1872), pp. 203-5.

228 in 1750-9.[44] The number of 'foreign' marriages performed in St Peter Port continued to grow through the rest of the century, and by 1790-9, more than two-thirds of Town Church marriages were between non-locals. In the nineteenth century, much of the foreign marriage business transferred to the rural parish of St Peters, where it continued for many decades.[45]

Almost a century after Hardwicke, Guernsey followed English precedent by also bringing marriage within the ambit of the civil law. This move was directly prompted by the passage in England and Wales of the 1836 Marriage Act, which had introduced the concept of civil marriage before a Registrar and permitted non-Anglican clergymen to conduct marriages in their own places of worship.[46] In 1837, a group of Guernsey Nonconformists had petitioned the Royal Court for the same rights as their co-religionists had been granted in England and Wales. Proposals for a new law were put before the States in 1838, but were not approved until 1840 owing to opposition from the Anglican rectors sitting in the legislature.[47] The new law, ratified by Order in Council of 3 October 1840 and applicable to Guernsey only (not the whole Bailiwick), introduced civil registration of births, marriages and deaths as well as setting out provisions for civil marriage and for the

---

[44] Town Church marriage registers (microfilm, PL).

[45] The business moved to St Peters during the rectorships of Thomas Brock and his son Carey Brock who also served as Anglican Deans and Commissaries and thus issuers of the special licences favoured by outsiders wishing to marry swiftly. For more on this matter, see Crossan, *Guernsey, 1814-1914*, p. 223.

[46] The 1836 Marriage Act was intended to operate in conjunction with the 1836 Births and Deaths Registration Act which had created the General Register Office and local Registrars, who, as well as being responsible for civil registration, were now also empowered to conduct marriages. In further allowing non-Anglican clergymen to conduct marriages, the Marriage Act stipulated that non-Anglican places of worship where marriages were to be performed should be formally registered as marriage venues with the local Superintendent Registrar, and that a Registrar should be present at non-Anglican marriage services. Notice of every marriage, unless by Anglican licence or under Anglican banns, was to be given in writing to the Superintendent Registrar and recorded in his Marriage Register. Parties wishing to marry on Anglican premises while circumventing the need for banns or licences were permitted to give notice to the Registrar in the same way as those opting for a civil ceremony or marrying in non-Anglican churches. Anglican churches were to send quarterly returns of marriages performed in them to the General Register Office in London.

[47] On this episode, see J. Duncan, *The History of Guernsey* (London, 1841), p. 576 and R. Hocart, *An Island Assembly: The Development of the States of Guernsey, 1700-1949* (Guernsey, 1988), pp. 31-2.

solemnisation of marriages in Nonconformist churches.[48] The law laid down that the Greffier of the Royal Court was henceforth to be Guernsey's Registrar General.[49] He was given authority to conduct civil marriages at the Greffe, and parties wishing to contract such a marriage, or marry in a Nonconformist church, were obliged to notify him in writing.[50] The 1840 law also stipulated that Nonconformist churches where marriages were to be performed were to be licensed by the Royal Court and required the presence of the Greffier or Deputy Greffier at their weddings. Anglican churches did not require licensing and were left free to continue marrying couples by banns or licence without prior notice to the Greffier. The foregoing suggests strong parallels with England and Wales' 1836 Marriage Act. However, Guernsey's 1840 marriage law differed from the English statute in two important respects. Firstly, it excluded Roman Catholic churches from being licensed for marriage. Secondly, it failed to ensure the central registration of Anglican marriages.[51]

Despite the new facility for civil and Nonconformist weddings, most marriages in Guernsey continued to be conducted by the Church of England for many decades after 1840. Analysis of marriage registers shows that, of the 17,055 marriages which took place in the island between 1850 and 1913, some 73 per cent were solemnised in Anglican churches.[52]

After 1840, no further local laws were enacted in respect of marriage until 1907, when a law was passed concerning marriage with a deceased wife's sister. The context in which this law was passed is complex and calls for explanation. Prior to the twentieth century, the marriage of persons related by consanguinity or affinity had been viewed as an ecclesiastical matter throughout most of Europe. In Guernsey, as in England and Wales, it was

---

[48] In Jersey, a similar law—*la Loi sur l'Etat Civil*—was passed in 1842. This also established a register of births, marriages and deaths and enabled civil marriages to take place.
[49] The Greffier was Clerk of the Court and already acted as the registrar of the Royal Court and the States.
[50] As under the 1836 Marriage Act, parties marrying by Anglican rites could also opt to give notice to the Greffier if they wished to circumvent the need for church banns or licences.
[51] Article 9 of the law placed an onus on Anglican clergymen to notify the Greffier of all marriages celebrated in their churches for a fee of 6d per marriage. However, the States made no funds available to pay for this service and it was never carried out.
[52] Church and civil marriage registers (microfilm, PL).

governed by the list of 'prohibited degrees' in the 1563 Anglican Book of Common Prayer. According to this document, marriage with one's late wife's sister was strictly prohibited.[53] Although a similar prohibition had obtained throughout Europe for centuries, advances in medical science had by the early 1900s led to the legalisation of such marriages in almost every western country.[54] Cognizant of this situation, the Westminster parliament had passed the Colonial Marriages Act in 1906 as a first step towards legalising marriage between a man and his late wife's sister. This Act granted full inheritance rights in England and Wales to children of marriages with deceased wives' sisters contracted in the colonies, where the law had not prohibited them. It was this law which was replicated in Guernsey by the 1907 *Loi relative au Mariage avec la Soeur d'une Femme Décédée (Possessions Britanniques)*.[55] Later in 1907, Westminster went on to pass the Deceased Wife's Sister Marriage Act. This statute put England and Wales on a par with the rest of western Europe by removing all remaining impediments to marriage in this jurisdiction between a man and his dead wife's sister. Two years later, Guernsey again followed suit with its 1909 *Loi relative au Mariage avec la Soeur d'une Femme Décédée* which similarly removed all impediments.[56]

---

[53] The Church based its policy on the Biblical 'one flesh' doctrine (Ephesians 5:31) and deemed man and wife to count as one person for the purposes of computing relationship, thus someone related to a wife by consanguinity was deemed to be related to a husband by affinity in the same degree.

[54] N.F. Anderson, 'The "Marriage with a Deceased Wife's Sister Bill" controversy: incest anxiety and the defence of family purity in Victorian England', *Journal of British Studies*, 21 (1982), p. 82.

[55] O in C, 26.3.1907.

[56] O in C, 3.7.1909. In 1921, Westminster passed another Act to remove the prohibition on marriage to deceased brothers' widows, and, in 1931 and 1960, it further extended the range of permissible relationships by means, respectively, of the Marriage (Prohibited Degrees of Relationship) Act and the Marriage (Enabling) Act. Guernsey brought its own law into line with the 1921 and 1931 Acts by means of its 1936 *Loi sur les Empêchements au Mariage à cause de Parenté et sur l'Etablissement de la Juridiction Civile dans les Causes Matrimoniales* (O in C, 3.3.1936) and into line with the 1960 Act by means of the Marriage (Enabling) (Guernsey) Law 1961 (O in C, 27.4.1961). As the full title of the 1936 *Loi sur les Empêchements* suggests, this statute also formally removed all remaining jurisdiction of Guernsey's ecclesiastical court in matters matrimonial save only the power of granting Anglican marriage licences.

Guernsey's two Edwardian laws on permissible relationships within marriage had left the primary marriage law of 1840 untouched. In England and Wales, by contrast, the law of marriage had undergone a long series of refinements since 1836.[57] These changes had been noted in Guernsey, and as the Edwardian period came to an end, demand for the modernisation of Guernsey's 1840 law reached a peak. In 1909, a group of States members and others (mainly Nonconformists) petitioned the Bailiff for a comprehensive overhaul of the 1840 law.[58] A States committee was set up to look into updating the legislation, but progress towards a new law was hampered by a number of factors, not least consistent opposition from the rectors. In the event, the formulation and passage of a new marriage law took a full ten years. An acceptable version was finally agreed in December 1918 and *la Loi ayant rapport aux Mariages célébrés dans l'île de Guernesey et dans les îles d'Auregny et de Serk* was ratified by the Privy Council on 15 April 1919.

The 1919 *Loi ayant rapport aux Mariages* replaced the 1840 marriage law and, as amended, remains the primary law under which marriages are conducted in Guernsey.[59] The law introduced a number of innovations based largely on changes already enacted in England and Wales. *Inter alia*, it removed the requirement that the Greffier (or Deputy Greffier) attend non-Anglican weddings, and allowed a third party (usually the non-Anglican clergyman) to assume the function of registrar. It also enabled marriages to take place in private houses, and empowered the Greffier to grant 'special' licences enabling parties resident in Guernsey for a month to marry twenty-four hours after notice had been given. In addition, the law brought Sark and Alderney within the scope of its provisions, as also the Roman Catholic church, whose marriages prior to 1919 it explicitly recognised as legally valid. Disappointingly for the Nonconformist petitioners, however, the law left untouched most of the privileges of the Anglican church as defined in 1840, with the one significant exception that notification of Anglican marriages to the Greffier was now to be enforced on pain of a fine.

---

[57] The most important of these refinements were embodied in the Marriage Act 1840, the Marriage and Registration Act 1856, the Marriages Validity Act 1884 and the Marriages Act 1886.
[58] *Billet*, 23.4.1909; *Gazette de Guernesey*, 24.4.1909.
[59] As at 2018.

Not long after the passage of the 1919 *Loi ayant rapport aux Mariages*, Guernsey's legislature turned its attention to another aspect of marriage. This was the matter of bigamy, which, although a statutory crime in England and Wales since 1604, had never been the subject of any statutory enactment in Guernsey.[60] By means of the 1923 *Loi relative à la Bigamie*, it was formally constituted a felony with a maximum penalty of seven years' penal servitude.[61]

The following decade, the 1930s, saw the passage of the last important law concerning marriage enacted during our period. This was the 1931 *Loi relative à l'Age du Mariage*.[62] Before the passage of this statute, the minimum age at which individuals could marry fell within the purview of Canon law, which, somewhat vaguely, permitted adolescents 'over the age of puberty' to contract marriages subject to parental consent. This was substantially the same situation as pertained in the United Kingdom before the passage of the Imperial Age of Marriage Act 1929. The Westminster statute set the minimum marriage age at sixteen for both sexes, and the Guernsey statute of 1931 did the same.

We have now covered all the laws which bore directly upon marriage in Guernsey during our period. The following sections will widen the focus by looking at laws which impacted more indirectly upon marriage (and upon which marriage had an impact). These include laws relating to settlement and nationality; to property-ownership; to inheritance; and to the guardianship and custody of children.

Settlement and nationality

We have seen that, under the Norman *Coutume* and hence Guernsey's customary law, a woman's legal personality was effectively subsumed into that of her husband. This carried serious implications for married women in the areas of both settlement and nationality. We will begin with settlement (or

---

[60] This had not however prevented prosecutions for bigamy under Guernsey's common law (see, for instance, 4.11.1858, GG, *Livres en Crime*, vol. 35; 4.6.1859, *Livres en Crime*, vol. 36).
[61] O in C, 29.1.1923.
[62] O in C, 13.6.1931.

établissement as it was called in Guernsey). This was a poor law concept by which a person's eligibility to receive benefits in a parish was determined by his or her ability to demonstrate that they belonged to that parish. It was important, because, prior to the mid-twentieth-century advent of States' benefits and pensions, parochial poor relief was the main public source of financial support in times of hardship. Anyone in need of poor relief who could not prove a settlement in the parish where they required it was generally removed to the parish where they did have a settlement.[63]

In Guernsey, as in England and Wales, settlement in a parish could be proven by the fulfilment of certain formal criteria. These criteria were laid down in ever more elaborate form through a series of laws passed between 1726 and 1867.[64] By 1867, they had become very complex.[65] Native islanders who had not been able to acquire a settlement in their own right simply inherited their fathers' settlement, while non-natives retained the settlement they had in their places of origin. This applied to both males and females, with the important proviso that, once married, a woman lost her original settlement and acquired that of her husband, retaining it even if he predeceased or deserted her. This put Guernseywomen who married non-natives at considerable risk of removal, since a large proportion of incoming residents never acquired a parochial settlement in Guernsey. Thus, in 1870, 29-year-old Marie Tucker (*née* Le Poidevin) found herself despatched to Netherbury in Dorset after her Dorset-born husband

---

[63] Or, in the case of non-natives, simply put on a boat to the French or English port closest to their home parish (Crossan, *Guernsey, 1814–1914*, pp. 161–8).
[64] R.-M. Crossan, *Poverty and Welfare in Guernsey, 1560–2015* (Woodbridge, 2015), pp. 62–5.
[65] Under *la Loi relative à l'Etablissement Paroissial* (O in C, 26.6.1867) applicants for relief in a parish would only receive it if they fulfilled one of the following criteria: having resided for an unbroken period of twenty years in the parish; having occupied as sole tenant for ten years a house or houses in the parish with a minimum annual rental of £12; having bought real estate in the parish worth a minimum of seven quarters (c.£140) and resided in it for three years; having served a five-year apprenticeship in the parish and resided in it for a further five years before reaching the age of 30; having worked as a domestic or farm servant in the parish for ten years after the age of 20, but only if unmarried.

absconded and left her in need.[66] Similarly, in 1890, 42-year-old Amelia Greening (*née* Le Noury) was removed to Lifton in Devon when the death of her Devonian husband reduced her to poverty.[67]

The fact that a married woman's legal personality was subsumed into that of her husband also impacted on her nationality, again even in widowhood or desertion. Between 1870 and 1948, Guernseywomen permanently lost their British nationality if they married non-British subjects.[68] This had its greatest impact in the late nineteenth and early twentieth centuries when French immigration to Guernsey was at its height and marriage between French and Guernsey spouses at its most common. For the poorer Guernseywomen who married Frenchmen and neither travelled nor bought property, loss of British nationality resulted in no further consequences than the loss of settlement rights. For the better-off, however, there could be more complex inconveniences—particularly after 1905, when the purchase of real estate by foreigners was restricted by law.[69] In 1910 Lavinia Allain, the Guernsey-born widow of a Frenchman, discovered that she had to go to the length of being *reçue habitante* (a form of denization) before she could purchase a house in her own native parish.[70]

---

[66] 8.10.1870, GG, *Livres en Crime*, vol. 41; 12.10.1870, IA, DC/HX 127-01. Acts of Court authorising the removal of some non-settled paupers (particularly women with children and the elderly) were passed by the Police Court and recorded in *Livres en Crime*. This does not imply that the subjects of the Acts had committed any offence (see Crossan, *Guernsey, 1814–1914*, pp. 161–4).

[67] 8.11.1890, GG, *Livres en Crime*, vol. 47.

[68] The matter of nationality in Guernsey was governed by United Kingdom law. Until 1870, British women who married foreign men had retained their maiden nationality. The position was however reversed by the Naturalisation Act 1870 which ruled that a married woman would henceforth be deemed a citizen of the state of which her husband was a citizen. This situation pertained until the British Nationality Act 1948 restored the pre-1870 *status quo* by stipulating that marriage would no longer have an effect on a woman's nationality.

[69] *Loi relative à l'Acquisition de Propriété Immobilière en cette Ile par des Etrangers ou Sociétés Etrangères* (O in C, 10.5.1905).

[70] Correspondence from June 1910, IA, LO 042-11. For the denization process, see Crossan, *Guernsey, 1814–1914*, pp. 141–3.

Married women's property

In this section we will deal with married women's property in its widest sense—that is, a woman's property in her person, as well as her belongings. The reason for this is that the Norman *Coutume* gave husbands ownership and control of both.[71] We will consider the issues of person and goods separately, beginning with the former.

First and foremost, marriage was regarded as conferring on a husband the right of exclusive and unrestricted sexual access to his wife. Thus, by virtue of the underlying marriage contract, a wife was legally assumed to have consented to each and every act of intercourse by her husband.[72] This was the case throughout the British Isles, whose common law shared an origin in the Norman *Coutume*. Sir Matthew Hale, a respected English legal authority, stated the position succinctly in 1736:

> the husband cannot be guilty of a rape committed by himself upon his wife, for by their mutual matrimonial consent and contract, the wife hath given herself up in this kind unto her husband which she cannot retract.[73]

A century later, the philosopher and feminist John Stuart Mill, taking the woman's perspective, expressed the matter somewhat differently:

> ... he can claim from her and enforce the lowest degradation of a human being, that of being made the instrument of an animal function contrary to her inclinations.[74]

A man's immunity from prosecution for the rape of his wife is now usually referred to as the 'marital rape exemption'. I have found no references to this concept in local historical records, but, just as in England, it would probably have been taken for granted in Guernsey that the crime of rape could not exist within marriage. When discussing the matter of rape in general,

---

[71] See nn. 31 and 32, above.
[72] J. Bourke, *Rape: A History from 1860 to the Present* (2007; London 2008 edn), pp. 307-8.
[73] Sir M. Hale, *History of the Pleas of the Crown*, 2 vols (London, 1736), 1, pp. 628-9.
[74] J.S. Mill, *On the Subjection of Women* (1869; Oxford, 1991 edn), p. 504. When Mill married Helen Taylor in 1851, he insisted on signing a legal instrument renouncing the powers that marriage conferred on him as a husband (J. Tosh, *Manliness and Masculinities in Nineteenth-Century Britain: Essays on Gender, Family and Empire* (Harlow, 2005), p. 17).

Guernsey's Bailiff, Peter Stafford Carey, told the Royal Commissioners investigating Guernsey's criminal law in 1846 'we should follow exactly the same principle as the English law'.[75]

The marital rape exemption was abolished in Scotland by a legal decision of 1989 and in England and Wales by one of 1991.[76] Expert legal opinion in Guernsey at the time of writing holds that, given United Kingdom precedents, no such exemption would now be recognised in Guernsey, assuming the evidence available for prosecution was sufficient and the public interest test was met.[77]

A man's property rights in his wife's person also extended to her physical presence in his home. This meant that, if she left him against his will, he could enforce her return by means of an action at law. This power was formalised and transferred to Guernsey's Matrimonial Causes Court by the Matrimonial Causes Law of 1939.[78] Historically, formal applications to the Court for restitution orders were however rare. More often than not, and particularly as regarded the less well-off, the power of restitution was exercised informally by the parochial police.[79] Accepting without question that husbands had a right to their wives' presence at home, constables usually responded positively to requests from aggrieved husbands to return wayward wives. In 1899, the police constable of the Vale travelled to town to bring back the wife of John Legg who had decided to go home to her mother.[80] Similarly, the St Martins constable crossed the island to St Sampsons in 1913 to retrieve John Robert's wife who had decamped with her children to her

---

[75] *Second Report of the Commissioners appointed to inquire into the State of the Criminal Law in the Channel Islands* (London, 1848), p. 276. Carey was a qualified English barrister and, prior to becoming Bailiff of Guernsey, had served as Recorder of Dartmouth, Judge of the Borough Court of Wells and Professor of Law at University College, London (*Star*, 19.1.1886).
[76] *Glasgow Herald*, 16.3.1989; *The Times*, 24.10.1991.
[77] Communication from Law Officers, 12.7.2017.
[78] Orders for the 'restitution of conjugal rights', as it was known, were also available in England and Wales, as were orders for 'adherence' in Scotland. They had largely fallen into obsolescence by the twentieth century but were not formally abolished until 1970 in England and 1984 in Scotland. In Guernsey, orders for the restitution of conjugal rights were abolished by the Matrimonial Causes (Amendment) (Guernsey) Law 1972.
[79] For the organisation of policing in Victorian and Edwardian Guernsey, see introduction to chapter 4.
[80] 29.8.1899, IA, AQ 0507/03.

father's.[81] In violent households, such forcible returns could have dangerous consequences. In one instance from 1936 a Forest parishioner attacked his wife with a breadknife when police returned her to him after she had originally fled his ill-treatment.[82]

A husband could also be ordered to render his wife her conjugal rights. Because of the implicit nature of the marital contract, however, the only right to which a wife could lay claim was the right to be maintained by her husband. In Guernsey, a man's obligation to maintain his wife and family was enshrined in statute law as early as 1856, when *la Loi relative à l'Application des Peines tant au Criminel qu'en Police Correctionnelle* made an able-bodied man who failed to maintain his wife and family liable to eight days' imprisonment.[83] In an extension of this principle, parochial authorities regularly used their police constables to retrieve husbands thought to be plotting desertion. In 1873, St Peter Port constable Flambe was sent as far as Jersey to intercept John Le Poidevin and Osmond Hale who had sailed for St Helier with the reported intention of abandoning their wives and children.[84]

For all that—and again consistent with the underlying contract—Guernsey's law held that, if a wife infringed her husband's right to a sexual monopoly over her by having intercourse with another man, she forfeited her own right to be maintained by him. As a Law Officer advised a St Peter Port official seeking to force a man to maintain his destitute wife in 1886, 'the Court has on several occasions held that a husband is not responsible for his wife's maintenance if she has been guilty of adultery.'[85]

A husband also enjoyed extensive rights over his wife's material belongings.[86] These were treated differently according to the form they took.

---

[81] 20.11.1913, IA, AQ 0227/10.
[82] 19.10.1936, 20.10.1936, 21.10.1936, IA, PC 189-01.
[83] O in C, 24.6.1856. This measure was primarily intended to protect parochial authorities from the burden of supporting abandoned wives and families.
[84] 6.10.1873, IA, AQ 0992/04.
[85] HM Procureur to St Peter Port Poor Law Board Vice-President, 3.3.1886, IA, DC/HX 062-03.
[86] Laurent Carey's *Essai sur les Institutions* contains a detailed summary of the status of married women's property in Guernsey at pp. 119–28. Though written in the eighteenth century, Carey's account remained applicable in our period, and this paragraph is largely based on his summary.

The ownership of all a woman's personal (or moveable) property, including money, was transferred absolutely and for all time to her husband upon marriage.[87] Because everything she had belonged to him, this also meant that he was liable for her debts. The position as regarded a wife's real (or immoveable) property was slightly different: although in a legal sense it remained hers, her husband became its sole administrator upon marriage and was also entitled to its usufruct. The main effect of her continued legal ownership was to ensure that he could not dispose of or charge such property without her assent, and that it reverted to her if he predeceased her.[88] However, a wife could not initiate litigation concerning her own real property without her husband's consent and participation, and neither could she make it the subject of a will without his prior authority.[89]

Owing to shared origins in Norman customary law, the common law position regarding married women's property elsewhere in the British Isles—England, Wales, Ireland, Scotland, Jersey—was very much the same: husbands owned their wives' personal property, and administered and enjoyed the usufruct of their real property.[90]

In England and Wales, a married woman's inability to own personal property and control real property was commonly overcome through the device of the trust, since the courts of equity regarded property held in trust for a wife as her separate estate.[91] While she was married, her property was under the control of trustees rather than her husband (though she could give them instructions for its use), and it reverted to her in its entirety upon widowhood.

In Guernsey, the primary device for circumventing common law restrictions on married women's property was not the trust, but the marriage

---

[87] Save what were termed her *paraphernaux* – traditionally, her bed, clothes, linen and personal accoutrements.
[88] A widow had the right to apply to the Court for the restitution of any property alienated or charged by her husband without her consent within a year and a day of his death.
[89] On the matter of wills, see n. 109, below.
[90] J. Perkin, *Women and Marriage in Nineteenth-Century England* (London, 1989), pp. 13–14; Barclay, *Love, Intimacy and Power*, p. 49; P. Matthews, 'The impact of matrimonial property on inheritance law', *Jersey & Guernsey Law Review* (October 2010).
[91] The English courts of equity (otherwise known as chancery courts) applied principles of equity as opposed to common law.

contract. Marriage contracts were used wherever a Guernsey bride had property or expectations of property, and they were ubiquitous in all ranks from small farmers and retailers upwards. In the period dealt with by this book, intending spouses would usually have a marriage contract drawn up well in advance of their wedding, and acknowledge it before the Royal Court prior to having a copy registered at the Greffe.

Typically, a Guernsey marriage contract would provide for a bride to retain the ownership of her present and future personal property and the administration of, and revenue from, her present and future real property.[92] It would also state explicitly that such property was not to be subject to a husband's control nor liable to his debts. Most contracts were accompanied by an inventory of the bride's possessions as at marriage. In the case of country-dwellers, inventories might include fields, furzebrakes, livestock and farming implements. In the case of town-dwellers, they might include cash at the bank, stock in trade, securities, and life insurance policies. In both cases, they also usually included an exhaustive list of the everyday household items a bride brought to the marriage: linen, crockery, furniture, pots and pans, even close-stools. This ensured that such items, which were traditionally provided by a bride's family, would revert to them if she died without issue.[93]

In the United Kingdom, the removal of married women's disabilities in respect of their property was one of the chief aims of the early feminist movement. Pressure exerted by this movement was largely responsible for the passage of the first Married Women's Property Act in 1870. This statute allowed wives in England and Wales to retain ownership of their earnings, their personal property, and money under £200 left to them in a will. Continued pressure from the feminist lobby after 1870 resulted in the passage of a second Married Women's Property Act in 1882. This finally gave English and Welsh wives the full range of rights and responsibilities enjoyed by their single or widowed contemporaries: the right to own, keep, administer and dispose of all of their own real and personal property; the right to sue and be

---

[92] For examples of nineteenth-century marriage contracts, see GG, *Contrats pour la Date*, 60–6 *et seq.*
[93] E.F. Carey (ed.), *Guernsey Folk Lore from MSS by the Late Sir Edgar MacCulloch* (London, 1903), p. 100.

sued, to enter into contracts in their own behalf, and to exercise responsibility for their own debts.[94]

These statutes had no impact on Guernsey, where the law remained resolutely frozen in Norman customary mode for many more decades. Only after World War I was the need for a change even suggested. With increasing numbers of middle-class English couples settling in Guernsey in the post-war period, local lawyers frequently found themselves asked to advise how the acquisition of a Guernsey domicile might affect the female spouse.[95] One such lawyer, Ambrose Sherwill, was elected to the States in 1920.[96] Sherwill (shown in plate 21, overleaf) had stood on a reformist platform, pressing among other things for the removal of married women's disabilities: 'it is little short of scandalous' he said in his election manifesto, 'that the personal property of a woman marrying in Guernsey should vest—in the absence of a *contrat de mariage*—entirely in her husband, and that all her realty should be under his control.'[97] In 1923, Sherwill and ten others submitted a petition for the introduction of a married women's property law broadly along English lines. They met a positive response, but progress in formulating and approving the new law was slow, and Jersey, which was subject to similar pressures, overtook Guernsey by passing its own married women's property law in 1925.[98] In 1927, however, the States finally approved *la Loi étendant les Droits de la Femme Mariée quant à la Propriété Mobilière et Immobilière*, and it was ratified by the Privy Council on 13 July 1928.

In line with the petitioners' aspirations, this law was modelled on Westminster's Married Women's Property Acts, and accorded married women in Guernsey the same rights as single and widowed women of full age to own, sell, enter into contracts with and otherwise dispose of their real and personal property (subject to the strictures of inheritance law). As a *quid pro quo*, the law also relieved husbands of responsibility for their wives' debts and

---

[94] Women north of the border were not so fortunate: the Scottish Married Women's Property Act of 1881 maintained husbands' curatorial rights over their wives' property, and these were not finally removed until 1920 (Barclay, *Love, Intimacy and Power*, p. 51).
[95] *Billet*, 28.4.1926.
[96] Advocate Sherwill went on to become HM Procureur in 1935 and Bailiff in 1946.
[97] *Star*, 22.12.1920.
[98] *Loi (1925) étendant les Droits de la Femme Mariée*.

obligations.[99] Interestingly, on the day the new law was approved by the States, a Law Officer remarked that the reform had been achieved without any 'agonised appeal from the married women themselves'.[100]

Plate 21. *Ambrose Sherwill*[101]
Island Archives Service, Guernsey

Inheritance law

Another of Guernsey's laws which remained set in Norman aspic well into the twentieth century was its law of succession. In this section, we shall consider the ways in which this law applied differentially to males and

---

[99] Similar legislation was introduced into Alderney in 1949 (Alderney Land and Property Law) and Sark in 1975 (Married Women's Property (Sark) Law 1975). Note that in France it remained illegal for a married woman to sell any of her own property without her husband's permission until 1981 (Wiesner-Hanks, *Gender in History*, p. 100).
[100] *Star*, 26.1.1927. This observation was reiterated in a Law Officers' memorandum on the legislation written two decades later: 'curiously enough, women appear to have taken little part in effecting the change' (IA, BF 026-17).
[101] Sherwill was knighted in 1949.

females, analysing first how widows and widowers were affected, and second, how male and female descendants were affected.

Guernsey's customary law gave widows and widowers fixed rights in their deceased spouses' property. *Douaire* entitled widows to a life interest in a third of their late husbands' real property, as well as half of their personal property if they had no children, and a third of their personal property if they did. *Franc-veuvage* gave widowers enjoyment for life (or until remarriage) of all of their deceased wives' real property, providing that a living child had been born of the marriage. As regarded a deceased wife's personal property, the situation before the passage of the 1928 Married Women's Property Law differed from that which pertained afterwards. Before 1928, marriage had already permanently transferred ownership of a wife's moveables to her husband, so her death altered nothing: the widower simply remained their owner until his own demise or until such time as he saw fit to dispose of them. After 1928, wives owned their own moveables, so an entirely new law was passed which laid down that widowers as well as widows would now be entitled to a third of the deceased spouse's personalty if there were children and half if there were none.[102]

Again, the common law position in these matters was similar in all parts of the British Isles. England and Wales had their own versions of *douaire* and *franc-veuvage* in dower and courtesy; Scotland in terce and courtesy; Jersey in *douaire* and *viduité*.[103] All these jurisdictions had their own methods of defeating or sidestepping these common law strictures where parties to a marriage desired it.[104] In Guernsey, the usual method, as with married women's property, was the marriage contract. By means of these contracts, it was not uncommon for a wife to renounce her customary right of *douaire* in return for a lifetime annuity, thus simplifying matters for the next generation.

---

[102] *Loi relative à la Portion Disponible des Pères et Mères* (O in C, 17.12.1929).

[103] In France, the situation was somewhat different. Following Napoleon's abolition of regional *coutumes*, his *Code Civil* of 1804 made no provision for the automatic succession of widows or widowers to any part of their late spouses' estate, as this was intended to be covered either in a marriage contract or a will. However, in 1891, a law was passed guaranteeing the surviving spouse a life interest in a quarter of the deceased spouse's property (https://www.loc.gov/law/help/inheritance-laws/France).

[104] For some of the means used in the various jurisdictions, see M. Thomas and B. Dowrick, 'The future of légitime – vive la différence', *Jersey & Guernsey Law Review* (October 2013).

Equally, some husbands chose to renounce their right of *franc-veuvage* so that their children might benefit immediately from their mothers' succession.

Turning now to the inheritance rights of descendants: from 1840 onwards these were governed in Guernsey not by customary law but by statute. The 1840 *Loi sur les Successions* arose out of a petition to the Royal Court in 1838. This petition was signed by six hundred ratepayers, and among their principal aims was to secure 'a greater share in real property for the female heirs in certain lineal successions and the admittance of female heirs to a share in collateral successions'.[105] This had been prompted by mounting frustration at the inequities to which daughters were subjected by Guernsey's customary law, which strongly favoured the male line, although it did not quite follow the old Norman *Coutume* in totally excluding daughters where there were sons.[106]

It is important to observe at the outset that the 1840 *Loi sur les Successions* did not change the basic character of Guernsey's inheritance regime, which was, and remained, one of modified primogeniture.[107] Under this regime, the eldest son was entitled to the lion's share of the parental estate in the form of his *préciput* (or eldership), and what was left was divided up by *partage* (deed of division) between his siblings—historically, two-thirds among brothers and one-third among sisters.

Notwithstanding the demand for greater equality, the law of 1840 did surprisingly little to mitigate injustices to females. Perhaps its greatest concession to them lay in its abolition of *vingtième*, a feature of customary law considered particularly prejudicial to daughters. This was applicable only to estates outside the urban area of St Peter Port and consisted in the right enjoyed by sons (whenever their number did not exceed double that of daughters) to take for themselves—before the eldest took his *préciput* and before the *partage*—one-twentieth in area of the estate in a single location of

---

[105] See preamble to O in C, 13.7.1840.

[106] Note that, in France, the inheritance rights of both sexes had been equalised by the revolutionary authorities in 1793, and this equality was preserved in the 1804 *Code Civil* (McMillan, *France and Women*, pp. 33-4).

[107] The following paragraphs are based on pp. 33-198 of Peter Jeremie's *On the Law of Real Property in Guernsey* (1862; Guernsey, 1866 edn), which contain a detailed exposition of the 1840 law.

their choosing, to be valued as bare land notwithstanding any buildings that might be on it.

For the rest, the 1840 law laid down that brothers should continue to take two-thirds of the post-*préciput* estate and sisters one-third—with the minor concession that brothers' portions would henceforth be capped at double those of sisters.[108] Within a specially demarcated area in St Peter Port which was deemed to be exclusively urban, the new law abolished the *préciput* on realty completely, laying down that the entire estate was to be divided by *partage*, but again this was to be two-thirds to sons and one-third to daughters, with sons' portions capped at double those of daughters.

The 1840 law also made new provisions for collateral successions, but again these only partly mitigated unfairness to females. Previously, no female had been allowed, with parity of degree, to inherit collaterally with males, which meant that, if a deceased unmarried person was survived by siblings of both sexes, only brothers were entitled to a share in the estate. Although the 1840 law finally admitted sisters to a share in the deceased's personalty and purchased realty, it was not on an equal footing with brothers. Instead, the principle observed in respect of lineal successions was applied, namely two-thirds to brothers and one-third to sisters, with brothers' portions capped at double those of sisters.

When the 1840 *Loi sur les Successions* is considered in the broadest terms, its most revolutionary innovation lay not in its concessions to females but in its provision for the testamentary devising of realty, which had previously been impossible in Guernsey. The new law opened the door to this, albeit in restricted form, by allowing individuals who had no descendants to dispose of a proportion of their real estate by will. In its treatment of women, however, the 1840 law was as inequitable here as in its other provisions: while it permitted a married woman to make a will of realty during marriage, this was on condition that her husband's consent was obtained and the will was attested by the Bailiff and two Jurats.[109]

---

[108] By way of *préciput*, the law of 1840 entitled the eldest son to a single enclosure of about one-sixth of an acre usually containing the main dwelling house and its appurtenances. Where the estate comprised only a single enclosure, the eldest son was granted the right to take the whole, giving his co-heirs credit for the excess of value over the *préciput*.
[109] O in C, 15.6.1852 dispensed with the need for attestation and consent.

The reason for the limited nature of concessions to women in the 1840 *Loi sur les Successions* was that its framers never intended to grant them equality, but to improve their lot where they could while ensuring that the traditional goal of preserving the integrity of holdings was adhered to. In this, the 1840 law satisfied property-owners in Guernsey for many decades. By the end of World War I, however, society was beginning to change: field-based agriculture was declining in importance, and home ownership, in the form of cottages and bungalows, was becoming more widespread. In many cases, a cottage or bungalow was the sole estate left at death, which made the eldest son's sole claim to it under *préciput* appear most unfair. Over the inter-war years, pressure built up for change. Ambrose Sherwill gave the matter equal prominence with married women's property in his 1920 election manifesto and pursued it vigorously on entering the States.[110] Partly through Sherwill's agency, the States appointed a committee to investigate possible reforms in the early 1920s. However, the subject proved so contentious that not one of the Inheritance Reform Committee's proposals between 1920 and World War II was translated into action.[111] During the Occupation, the matter was put on hold, but when it was addressed again afterwards, more indecision ensued.[112] Finally, three decades after the subject was first mooted, the States passed a new inheritance law in 1954.[113] In general terms, this law did not represent as radical a break with the past as might have been expected, for although it provided for a general right to devise real estate by will, this right was constrained by the stipulation that testators with close relatives could only bequeath their realty to family members.[114] From a female perspective, however, the 1954 law was truly ground-breaking in that—by and large—it established successoral equality between the sexes. *Douaire* and *franc-veuvage* were abolished and replaced by an egalitarian provision giving both widows

---

[110] *Star*, 22.12.1920.
[111] For the various reports and proposals of the States' Inheritance Reform Committee, see *Billets*, 7.3.1928, 30.11.1938, 20.9.1939, 10.1.1940.
[112] *Billets*, 22.2.1949, 18.7.1950, 13.2.1951; *Guernsey Evening Press*, 25.1.1949, 19.7.1950, 14.2.1952.
[113] O in C, 13.4.1954.
[114] Specifically, to their spouse and/or one or more of their legitimate, illegitimate or step-children (and descendants of these). Ultimately, an unfettered power of testamentary disposition was granted by the Inheritance (Guernsey) Law 2011. Note that England and Wales had substantially reached this position by the mid-nineteenth century.

and widowers enjoyment until death or remarriage of one-half of the deceased's realty. The *préciput* enjoyed by the eldest son was abolished, and no sex distinctions were made in the new provisions for wills and legatees. Most importantly, the two-thirds/one-third formula set out in respect of sons and daughters in the 1840 *Loi sur les Successions* was revoked, which meant that, where no will was made (perhaps the commonest state of affairs over the next few decades), brothers' and sisters' entitlements would henceforth be completely equal.[115] For Guernseywomen, who had long been gravely disadvantaged by the island's succession law, this was a major, if belated, achievement.

Guardianship and custody

Many of the successoral disadvantages historically suffered by women derived from the primacy accorded to the male line by the old Norman *Coutume*. As noted above, transmission of the male name and the property associated with it were all-important, and the main role of women was to act as vehicles for perpetuating the line. An important concomitant of this was that all the children produced by a marriage were regarded as belonging to their father alone until they reached the age of majority. In legal terms, this gave fathers sole rights to their children's guardianship and custody, and denied mothers any legal claim to them.[116] This principle was observed not only in Guernsey, but in other jurisdictions influenced by Norman customary law, including England and Wales. Where Guernsey stands out is in the length of time for which this principle persisted.

The situation which most clearly illustrates a Guernsey mother's lack of rights is that which arose when her husband died without having appointed a guardian to their children. Though not debarred from becoming their guardian, the mother had no *a priori* claim to this, as the ultimate choice lay with a council of senior family members (or friends and neighbours in default).[117] Whomever the council selected as guardian (*tuteur* in local legal

---

[115] Surprisingly perhaps, Jerseywomen had enjoyed equality of treatment since the passage of Jersey's *Loi sur les Partages des Successions* in 1851.
[116] Terrien, *Commentaires du Droict Civil*, p. 19.
[117] Carey, *Essai sur les Institutions*, pp. 172–3.

parlance) had then to be sworn in before the Royal Court—and perusal of Court registers shows that mothers were by no means the only or even the primary choice.[118]

In practice, this procedure was invoked only in the case of children from better-off backgrounds whose maintenance and education required special financial provision, or who owned property which needed to be managed until they were of age. Where money and property were not an issue, measures of this sort were unnecessary, and widows from lower social strata continued to care for their children without being subjected to them.

Of course, guardianship was not the same thing as custody, which was more closely linked to co-residence, and usually came to the fore when conjugal households broke up for reasons other than death. In England and Wales, the first encroachment on a father's exclusive rights to his children was made in respect of custody rather than guardianship. Here, the subject came to prominence in the early nineteenth century through a number of high-profile separations where courts had been unable to grant custody to mothers even when fathers were demonstrably unfit. Largely owing to a campaign by the novelist Caroline Norton, whose three young sons were taken from her on separation from her dissolute husband, this situation changed in 1839 when the Custody of Infants Act became the first statute to recognise a maternal right to custody, albeit limited, by allowing separated wives to petition for custody of children under seven. Further inroads were made in 1873 when a second Infant Custody Act allowed mothers to petition for children up to sixteen, and again in 1886 when the Guardianship of Infants Act allowed them to petition for children up to twenty-one.

As its name would suggest, the 1886 Act also finally tackled the issue of guardianship. In one revolutionary move, this Act placed mothers on almost the same footing as fathers by laying down that, on the death of a father, a mother would henceforth automatically become her children's legal guardian, either alone when no guardian had been appointed by the father, or jointly with any guardian appointed by him.[119]

---

[118] Nineteenth- and early twentieth-century swearings-in are recorded in *Plaids de Meubles* registers at the Greffe.
[119] During his lifetime, however, a father's authority over his children continued to trump that of their mother.

In Guernsey, child custody issues also came up from time to time in marital separation cases.[120] Prior to 1890, if a separated mother gained custody of her children, this was invariably by negotiation, since mothers lacked any legally enforceable rights. In 1890, however, Guernsey enacted its first law on summary separation in the form of *la Loi relative à la Séparation de Mari et Femme en Police Correctionnelle*. This law, which was based on an English statute of 1878, permitted the Court to order the separation of a wife from her husband if he had been convicted of a serious assault on her, or of desertion or neglect.[121] In also permitting the Court to assign custody of children to a wife, this law represented the first legal dent in a Guernsey father's exclusive rights to his children.

In matters pertaining to guardianship, however, the principle of paternal supremacy remained intact and unassailed in Guernsey until the late twentieth century. It was only in 1978 that a law was enacted providing for a mother's automatic assumption of guardianship under terms similar to those of Westminster's 1886 Guardianship of Infants Act.[122] In words reminiscent of the 1886 statute, this law provided that, on one of the parents' death, the surviving parent, irrespective of sex, would automatically become the legal guardian of their children, either alone or jointly with any guardian appointed by the deceased parent.[123]

By this point, the rights of English mothers and fathers had been equalised not only in death but also during their lifetimes. This had been achieved by means of the 1973 Guardianship of Minors Act which made the rights and authority of a mother over her minor children fully equal and interchangeable with those of a father.[124] Guernsey's 1978 Guardianship of Minors Law

---

[120] See, for instance, Stephen Foster's fictionalisation of a historical case in *Zoffany's Daughter: Love and Treachery on a Small Island* (Cookham, 2017).
[121] O in C, 30.6.1890. For more detail on this specialised form of separation (which should not be confused with ordinary judicial separation), see section on Separation, below.
[122] The Law Reform (Age of Majority and Guardianship of Minors) (Guernsey) Law 1978 (O in C, 21.3.1978). This law also lowered the age of majority from 20 to 18.
[123] If the surviving parent did not wish to share guardianship, the law also permitted him or her to apply to the Court to remain the sole guardian.
[124] In France, women's equal parental rights were officially recognised in 1970 (C.L. Blakesley, 'Child custody and parental authority in France and Louisiana', *Boston College International and Comparative Law Review*, 4 (1981), p. 295).

severed the island's last link with the *Coutume* in matters of paternal preference by also replicating this development.

This brings us to the conclusion of this section and the end of our analysis of Guernsey laws which had an indirect bearing upon marriage, and *vice versa*. In the remainder of this chapter we will examine what recourses were available to women (and men) when the marriages they had contracted broke down.

Separation and divorce

Separation

According to the apostle Mark, Jesus decreed that no man should put asunder what God had joined together.[125] This, together with similar scriptural pronouncements, led to the development of the Christian view of marriage as indissoluble. As we saw earlier, the church exercised jurisdiction over matrimony from the twelfth century on, so it was initially to ecclesiastical rather than civil courts that couples resorted in cases of marital difficulty. The power of these courts was severely restricted. Although they could declare marriages void where Canon law had been contravened (in cases of consanguinity, affinity, incapacity, minority, etc.), the most they could do where there had been no such contravention was to grant a separation *a mensa et thoro*.[126] However, separations *a mensa et thoro* were only granted where there was evidence of serious abuse, and they did not dissolve a couple's marriage, nor allow them to remarry.

In Normandy, the power to grant separations *a mensa et thoro* was transferred from the ecclesiastical to the civil courts in the second half of the sixteenth century.[127] In England and Wales, it remained with the ecclesiastical courts until the passage of the 1857 Divorce Act. The English ecclesiastical courts' powers with regard to separation were defined in detail in the Anglican Canons of 1604. In 1623, the island of Jersey acquired a set of Anglican

---

[125] Mark 10:8-9.
[126] *A mensa et thoro* = from bed and board.
[127] Schneider, *King's Bench*, p. 13; Musset, *Régime des Biens entre Epoux*, p. 92.

Canons as part of the constitution given to its ecclesiastical court by James I, and these Canons authorised the court to grant separations *a mensa et thoro* on the three grounds of adultery, cruelty, and danger to life.[128] Guernsey, for its part, never adopted any Anglican Canons.[129] From this circumstance, the island of Guernsey evolved a policy on marital separations which differed from that of both Jersey and England and Wales. This policy confined Guernsey's ecclesiastical court solely to the annulment, or voiding, of marriages contracted contrary to the technicalities of Canon law, and put the matter of separation—as one which partook of the temporal—squarely within the purview of the Royal Court. Laurent Carey described the situation thus:

> Le Juge d'Eglise a la connaissance de toutes les choses qui sont purement spirituelles ... et de toute spiritualité où il n'y a point de temporalité annexée ... Quand on prétend [les mariages] nuls par cause d'impuissance ou de parenté ou d'alliance en degrés prohibés ... ces questions sont de la compétence du Juge d'Eglise ... [mais] il ne peut connaître ni prononcer ... sur la séparation de corps et de biens des maris d'avec leurs femmes, ni sur les conventions matrimoniales, non plus que sur les provisions demandées pour nourriture et aliments: de sorte que toute contestation qui nait à l'occasion d'un mariage ne peut être décidée que par le Juge séculier.[130]

The ecclesiastical court retained the power to annul marriages on Canon law grounds until 1936, and there are several instances of its use during our period. Civil separations were, however, much more common than ecclesiastical annulments, and it is thus on the civil court's role in granting separations that we will concentrate here.

The system which Guernsey's secular authorities evolved for separating spouses owed much to that which had been established in the Norman civil courts in the sixteenth century. Indeed, the wording of a 1631 ordinance regulating separations followed that of the judicial decree setting out the

---

[128] Jersey's Canons are reproduced in E. Durell (ed.), *An Account of the Island of Jersey by the Rev. Philip Falle to which are added Notes and Illustrations* (Jersey, 1837), pp. 246-61. Numbers 12 and 54 dealt with separations *a mensa et thoro*.

[129] See n. 41, above.

[130] Carey, *Essai sur les Institutions*, pp. 18-19.

procedure adopted in Normandy after 1555.[131] Terrien reproduced this decree in his *Commentaires*, and, in the mid-eighteenth century, Laurent Carey identified it as authoritative in Guernsey.[132]

We should note that both the 1631 ordinance and the decree reproduced by Terrien dealt only with *séparations quant aux biens* (separations of property). We should also note that Jersey's civil court adopted a very similar procedure, also based on the Norman model. In Jersey, however, the ecclesiastical monopoly over separations *a mensa et thoro* meant that the civil court was confined to separating couples *quant aux biens* only. On this basis, civil *séparations quant aux biens* evolved a very special role in Jersey; they came to be the means by which Jersey couples achieved what Guernsey couples achieved through marriage contracts. In Jersey, where marriage contracts were rare, a civil *séparation quant aux biens* was the usual device for giving a wife ownership and control of her property.[133]

In Guernsey, the procedure outlined in the 1631 ordinance was used to effect both separations *quant aux biens* and separations *a mensa et thoro*. While Laurent Carey reported that the courts of his day dealt with more separations *quant aux biens* than *a mensa et thoro*, by our period, the majority of separations were in the latter category.[134] In spite of this, court registers continued to record all separations as *séparations quant aux biens* until September 1920, when they silently and without explanation replaced the old term with *séparation de corps et de biens*.[135]

After 1631, no further laws were passed with regard to judicial separation in Guernsey,[136] but practices surrounding it gradually evolved as successive courts built on the innovations of their predecessors. The separations granted by Guernsey's courts during the century covered by this book are best described as an amalgam of the private separations which came into being as

---

[131] Ord, 3.10.1631 (I am grateful to Dr Darryl Ogier for drawing my attention to this ordinance).
[132] Terrien, *Commentaires du Droict Civil*, p. 18; Carey, *Essai sur les Institutions*, p. 119.
[133] *Report of the Commissioners appointed to inquire into the Civil, Municipal and Ecclesiastical Laws of Jersey* (London, 1860), pp. xix, xxxi–xxxii.
[134] Carey, *Essai sur les Institutions*, p. 119.
[135] Separations are recorded in *Plaids de Meubles* registers at Guernsey's Greffe.
[136] With the exception of the more narrowly specialised Police Court separation laws, for which see below.

an alternative to ecclesiastical separations in England and Wales and the judicial separations available from England's newly-established Divorce Court after the ecclesiastical courts lost their powers of separation in 1857.[137] Spouses applying to be separated in Guernsey had to submit a formal petition and appear before the Ordinary Court, who granted (or refused) the separation and made arrangements for the custody of children, maintenance payments, and the division of assets.[138] Public notice was then given of the separation in order that tradesmen, creditors and other interested parties might be apprised of the spouses' change of circumstances.

The grant of a separation gave a married woman all the legal rights and responsibilities of an unmarried woman as regarded her realty and personalty, and released her husband from liability for her debts. However, a separated couple could not remarry, and they were treated as a married couple upon their death, i.e., a widower was entitled to his *franc-veuvage* as also to his wife's personalty, and a widow was entitled to her *douaire*.[139]

In recording a separation, Court registers used the standard formula *séparés de leur consentement mutuel*. Technically, the agreement of both spouses was required, and the procedure involved negotiation. Nevertheless, separations were normally initiated by one spouse only. In most cases in our period this was the wife. Grounds commonly adduced by wives in the late nineteenth century included their husbands' profligacy, violence, cruelty, habitual drunkenness, neglect, and desertion.[140] Adultery was not often adduced by a wife, and, when it was, her petition might be rejected if there

---

[137] Private separations under the English law of contract first arose when ecclesiastical courts closed during the Interregnum. They usually took the form of an agreement indemnifying the husband against any future responsibility for his wife's debts in return for providing her with a maintenance allowance, and they usually also contained provisions for the custody and maintenance of children. A well-known example of separation by private deed was that between Charles Dickens and his wife. The judicial separations available after 1857 required the petitioning party to prove adultery, cruelty or two years' desertion on the part of the respondent. Any wife obtaining a judicial separation was treated as if she were unmarried with respect to any property she subsequently acquired, as also with respect to entering into contracts and suing and being sued (Stone, *Road to Divorce*, pp. 149–82; O. Anderson, 'Civil society and separation in Victorian marriage', *Past & Present*, 163 (1999), p. 167).

[138] The Ordinary Court was a division of the Royal Court composed of the Bailiff (or his Lieutenant) and at least two Jurats.

[139] Carey, *Essai sur les Institutions*, pp. 121, 124, 133.

[140] Some petitions, though not all, can be found in registers of *Requêtes* at the Greffe.

were no evidence of compounding abuse. Thus, while Patty Le Page was granted a separation from Daniel Le Cheminant in 1888 on the basis of his persistent violence, Sarah De La Mare's petition for a separation from James Renouf in 1914 was refused because she could adduce nothing further than his persistent faithlessness.[141] Adultery was considerably more likely to be accepted as a sole ground for separation in the case of a petitioning husband, thus George Simpson's petition for a separation from Amy Brown in 1898 was successful, even though it was based on her adultery alone.[142] Other grounds successfully adduced by men were habitual drunkenness on the part of a wife, and a wife's neglect of her duties in respect of home and family.

Couples from a wide range of social backgrounds applied to the Court for separation. Where a separating couple were wealthy and their finances complex, they might come to Court with a ready-made agreement apportioning assets and settling maintenance.[143] Those with less complex finances typically left the arrangements to the Court. In these cases, the Court would either divide assets and allocate maintenance at their sitting, or, alternatively, appoint a Jurat as a Commissioner to negotiate a settlement between the spouses in private.[144]

The question of child custody was settled via negotiation, and, notwithstanding customary law strictures, wives were fairly often granted custody of their offspring. This happened most frequently when a husband was violent or a drunkard. If a husband was of good character and insisted on retaining his children, however, his wife had no choice but to relinquish them if she wished to proceed with the separation. Thus when Mary Ann Wright separated from Edwin Hoskins in 1888, he retained their two children, and she was obliged to content herself with a share of the household furniture and 8s 4d a week.[145]

---

[141] 11.8.1888, GG, *Requêtes*, vol. 2; 6.12.1913, 9.2.1914, *Requêtes*, vol. 3. See also Note 5, p. xiii, above.
[142] 11.6.1898, GG, *Requêtes*, vol. 2.
[143] See, for instance, the separation of Henry Le Mesurier Dobrée and Ann Paley, 31.3.1887, GG, *Plaids de Meubles*, vol. 9.
[144] As in the case of Abraham Paint and Marie Hallouvris, 8.9.1883, GG, *Plaids de Meubles*, vol. 8.
[145] 6.10.1888, GG, *Plaids de Meubles*, vol. 9.

As noted above, separations granted by Guernsey's Ordinary Court had affinities with English private separations and Divorce Court separations. In England, however, the complaint was commonly heard that the high cost of both of these types of separation put them beyond the reach of the poor. From the 1850s onwards, English feminists had therefore lobbied for the institution of a cheaper and more expeditious form of separation, particularly in cases where a wife was experiencing domestic violence. Eventually, feminist lobbying paid off in the form of the 1878 Matrimonial Causes Act. This law opened a quite different channel by which separation could be obtained, and one which in time became largely the preserve of the poor.

Initially, this mode of separation was available only to wives, and, although it was not technically an injunction or restraining order against an offending husband, it had many of the same characteristics. The 1878 Matrimonial Causes Act empowered a magistrate sitting at petty sessions to grant a summary order of non-cohabitation to a wife whose husband had been convicted of aggravated assault upon her. The separated wife was entitled to the custody of all children under ten, as well as a maintenance allowance from her husband. She was also permitted to retain any property gained after separation.[146]

This set an example for Guernsey, where separations granted by the Ordinary Court were also largely beyond the budgets of the poor. Twelve years after the passage of the English Matrimonial Causes Act, the States passed a very similar piece of legislation. The 1890 *Loi relative à la Séparation de Mari et Femme en Police Correctionnelle* made it possible for a woman to apply to the Police Court for a summary order of non-cohabitation against her husband if he had been convicted of a serious assault on her, or of desertion or neglect.[147] The law specifically stated that this order would have the same effect as a *séparation quant aux biens* granted by the Ordinary Court. The law also empowered the Court to give custody of any children under fourteen to wives, and to order husbands to pay a fixed weekly sum for maintenance. Adulterous wives were ineligible to apply for a separation under

---

[146] G. Behlmer, 'Summary justice and working-class marriage in England, 1870-1940', *Law and History Review*, 2 (1994), p. 242.

[147] O in C, 30.6.1890. The Police Court, composed of the Bailiff (or his Lieutenant) and at least two Jurats, was an iteration of the Ordinary Court responsible for trying petty criminal offences.

the new law, unless their adultery had been condoned by their husbands. The first such separation was granted on 19 July 1890 and several others followed in short order.[148]

For forty years the 1890 *Loi relative à la Séparation de Mari et Femme* was the principal recourse available to working-class Guernseywomen who wished to free themselves of violent or abusive husbands. In practice, however, it was not very effective, not least because it provided no mechanism for enforcing maintenance payments, so that wives were often forced to resume cohabitation for purely economic reasons. To some extent, this defect was addressed by a second summary separation law passed in 1930.[149] By this date, the work of the Police Court had been transferred to a new Magistrate's Court, and the 1930 law was drawn up at the request of the stipendiary magistrate, an English barrister.[150] It incorporated many of the features introduced into this area of the law in England and Wales in the forty years since 1890.[151] Repealing and replacing its predecessor, the new law empowered the magistrate to imprison a husband for up to three months if he failed to pay maintenance, and added two further grounds on which a wife could apply for a separation, namely if her husband had had intercourse with her while knowingly suffering from a sexually transmitted disease, and if her husband had forced her to engage in prostitution. Unprecedentedly, the 1930 law also empowered the magistrate to grant a man a separation, although men could only apply on the grounds of their wives' habitual drunkenness or persistent cruelty towards their children. If the husband's application for separation was successful, he was entitled to custody of the children but he could also be ordered to pay his wife up to £2 in maintenance per week.

Between 1930 and the end of our period, the only further change to the law governing separation by summary order came in 1939, when the Matrimonial Causes (Guernsey) Law added the adultery of either spouse as a

---

[148] 19.7.1890, GG, *Livres en Crime*, vol. 47; *Gazette de Guernesey*, 26.7.1890.
[149] *Loi relative à la Séparation de Mariés en Police Correctionnelle* (O in C, 28.7.1930).
[150] The Magistrate's Court had been created in 1925, and the magistrate was Henry Casey, who served from 1925 to 1940, and again from 1945 to 1957.
[151] Westminster legislation on which elements of the 1930 law were based included the 1895 Summary Jurisdiction (Married Women) Act; the 1902 Licensing Act; and the 1925 Summary Jurisdiction (Separation and Maintenance) Act.

further ground for summary separation.¹⁵² The 1930 law was itself finally repealed and replaced by the Domestic Proceedings and Magistrate's Court (Guernsey) Law 1988 which consolidated all existing legislation relating to summary separations, as also to domestic violence, while instituting full equality between the sexes.¹⁵³

Neither separation by summary order nor separation by the Ordinary Court dissolved an existing marriage, and in neither case were spouses free to remarry. The only way to attain this freedom (aside from Canon law annulment) was full-blown divorce. However, for all but a few years at the end of our period, this option was unavailable in Guernsey. The next section will discuss local attitudes to divorce and chart Guernsey's hesitant steps towards its first divorce law.

Divorce

Given Guernsey's Calvinist past, it is in some ways surprising that divorce was so late in coming to the island. Calvin, who rejected the Catholic view of marriage as a sacrament and conceived of it purely as a contract, was in favour of divorce, as were most leading figures of the Protestant Reformation.¹⁵⁴ Thus, while Catholic countries such as Spain, Portugal and Italy eschewed divorce throughout the nineteenth century, it was available in much of Protestant Europe, including Switzerland, Germany, the Netherlands, Sweden and Norway.¹⁵⁵

The picture as regarded divorce in Britain and France was more complex. In France, divorce on easy terms was introduced by the revolutionary authorities in 1792. However, in 1803 Napoleon instituted a much less liberal divorce law, and in 1816 divorce was removed from the *Code Civil* altogether. For seventy years it was impossible to obtain a divorce in France, and it was only in 1884 that divorce was reintroduced, on the four grounds of adultery, physical violence, moral cruelty and receipt of a sentence to life

---

[152] This was based on a similar provision in the 1937 Matrimonial Causes Act of England and Wales.
[153] G. Dawes, *Laws of Guernsey* (Oxford, 2003), pp. 80–6.
[154] Stone, *Road to Divorce*, p. 301.
[155] L. Abrams, *The Making of Modern Woman: Europe, 1789–1918* (Harlow, 2002), p. 85.

imprisonment.[156] In Scotland, divorce on grounds of adultery or desertion was available from the Court of Session from 1560, and later from the Commissary Court in Edinburgh. The procedure involved was however quite expensive and hence infrequently used.[157] In England and Wales, divorce was completely unavailable until the late seventeenth century. After that date, it became possible for very wealthy people (usually aristocrats) to procure a divorce by private Act of Parliament. For obvious reasons, this was available only to the privileged few, and only just over two hundred such divorces were ever granted.[158] By the early nineteenth century, demand had mounted throughout England and Wales for a widening of access to divorce. This, together with concern over the incidence of bigamy among the separated, led to the establishment of a Royal Commission on Divorce and Matrimonial Causes in 1850, which itself ultimately led to the passage in 1857 of the Matrimonial Causes Act. In theory, this Act finally made divorce available to everyone in England and Wales. In practice, a number of logistical and financial hurdles were built into the Act which continued to restrict access. Suing for divorce had to be done before a single specialised Divorce Court in London and cost a minimum of £50 even if uncontested.[159] This placed it largely beyond the means of working-class people, many of whom did not earn this much in a year. Further, petitioners had to prove fault in respondents, and the criteria were for this were not only very narrow but unequal between the sexes. Adultery was enshrined as the principal ground, but, whereas a man could divorce his wife for adultery alone, a woman needed to prove adultery with the compounding offence of desertion, cruelty or incest.[160] This situation persisted unaltered until after the First World War, when the Matrimonial Causes Act of 1923 finally levelled the playing-field by making simple adultery a ground on which both women and men could petition. In 1937, a third Matrimonial Causes Act added cruelty, desertion,

---

[156] McMillan, *France and Women*, pp. 33–4, 37, 43, 152–3.
[157] Barclay, *Love, Intimacy and Power*, p. 48.
[158] Stone, *Road to Divorce*, pp. 309–46.
[159] J. Burnett, 'Exposing "the inner life": the Women's Co-Operative Guild's attitude to "cruelty"', in S. D'Cruze (ed.), *Everyday Violence in Britain, 1850–1950: Gender and Class* (Harlow, 2000), p. 140.
[160] In the rare cases where a woman could prove that her husband had committed the crime of rape, sodomy or bestiality, the Act also treated this as sufficient evidence to justify a divorce. This remained the case in subsequent Matrimonial Causes Acts.

and incurable insanity to the list of grounds on which divorces could be granted. As per the 1923 precedent, these new grounds were applicable to both sexes. The Matrimonial Causes Act of 1937 was the last substantive enactment on divorce in England and Wales during the period covered by this book.

After 1857, people from Guernsey very occasionally availed themselves of the facilities for divorce in England. One such person was the Jurat John Thomas Ross De Havilland who in 1891 obtained a divorce from his American wife Louisa Young from the English Divorce Court on grounds of her adultery with Lieutenant William Bell.[161] De Havilland was resident in Guernsey at the time, and this only seems to have been possible because the 1857 Matrimonial Causes Act did not set out any clear requirements as to domicile, a situation which was later rectified.

De Havilland sat in Guernsey's States between 1881 and 1907, and at no time during his tenure did the question of enacting a local divorce law ever arise. The first time the possibility was mooted was in the 1920s when reforms to the inheritance law and married women's property law were under discussion. Ambrose Sherwill took a close interest in divorce, as he had in the reform of inheritance and married women's property laws. The matter was not however formally pursued at this time. It was raised again in 1933, when twelve States members submitted a petition asking that the assembly approve the introduction of divorce in principle.[162] The petition resulted in a formal debate on the subject on 12 July 1933. Those advocating divorce rested their case on an argument repeatedly heard in England since the 1850 Royal Commission: bigamy among the separated was on the rise, and the only way to eliminate it was divorce. Notwithstanding that this was an eminently respectable argument, all save one of the rectors present at the 1933 debate voted against, and the petition was rejected by a margin of seven.[163]

Guernsey society was changing rapidly in the inter-war period. Hollywood movies, glossy magazines and popular radio shows were introducing locals to values very different from those of the Victorian

---

[161] *Star*, 14.11.1891.
[162] *Billet*, 12.7.1933. The petitioners were led by Deputy William Arnold, a lawyer who went on to become HM Procureur in 1946 and Bailiff in 1959.
[163] *Star*, 13.7.1933. The rector who voted in favour was Edward Frossard of St Sampsons, who had been one of the petition's signatories.

generation. Increasing numbers of settlers from England, where divorce had been available for eighty years, were also bringing their values with them. While the rectors might have hoped the matter would go away, public demand for divorce was intensifying. Thus, in 1935, a second petition on divorce was submitted to the States.[164] The petition repeated the argument used in 1933, laying renewed stress on the 'lives seared with disrespect and discontent' which separated partners in new unions experienced owing to the indissolubility of their previous marriages. If the argument was the same, the outcome of the vote was this time very different. Although only one more rector was converted to the cause, sufficient other members changed their minds to allow divorce at last to be approved in principle.[165] The next logical step was to investigate what this might mean in terms of legislation. An eight-man committee (including three rectors) was set up to deal with the task.[166] The following year, the States resolved to extend the committee's mandate to cover not just divorce but all matrimonial causes.[167]

Under the chairmanship of Deputy Aylmer Drake and with the technical assistance of Ambrose Sherwill, who was now HM Procureur, the committee met thirty-seven times.[168] It used the official report of Westminster's 1912 Royal Commission on Divorce and Matrimonial Causes as a basis for its deliberations. In 1937, the committee followed the example set by the Royal Commission by issuing a majority and a minority report.[169] The latter, signed by two of the rectors, expressed an implacable opposition to divorce of any sort on grounds of religious principle. The former not only pronounced itself in favour of divorce but proposed legislation along lines recommended by the 1912 Royal Commission which had later been embodied in Westminster's 1923 Matrimonial Causes Act.

As events turned out, the States debated these reports just as the Westminster parliament were discussing their 1937 Matrimonial Causes Act.

---

[164] *Billet*, 27.3.1935.
[165] The petitioners won the day by a margin of twelve, largely because all the Deputies but two were in favour, as were all but three of the Jurats (*Guernsey Evening Press*, 27.3.1935).
[166] One of the rectors was Reverend Frossard (*Billet*, 24.4.1935).
[167] *Billet*, 18.2.1936. This coincided with the States' decision to remove the ecclesiastical court's remaining jurisdiction in matrimonial affairs (see n. 56, above).
[168] A record of the committee's meetings is preserved in IA, AS/MB 026-01 and LO 023-08.
[169] *Billet*, 30.6.1937.

While the States' reaction to the majority report was overwhelmingly positive, they nevertheless deemed it prudent to instruct the committee to consult Westminster's 1937 Act and revise their proposals if necessary.[170] Four months later, the committee reverted to the States with amended proposals. The States maintained their positive stance, and these proposals were duly approved.[171] A *projet de loi* was then drafted by the Law Officers and ratified by the Privy Council on 3 July 1939.[172]

The Matrimonial Causes Law (Guernsey) 1939 was applicable to the whole Bailiwick with the exception of Sark, which had asked to be excluded.[173] It established a new division of the Royal Court in the form of the Court for Matrimonial Causes. This Court, to be composed of the Bailiff and four Jurats, was henceforth to exercise jurisdiction over suits for divorce. The law set out seven separate grounds for divorce, applicable (within the limits of the possible) to both sexes: adultery; desertion for three years; persistent cruelty since marriage; incurable insanity for at least five years; the commission of sodomy, bestiality or rape; habitual drunkenness for at least three years; and life imprisonment under a commuted death sentence.[174] The first five of these grounds replicated those in England's 1937 Matrimonial Causes Act.[175] The last two, though recommended by the 1912 Royal Commission on Divorce, were not included in the 1937 Act.

A further difference with England lay in Guernsey's decision not to replicate the 1937 Act's bar on the filing of divorce petitions within the first three years of marriage. In this the Guernsey law resembled the Divorce (Scotland) Act 1938. The lack of such a bar was intended to be counterbalanced by a provision for appointing mediators, as also the faculty

---

[170] *Billet*, 30.6.1937.
[171] *Billet*, 29.10.1937.
[172] The drafting team consisted of HM Procureur Ambrose Sherwill, HM Comptroller George Ridgway and legislative draftsman G.F. Griggs. Correspondence between Sherwill and the Home Office on technical matters concerning the *projet* is preserved in NA, HO 45/21143.
[173] Divorce was eventually made available to those domiciled in Sark by the Matrimonial Causes (Amendment) (Guernsey) Law 2002.
[174] Or confinement as a criminal lunatic or imprisonment for a term of not less than fifteen years.
[175] Save that the Guernsey law included female as well as male bestiality.

given the Court to adjourn proceedings until it was satisfied that an adequate attempt at reconciliation had been made.

In addition to its powers over divorce, Guernsey's 1939 law gave the island's new Matrimonial Causes Court jurisdiction over suits of nullity of marriage; applications for decrees of presumption of death and attendant dissolution of marriage; suits for restitution of conjugal rights; and, perhaps most importantly, suits for separation.[176] The grounds for separation specified by the new law were similar to those required for a divorce. In addition, they also included failure to comply with a decree for restitution of conjugal rights, and, in a wife's case, her husband's failure to maintain her.

When granting both divorces and separations, the Court was empowered to make maintenance orders, settle property, and allocate custody of children. The Court also had the power to order co-respondents in proceedings for divorce or separation on grounds of adultery to pay compensatory damages to petitioners.

Unfortunately for the islanders who had already waited so long for divorce, the outbreak of World War II within weeks of the law's passage prevented its immediate implementation. The delay was continued through Guernsey's five years of Occupation, and it was only on 31 August 1946 that the law was made operational.[177] Shortly before the law came into force, the States passed an amendment empowering the Royal Court to appoint a Commissioner to exercise concurrent jurisdiction over matrimonial causes with the Bailiff and Jurats.[178] This was ostensibly to allow an experienced practitioner to deal with the anticipated post-war avalanche of divorces while the Bailiff and Jurats learned how to handle them. Henry Casey, Guernsey's stipendiary magistrate, was chosen to fill this position. Mr Casey was to

---

[176] Although the Magistrate's Court remained responsible for separation by summary order, and the Ordinary Court retained concurrent jurisdiction over uncontested separations.
[177] Jersey's intending divorcees had to wait even longer, since the States of that island did not pass a Matrimonial Causes Law until August 1949, which did not become operational until 1950. The Jersey law was more narrowly based on England and Wales's 1937 Matrimonial Causes Act than the Guernsey law, including among other things a bar on divorce petitions within three years of marriage.
[178] O in C, 2.8.1946.

exercise sole jurisdiction in the Matrimonial Causes Court until his retirement in 1957.[179]

Guernsey's first ever divorce was granted on 14 November 1946.[180] Ten years later, a report on the new law's first decade of operation showed that 566 divorce petitions had been filed, of which 494 had been successful, 35 withdrawn and 21 refused. Of the 494 divorces granted, 263 had been petitioned for on grounds of adultery, 182 on grounds of desertion, and 25 on grounds of cruelty. The year of peak demand was 1947, when a total of 98 divorces were granted.[181] As the 1940s came to an end, demand for divorce dropped sharply, and the 1950s saw an average of only 33 divorces a year.[182] This figure represented a rate of 0.75 divorces per thousand inhabitants,[183] which—interestingly—was higher than the rate of just over 0.50 per thousand over the same period in England and Wales.[184] We can only speculate on the reasons for Guernsey's higher divorce rate, but contemporary sources suggest an overhang from wartime evacuation and its consequences on couples separated for five years.[185]

The 1939 Matrimonial Causes Law remains in force at the time of writing. Since 1946, it has undergone a number of amendments. The most significant of these occurred in 1972, when the Matrimonial Causes (Amendment) (Guernsey) Law repealed the article in the 1939 law setting out the seven separate grounds for divorce and replaced it with an article specifying 'irretrievable breakdown' as the sole ground.[186] This was done to reflect changes instituted by the 1969 Divorce Reform Act of England and Wales, and—like its English counterpart—Guernsey's 1972 law stipulated that 'irretrievable breakdown' had to be proven by the establishment of one or more of five facts. Two of these facts consisted in prolonged periods of separation (five years where only one spouse wanted a divorce, and two years

---

[179] *Star*, 17.4.1957.
[180] *Guernsey Evening Press*, 12.2.1947.
[181] *Guernsey Evening Press*, 18.2.1958.
[182] Calculated from figures in *Guernsey Evening Press*, 18.2.1958 and 14.1.1965.
[183] Based on an average of population totals in the 1951 and 1961 censuses.
[184] Stone, *Road to Divorce*, pp. 401–2.
[185] Some 17,000 people were evacuated from Guernsey in June 1940. The majority of these were children, but there were also a large number of accompanying mothers. The impact of this on local marriages is discussed in *Guernsey Evening Press*, 22.10.1945.
[186] O in C, 23.10.1972.

where both did), and this was said to have introduced the concept of 'no-fault' divorce. Establishing breakdown by this means was however time-consuming, and parties seeking a quicker divorce could still only do so by proving fault on the part of the respondent in the form of adultery, unreasonable behaviour or desertion. Perhaps more significant in a Guernsey context than the 'no-fault' provisions was therefore the fact that the 1972 amendment law also abolished the ability to claim damages for adultery and to petition for the restitution of conjugal rights. In breaking with the tacit view of marriage as conferring property rights over a spouse's person, the abolition of these provisions arguably had greater symbolic value than the 'no-fault' clauses. It should be noted, however, that vestiges of the old view of marriage still survived in the grounds for annulment set out in the Matrimonial Causes Law, which included impotence, wilful refusal to consummate a marriage, and pregnancy at the time of marriage by a person other than the petitioner.

This excursion into the 1970s has taken us somewhat beyond our brief. In the next chapter, we will return to the 1850s to investigate the nature and incidence of violence perpetrated by men upon women—not only within marriage, but in the family more generally, as also in informal unions and casual encounters.

4

Domestic Abuse and Sexual Violence

Since this chapter focuses on the work of Guernsey's police and judiciary, it will be necessary to preface it with a brief account of their organisation, as also of their record-keeping. Before 1915, Guernsey was policed on a parochial basis, with some parishes relying solely on their unpaid elected Constables and others employing additional salaried constables.[1] St Peter Port's two parish Constables were assisted by a force of salaried constables from 1853, and the relatively populous parishes of St Sampsons, the Vale and St Martins each employed a paid assistant constable from 1896. In wartime conditions in 1915, the States set up a temporary all-island Police Force. When this was made permanent in 1919, Guernsey's parochial policing system came to an end.[2]

From their inception, the salaried assistant constables kept a daily log of their activities in what they termed 'Occurrence Books'. Use will be made in this chapter of Occurrence Books kept by the salaried constables of St Peter Port from 1853, and of the Vale and St Martins from 1894 and 1909 respectively. The Island Police Force kept their own set of Occurrence Books from 1915, and for the period up to 1959 these will also be referred to.

As regards the court system: until 1925 lesser criminal offences were tried summarily by the Police Court (*Cour de Police Correctionnelle*) which was an iteration of the Ordinary Court composed of the Bailiff (or his Lieutenant) and at least two Jurats. After 1925, such offences were tried by the

---

[1] Each parish had two elected Constables; for more detail see section on Governance, chapter 1.
[2] R. Hocart, *An Island Assembly: The Development of the States of Guernsey, 1700–1949* (Guernsey, 1988), pp. 68, 90, 97.

stipendiary magistrate in a newly created Magistrate's Court.[3] Criminal offences of a more serious nature were tried on indictment by the Full Court, which was composed of the Bailiff or his Lieutenant and at least seven Jurats.

Proceedings concerning both petty and serious crime were recorded in the series of Greffe registers labelled *Livres en Crime* until the end of 1948.[4] From January 1949 however, *Livres en Crime* recorded only crimes tried by the Full Court, and offences dealt with by the magistrate were recorded in a separate series of Magistrate's Court Books. It is important to note that few crimes were statutorily defined in the period covered by this book, so most offences were tried under customary law. Because local charges and indictments often took the form of what stipendiary magistrate Henry Casey called in 1946 'a setting out of facts',[5] it is not always possible to put an English-style legal name to the misdeed which has been recorded in court registers.[6]

The statistics which will be used from time to time in this chapter are derived from a systematic study of Police Occurrence Books and court registers.[7] In the case of the former, I have analysed in detail the records of thirty individual years spanning the period under study, and, in the case of the latter, I have analysed records for twenty-eight individual years. In the interests of ensuring even coverage, I have spread my analysis over alternate years in alternate decades. The court register sample begins in 1850 and the Occurrence Book sample in 1854. The final year in both samples is 1958.

---

[3] The Ordinary Court retained concurrent jurisdiction with the Magistrate's Court until 1954, but never exercised this jurisdiction after 1925 (F. Gahan, 'The law of the Channel Islands, IV: criminal law in Guernsey', *The Solicitor Quarterly*, 2 (1963), p. 155).
[4] Court verdicts and sentences were also recorded in Police Occurrence Books when reported incidents progressed to a trial.
[5] *Evidence given before the Privy Council Committee on Proposed Reforms in the Channel Islands: Guernsey* (London, 1946), p. 212.
[6] This matter is discussed in greater detail in the introduction to chapter 5.
[7] For a full list of references to these, see under Primary Sources in Bibliography.

Domestic abuse

Prior to the twentieth century, violence in the form of corporal punishment was considered an appropriate means of enforcing discipline in all sorts of contexts, including the home, schools and reformatories, the armed forces, the merchant navy, poor law institutions, and the penal system. In the context of the home, men were traditionally seen as masters of their own domains, with absolute authority over their wives and families. This view was enshrined in religious doctrine. 'Wives, submit yourselves unto your own husbands', the apostle Paul instructed the Ephesians; 'for the husband is the head of the wife, even as Christ is the head of the church.'[8] Until 1928, women marrying in one of Guernsey's Anglican churches were obliged to promise not only to love and to cherish, but also to obey their husbands.[9] If the couple were Methodists, they might also have been familiar with John Wesley's famous dictum:

> whoever, therefore, would be a good wife, let this sink into her inmost soul: "My husband is my superior, my better: he has the right to rule over me. God has given it to him, and I will not strive against God."[10]

With authorities such as these to support them, and evidence of women's second-class status all around them—in schools, the workplace, civic life—it is little wonder that many men grew up with the assumption that they had an absolute right to the submission of the opposite sex. 'Think what it is to be a boy,' observed the philosopher and feminist John Stuart Mill:

> to grow up to manhood in the belief that ... by the mere fact of being born a male he is by right the superior of all and every one of an entire half of the human race ... how it grows with his growth and strengthens with his strength; how it is inoculated by one schoolboy upon the other.[11]

---

[8] Ephesians 5:22-24. See also Colossians 3:18.
[9] Bridegrooms promised only to love and to cherish. In 1928, the Church permitted the word 'obey' to be dropped from brides' vows where couples wished it.
[10] J. Emory (ed.), *The Works of the Rev. John Wesley*, 14 vols (London, 1829-31), 9, p. 82.
[11] J.S. Mill, *On the Subjection of Women* (1869; Oxford, 1991 edn), pp. 558-9.

Where submission was not forthcoming, the Norman *Coutume* explicitly accorded a husband the right to use physical violence to chastise his wife (as also his children and servants), provided it was within reasonable bounds.[12] This right was re-stated in Terrien's *Commentaires* and in *L'Approbation des Lois*, and it was confirmed as being part of insular law in Le Marchant's commentary (c.1660) and Carey's commentary (c.1750).[13] It proved a very durable part of insular law. As late as 1846, Guernsey's Bailiff Peter Stafford Carey told Royal Commissioners enquiring into the island's criminal law that it remained legally permissible for a Guernseyman moderately to 'correct' his wife.[14] In this, Guernsey's position was at least clearer than that of England. It was a common belief among contemporary Englishmen that a man had the right to chastise his wife, but, by the mid-nineteenth century, English legal authorities were questioning whether this had any firm basis in law.[15]

There have been many historical studies of domestic violence in England and Wales. For want of better sources, these studies have also relied on police and court records. Almost all of them have however observed that such records never represented more than a small fraction of the everyday violence which took place in past communities.[16] The St Peter Port Occurrence Books for the 1850s contain comparatively few reports of domestic violence: on average about twenty to thirty a year. By the 1950s, the number of reports had increased to an average of fifty to sixty a year for the entire island. In neither case should these low numbers be taken as evidence of a low incidence of abuse. As historians of domestic violence point out, such incidents were so

---

[12] W.L. De Gruchy (ed.), *L'Ancienne Coutume de Normandie* (Jersey, 1881), pp. 194, 241.
[13] G. Terrien, *Commentaires du Droict Civil tant Public que Privé Observé au Pays et Duché de Normandie* (1574; Rouen, 1654 edn), p. 16; *Approbation des Lois, Coutumes, et Usages de l'Ile de Guernesey ratifiée au Conseil Privé le 27 Octobre 1583* (Guernsey, 1822), p. 1; T. Le Marchant, *Remarques et Animadversions sur l'Approbation des Lois et Coustumier de Normandie usités ès Jurisdictions de Guernezé*, 2 vols (c.1660; Guernsey, 1826 edn), 2, pp. 198-9; L. Carey, *Essai sur les Institutions, Lois et Coutumes de l'Ile de Guernesey* (c.1750; Guernsey, 1889 edn), pp. 119, 123.
[14] *Second Report of the Commissioners appointed to inquire into the State of the Criminal Law in the Channel Islands* (London, 1848), p. 276.
[15] A. Clark, 'Domesticity and the problem of wifebeating in nineteenth-century Britain: working-class culture, law and politics', in S. D'Cruze (ed.), *Everyday Violence in Britain, 1850-1950: Gender and Class* (Harlow, 2000), pp. 27-32.
[16] J. Rowbotham, '"Only when drunk": the stereotyping of violence in England, c.1850-1900', in D'Cruze (ed.), *Everyday Violence in Britain*, p. 155.

much a part of daily life that few people thought them worth reporting.[17] Moreover, communities had their own ways of dealing with such violence, which ranged variously from ostracising offenders to providing victims with shelter and support.[18]

Of the reports which did find their way into Guernsey's Police Occurrence Books, some emanated from relatives, some from neighbours or passing witnesses, and some from the victims themselves. Spousal violence as it appears in these Books was most commonly associated with drinking. Local duties on alcohol were low, and spirits (which were sold at higher strengths than in Britain) were cheap.[19] Excessive drinking seems to have been widespread, and many a drunken husband took out his frustrations on his wife and children. The underlying causes of masculine ill-temper probably differed with each individual and can only be guessed at, but, once violence had begun within the home, it seems quickly to have become a habit. Most of the offenders who figured in Police Occurrence Books were reported not just once but many times. Their violence took many forms and often a combination of forms. It might involve smashing windows, breaking furniture and throwing crockery. Frequently it involved turning wives and children out of doors. Most often of all it involved blows—slapping, punching, kicking—and the use of domestic implements as offensive weapons: pokers, brooms, frying-pans, even teapots and kettles (sometimes with their contents).

Another reason why domestic violence incidents were not reported must have been the knowledge that reporting them would achieve little. Throughout our period, duty constables, who exercised considerable discretion, would make a *prima facie* assessment of a reported incident, and,

---

[17] Rowbotham, '"Only when drunk"', p. 157.
[18] In both France and England, a practice known *inter alia* as *charivari*, 'rough music' and 'riding the stang' was also used as a community punishment for excessive wife-beating. It involved the shaming of an offender by creating a disturbance outside his home. This practice also existed in Guernsey, where it was known as *la chevaucherie d'âne* or *la fauch'rie d'âne*. There are records of *fauch'ries* as late as 1947, but by then – and probably throughout the whole of our period – they were only performed as youthful pranks (*Star*, 12.6.1935, 18.9.1947; see also W. Gallienne, 'La fauch'rie l'âne: a description of the last fauch'rie l'âne to be enacted in the island', *TSG*, 23 (1992), pp. 319-21).
[19] R.-M. Crossan, *Poverty and Welfare in Guernsey, 1560-2015* (Woodbridge, 2015), pp. 32-4.

if they deemed it trivial (or spurious), would decline to take the matter further. As late as the 1930s, a woman who had come to the police station complaining that her husband had grabbed her by the throat and pushed her across the room was simply told to 'go away'.[20] The ostensible reason for this was that the woman bore no marks. But even when there were obvious marks, police might still dismiss a complaint if they considered the husband's actions 'justified'. When police were summoned to a house in St Sampsons in July 1916 to deal with reports of a husband assaulting his wife, the wife's plight was quickly forgotten when it was discovered she had been drinking. No action was taken against the man, but she herself was escorted to the elected Constable of the parish to receive an admonition for her laxity and a warning not to indulge again.[21] As a scholar of English domestic violence has observed, any substantiated accusation of drunkenness or neglect of home duties automatically placed a woman in the wrong.[22]

On other occasions, police might decline to follow up a report of domestic abuse because of the social standing of the accused. In June 1856, the neighbour of a well-to-do farmer from the outskirts of St Peter Port came to the police to complain of having witnessed the farmer ill-treating his wife. Later in the day, the neighbour was visited at his home by one of the assistant constables and advised 'to drop the matter'. No reason was given for this in the Occurrence Book, but it could well have been related to the fact that this farmer was a respected member of the community who was himself later to serve as Constable of St Peter Port.[23] Sometimes, of course, it was the victim herself, rather than the police, who pressed for the case to be dismissed. Many wives understandably feared retribution if their husbands were prosecuted, and Occurrence Books throughout our period abound with records of their pleas to let the matter rest.[24]

Such insistence was not usually necessary, however. Even when they did feel there was a case to answer, police constables often stopped short of initiating court action. On many occasions, they simply issued the offender

---

[20] 13.2.1934, IA, PC 186-06.
[21] 21.7.1916, IA, PC 181-01.
[22] Rowbotham, '"Only when drunk"', p. 167.
[23] 11.6.1856, IA, AQ 0991/02.
[24] See, for instance, 4.8.1857, IA, AQ 0991/03; 13.11.1872, IA, AQ 0992/03; 7.5.1910, IA, AQ 0995/01; 9.12.1934, IA, PC 187-04.

with a verbal reprimand, or consigned him to a cell to cool down. Thus Thomas Domaille experienced nothing worse than a night behind bars on no fewer than six occasions in the 1850s when he had assaulted his wife.[25] Clearly, however, this was no deterrent to a habitual perpetrator of violence.

Usually, the only domestic violence cases which did reach court were ones where the injuries sustained had been particularly severe, or where serious violence had been repeated with particular frequency. Such cases were usually referred by St Peter Port's post-1853 salaried constables to one of their elected superiors. If the elected Constable decided to proceed, he either ordered the accused to appear in court at the next sitting or, more commonly in serious cases, took him into custody and consulted the Bailiff and Law Officers for further instructions.[26] After the establishment of the Island Police in 1915, constables' first point of reference was the Police Inspector.[27]

About 25 per cent of reported incidents reached court in the 1850s, and convictions for domestic violence comprised some 3 per cent of all Police Court convictions. Surprisingly, the proportion of cases reaching court declined in the twentieth century, so that, by the 1950s, only 5 per cent of reported domestic violence incidents were prosecuted, and convictions for domestic violence constituted no more than 1 per cent of convictions in the Magistrate's Court. It is impossible to assess whether this declining proportion arose because greater numbers of 'trivial' domestic incidents were reported in the 1950s, or because the police had become even more disinclined to take action.

Domestic violence cases were usually prosecuted as common assaults. Perhaps surprisingly, given the rigorous prior *triage*, many cases which were brought to court were dismissed. Often this was because the court deemed the evidence insufficient to convict. This was a particular problem in the earlier part of our period, when a wife was prohibited from giving evidence in court to prove ill-treatment of herself on the part of her husband.[28] The

---

[25] 20.10.1854, IA, AQ 0991/02; 21.3.1857, 20.8.1857, 15.12.1857, 24.4.1858, 19.8.1858, IA, AQ 0991/03.
[26] The police initiated proceedings but the Law Officers conducted prosecutions in court. At this time there were no private criminal prosecutions in Guernsey.
[27] Memorandum on Criminal Procedure in Guernsey, 20.11.1922, NA, HO 45/24658.
[28] *Second Report of the Commissioners*, p. 233.

situation eased somewhat with the passage in 1865 of *la Loi relative aux Preuves* which allowed spouses of both sexes to be heard as witnesses in criminal proceedings relating to offences of violence committed against them by their spouse.[29] This law was however permissive only, and it was not until the passage of the 1923 *Loi relative aux Preuves au Criminel* that spouses could be compelled to testify against one another in such cases.[30]

In the mid-Victorian period, the Police Court also dismissed many domestic violence cases in return for a husband's promise not to oppose his wife's application for a separation.[31] This practice ceased after the passage in 1890 of *la Loi relative à la Séparation de Mari et Femme en Police Correctionnelle*, which allowed the Police Court itself to grant non-cohabitation orders to victims of violence.[32]

Where convictions were obtained, sentences in cases of domestic abuse tended to be light. In the 1850s, most of those convicted received short custodial sentences of two or three days. By the 1950s, the great majority of men convicted for spousal assault were simply bound over. Historical studies of domestic violence have drawn attention to lax sentencing for domestic assaults in the United Kingdom. One scholar has observed that 'violence to a wife could be punished less severely than violence to a cat or even a municipal park bench!'[33] The same was undoubtedly true of Guernsey. In a single Police Court session in May 1914, Ernest Ogier was sentenced to one month in prison for working a sick donkey, while Richard Wyatt got away with a token fine for assaulting his wife.[34] Four years earlier, Frederick Frampton had received one month in prison for striking a constable, but only one week for beating his cohabitee.[35] As the above-mentioned scholar concluded, the courts' 'failure to crack down hard on wife-abuse suggests a general acquiescence in the practice.'[36]

---

[29] O in C, 29.6.1865.
[30] O in C, 10.2.1923.
[31] For instance, 14.9.1857, 15.12.1857, IA, AQ 0991/03; 18.9.1873, IA, AQ 0992/03.
[32] See section on Separation, chapter 3.
[33] M.E. Doggett, *Marriage, Wife-Beating and the Law in Victorian England* (Columbia, 1993), p. 127.
[34] 14.5.1914, GG, *Livres en Crime*, vol. 55. See also Note 5, p. xiii, above.
[35] The constable had been called to Frampton's home to deal with the assault (29.12.1910, GG, *Livres en Crime*, vol. 55).
[36] Doggett, *Marriage, Wife-Beating and the Law*, p. 128.

Even where beatings had resulted in a wife's death, Guernsey's courts tended to err on the side of caution. In the mid-1850s, there were three particularly unpleasant such trials. Only in one of them, where the evidence was incontrovertible, was the husband convicted of his wife's murder.[37] In the other two cases, both involving men already known to the police for wife-beating, Jurats sitting in full court rendered unanimous acquittals. The first of these cases concerned the wife of Robert Street who died of a ruptured kidney at her home in St Peter Port on an autumn night in 1856. Street was charged with her murder, as the doctors who conducted her autopsy considered the rupture likely to have resulted from violence. At Street's trial, the Bailiff, Peter Stafford Carey, observed that, although it was apparent that Mrs Street 'had died of injuries inflicted by someone very recently', there was no proof that her husband, who had been in the house with her, had inflicted them. The previous year, Street, a hawker, had spent a night in police cells for assaulting his wife but was released without charge.[38] A majority of the Jurats at Robert Street's trial agreed that Mrs Street 'had died a violent death'. However, they also agreed with the Bailiff that 'there [was] a link wanting in the chain of evidence,' and therefore 'they preferred discharging the prisoner to condemning him with any doubt, however slender, lingering in their minds.'[39] While we might agree that the evidence presented against Street in court does not appear to have been conclusive, what strikes a modern researcher is the apparent absence of any effort on the part of either the police or court to establish whether there was anyone else in the house who could have inflicted the violence.[40]

A matter of months later, William Trachy was acquitted in very similar circumstances. This time, the unfortunate wife had died from injuries sustained during a drinking bout in which both had participated in their St Peter Port garret. Trachy, a seaman, had a long record of domestic violence.[41]

---

[37] An Irishman from County Kilkenny was sentenced to transportation for life for kicking and punching his wife to death at their home in St Peter Port (9.5.1853, 6.6.1853, GG, *Livres en Crime*, vol. 34).

[38] 24.12.1855, IA, AQ 0991/02. See also Note 5, p. xiii, above.

[39] 18.10.1856, 20.10.1856, 18.11.1856, GG, *Livres en Crime*, vol. 35. The trial is reported in *Comet*, 17.11.1856, 20.11.1856.

[40] This, at least, is the impression given by newspaper reports. Surviving police and court records are too perfunctory to provide further enlightenment.

[41] See incidents reported on 30.7.1853, 8.2.1855, 9.2.1855, 4.3.1856, IA, AQ 0991/02.

The couple had been drinking alone, and neighbours testified to having heard shouting and scuffling in their garret on the day the woman died. Nevertheless, Trachy was allowed to walk out of the Royal Court free. As with Robert Street, the grounds given for his acquittal were that there was no proof his wife's injuries had been inflicted by him, but again neither police nor court appear to have made much effort to find it.[42]

In the Trachy case, the fact that the wife was a known drinker may have disposed the authorities to view her fate as understandable, if not deserved. The exculpatory effect of female errancy lingered well beyond the 1850s. Just short of seven decades after Trachy's acquittal, Ambrose Sherwill, acting as defence counsel for a man accused of attempted wife murder, argued for his client's acquittal on the basis that

> the wife was neglectful and was living in a loose manner, causing considerable grief to her husband, and providing such provocation as to make any violence used towards her at least less blameworthy.[43]

In this case, evidence against the husband was so overwhelming that the court found him guilty as charged.[44] The issue here, however, is not so much the court's verdict as the fact that such an apparently enlightened figure as Ambrose Sherwill could have used so crude an argument.[45] It is an illustration, if nothing else, of the universality and persistence of patriarchal attitudes.

Sexual violence

As with domestic abuse, traditional attitudes to sexual violence had a surprisingly enduring purchase. In order to identify these, we shall turn, to begin with, to the customary law. The thirteenth-century *Grand Coutumier* stated that the forcible deflowering of a virgin was a felony and therefore liable

---

[42] *Comet*, 1.6.1857.
[43] *Star*, 30.6.1926. My italics.
[44] *Star*, 1.7.1926.
[45] Notwithstanding his duty to adduce what evidence he could to defend his client.

to the death penalty.[46] However, Guillaume Terrien, citing a legal decision of 1518, added a rider—namely, that men who raped females who had already 'abandoned themselves' to others would not be liable to the death penalty but a lesser punishment.[47] The prime consideration underlying both of these provisions was not the harm done to the women themselves, but to the males who had property in them. The rape of a virgin was seen as a form of theft. Virginity was a *sine qua non* for respectable matrimony, and its forcible removal nullified a woman's value in the marriage market. Hence a man who raped a virgin merited serious punishment. A non-virgin who bestowed her favours freely was of no marketable value to anyone and, as no male interests were injured by her violation, punishment need not be so severe. As Nicola Lacey has observed, the law was 'coded masculine through and through'—'male interests masquerading as human interests'.[48]

Terrien's statements on rape were accepted as part of Guernsey law in the *Approbation des Lois*.[49] They were also repeated and reaffirmed by Thomas Le Marchant (c.1660) and Laurent Carey (c.1750).[50] In 1846, however, Peter Stafford Carey told the visiting Royal Commissioners that Terrien's distinction with regard to 'women of bad fame' was no longer observed in Guernsey rape cases.[51] He also told the Commissioners, that, even though Guernsey's legislature had never made any statutory enactments on rape, the crime would now be handled in precisely the same way as in England and Wales where rape had long been a statutory offence and the subject of much case law.[52] Carey was speaking just four years before the start of our period so we may take this as the official position as our period began. The extent to which it pertained in practice will become apparent below.

---

[46] De Gruchy (ed.), *L'Ancienne Coutume*, p. 162.
[47] Terrien, *Commentaires*, pp. 483–4.
[48] N. Lacey, *Unspeakable Subjects: Feminist Essays in Legal and Social Theory* (Oxford, 1998), pp. 14, 189.
[49] *Approbation des Lois*, p. 23.
[50] Le Marchant, *Remarques et Animadversions*, 2, p. 183; Carey, *Essai sur les Institutions*, pp. 126, 228.
[51] *Second Report of the Commissioners*, p. 276.
[52] *Second Report of the Commissioners*, p. 276. At the time of writing, rape remains a common law offence in Guernsey. For the law in England and Wales, see L.A. Jackson, *Child Sexual Abuse in Victorian England* (London, 2000), p. 13.

Reports of sexual assaults featured even more rarely in Police Occurrence Books than reports of domestic violence, especially in the earlier part of our period. In 1850s St Peter Port, they averaged as few as one or two a year. In Guernsey, as elsewhere, issues of family honour, respectability, and shame militated against the reporting of sexual assaults, since victims were invariably perceived as tainted by the nature of the crime itself. Reporting therefore remained at a low level throughout the nineteenth century, and it was only after c.1910 that there was any perceptible rise. This rise was chiefly due to Edwardian legislation establishing new categories of sexual offence.[53] The rising trend in reporting was sustained through subsequent decades, and, by the 1950s, the number of reported male-on-female sexual assaults stood at between twenty and thirty per year.

As in cases of domestic violence, few reports of sexual assaults ever went beyond the police station, and, when they did reach court, they did not always result in convictions. In the 1850s, convictions for sexual offences of all kinds comprised on average only 0.3 per cent of all criminal convictions in Guernsey each year. This situation, which persisted for the rest of the century, mirrored that in Victorian Britain, where a county as large as Cornwall might see only a handful of such convictions annually.[54] In the post-Edwardian period, numbers of convictions increased in tandem with increased reporting, such that by the 1950s convictions for sexual offences accounted for an average of 5 per cent of annual criminal convictions. This substantial increase in convictions in comparison with the 1850s is the more noteworthy in light of the fact that domestic violence cases followed an opposite trajectory, declining from an average of 3 per cent to 1 per cent of convictions over the same period.

Sexual assaults on adults[55]

Reports to Guernsey's police of sexual assaults on adult women were particularly few in the nineteenth century, and—because of the issues of honour and taint highlighted above—a majority of the small number of rape

---

[53] This legislation will be dealt with below.
[54] Jackson, *Child Sexual Abuse*, p. 24.
[55] Any assault victim over sixteen will be considered an adult for the purposes of this section.

reports logged by St Peter Port's Victorian police did not come from ordinary members of the public, but rather from prostitutes who had no 'honour' to lose. The police's response to a rape allegation by a prostitute was predictably dismissive. Most constables seemed to feel that, merely by engaging in the trade, prostitutes forfeited any right to protection or redress. The behaviour of the St Peter Port police towards a well-known prostitute in 1857 is fairly typical: when she came to the desk one April night with a complaint that a punter had attempted to rape her, the duty constable refused to entertain it and instructed her to decamp.[56]

The handful of rape reports which did come from ordinary members of the public were taken more seriously, and from time to time such cases reached court. Peter Stafford Carey's remarks to the 1846 Commissioners notwithstanding, however, the exculpatory effect of a 'bad fame' aspersion remained strong. A case in point was the 1854 trial of William Strachan for 'attempting the chastity' of seventeen-year-old Catherine Falla.[57] Strachan, a Royal Artillery Private, had attached himself to Catherine and another girl as they walked up Mill Street in St Peter Port one spring evening. The girls were on their way to the Charroterie where Catherine's friend intended to pay a visit to an acquaintance. After the friend had reached her destination, leaving Catherine alone with the soldier, Catherine expressed a wish to return to her home in Hauteville, and Strachan suggested he accompany her up Park Lane Steps, a quiet stairway linking the two thoroughfares. Catherine declined his offer, and set off down the adjacent lane, Strachan still following her. The soldier set upon her towards the end of the lane, from whence her screams attracted a nearby constable who, with another witness, appears to have found Strachan *in flagrante*.

According to the press report, Catherine's claims as to rape were undermined by her admission that she had in the past kept company with other soldiers, for whom it was claimed she had 'a predilection'. Advocate Gallienne, for the defence, asked 'if it was not inconsistent ... to charge a man with attempting the chastity of a female who proved to be entirely destitute of chastity?' HM Procureur countered that 'even though her previous

---

[56] 3.4.1857, IA, AQ 0991/03.
[57] The paragraph which follows is drawn from *Comet*, 22.5.1854 and 11.5.1854, 13.5.1854, 20.5.1854, GG, *Livres en Crime*, vol. 34. See also Note 5, p. xiii, above.

character would raise a contrary presumption', Catherine's refusal to accompany the soldier up Park Lane Steps showed that she had wished to avoid potential danger. In light of her 'tainted' reputation, however, he suggested a penalty of just six weeks' imprisonment. Summing up the case, the Bailiff, Peter Stafford Carey, confirmed 'that the degree of criminality' inherent in Strachan's actions 'would be diminished by the previous character of the girl'. Other Jurats were of the same mind and found Private Strachan 'guilty, with extenuating circumstances'. They then passed a sentence of three weeks' imprisonment.[58]

Plate 22. Peter Stafford Carey[59]
Guernsey Museums & Galleries (States of Guernsey) 2018

A generation or two after Carey, matters were not quite so stark. A similar case from 1903 had a very different outcome. This case involved the rape of another seventeen-year-old by two young men near the military camp at Fort Le Marchant in the Vale.[60] According to a newspaper report, attempts were

---

[58] It was the task of HM Procureur, acting as prosecutor in criminal trials, to suggest an appropriate sentence in his closing speech. The Bailiff then summed up the evidence, and each Jurat gave his personal opinion on it. The sentence was decided by majority vote of the Jurats, the Bailiff having a casting vote in case of a tie (J. Duncan, *The History of Guernsey* (London, 1841), p. 494).
[59] Carey was knighted in 1863.
[60] 23.10.1903, GG, *Livres en Crime*, vol. 53.

made by the men's defence counsel to discredit the seventeen-year-old by suggesting 'she was often seen walking round the camp'.[61] However, the Bailiff, Sir Henry Giffard, concluded that even though she 'was not a steady girl [and] was seen in the camp oftener than she ought to have been [she] should still have the protection of the law.'[62] On this occasion, the two assailants were unanimously found guilty and sentenced to ten years' penal servitude.

During the course of the Fort Le Marchant rape trial, defence counsel Harold Randell had reminded Jurats of the 'cautionary instruction' famously issued by the English jurist Sir Matthew Hale:

> rape is an accusation easily to be made and hard to be proved, and harder to be defended by the party accused, tho' never so innocent.[63]

It was probably not difficult for Jurats to put themselves in the place of the accused, since the defendant in a rape case was always male and Jurats hearing the case were also invariably male. The historian Carolyn Conley has contended that this state of affairs all too frequently led English judges and juries to give defendants the benefit of the doubt, or to trivialise or minimise assaults.[64] That this was also the case in Guernsey certainly seems to have been the impression of a 21-year-old hotel receptionist who took her alleged rapist to court in Guernsey in 1949.[65] Even though there was evidence of physical injury, the defending advocate urged a cautionary approach: 'it is not quite enough to convict a man just because a complaint has been made ... For a variety of reasons a person might make a complaint which is not reliable.'[66] Nine out of the twelve male Jurats hearing the trial agreed and the alleged perpetrator was allowed to go free. Expressing her disappointment at the acquittal, the receptionist (who was from England) later wrote to Guernsey's Law Officers:

---

[61] *Guernsey Evening Press*, 23.10.1903.
[62] Like Peter Stafford Carey before him, Giffard (knighted in 1903) was an English-trained barrister.
[63] Sir M. Hale, *History of the Pleas of the Crown*, 2 vols (London, 1736), 1, p. 634. For Advocate Randell's words, see *Guernsey Evening Press*, 23.10.1903.
[64] C.A. Conley, 'Rape and justice in Victorian England', *Victorian Studies*, 29 (1986), p. 532.
[65] The trial is reported in *Star*, 19.3.1949, 25.4.1949, 26.4.1949.
[66] *Star*, 26.4.1949.

> ... it is not my place to criticize the administration of Guernsey law, but I would like to say that, in cases such as mine, it seems hardly right that those who sat in judgement should all be men of the same age and outlook.[67]

The philosopher and feminist John Stuart Mill had once observed that

> it is one of the fundamental doctrines of the British Constitution that all persons should be tried by their peers; yet women, whenever tried, are tried by male judges and a male jury.[68]

In rape and sexual assault cases, women were arguably as much on trial as their assailants, and the presence of females on the bench might have produced different outcomes. By the time the hotel receptionist wrote her letter, women had been serving on juries in England and Wales for nearly three decades, and nearly a quarter of magistrates were female.[69] In Guernsey, the Royal Court remained unmitigatedly masculine until the final quarter of the twentieth century. There were no female advocates until 1973 and no female Jurats until 1985. A further eleven years were to elapse before the first female acting magistrate was appointed, and there was no female stipendiary magistrate until 2004.[70]

Sexual assaults on girls

Few reports of child molestation were made to Guernsey's police in the nineteenth century, and when cases did come to police attention, they were usually not followed up.[71] One reason for police inaction was the problem of evidence. Little could be achieved if the child was young and inarticulate and there were no witnesses to an alleged incident. A further reason, harder to understand from a twenty-first-century perspective, was the widespread

---

[67] 30.4.1949, IA, LO 038-03.
[68] J.S. Mill, *Dissertations and Discussions Political, Philosophical and Historical*, 2 vols (London, 1859), 1, p. 418.
[69] S. D'Cruze and L.A. Jackson, *Women, Crime and Justice in England since 1660* (Basingstoke, 2009), pp. 114–15.
[70] See Appendix 2.
[71] St Peter Port constables' handling of a reported molester in 1859 is typical. Although the man was held for a few hours at the police office, the case was ultimately not pursued and he was allowed to go free (8.4.1859, 9.4.1859, IA, AQ 0991/03).

feeling that assaults on such lower-class girls as came within the police's ambit were of no great consequence. Juvenile prostitution was a fact of life in nineteenth-century St Peter Port, and when the police dealt with child prostitutes, their response was to have them checked for sexually transmitted diseases, not to enquire who paid for their services.[72] This was compounded by a generally shared view that young girls from very poor backgrounds seldom remained innocent for long and might well exercise a degree of agency in sexual cases.[73]

These attitudes are neatly encapsulated by a child sexual assault case from the 1870s so serious that it did overcome police and judicial barriers. In the autumn of 1871, a 75-year-old retired master mariner working as a porter at the Town Hospital, was charged with sexually assaulting two little girls aged eight and ten. The nature of the assault is unclear, but evidence from the Police Occurrence Book suggests that under contemporary English law it would probably have been prosecuted as 'unlawful carnal knowledge'.[74] The porter had first met the girls when they came to the Hospital to fetch prescriptions from the dispensary. He made friends with them and, when they came to the Hospital again,ptsinvited them into his lodge. The girls began to visit the man regularly, and it was during these visits that his behaviour took on a sexual dimension. According to newspaper accounts, the porter's assaults on the girls were carried out 'with, as it appears, the *willing assent of the wretched little creatures*, the prisoner bribing them with small presents of money, sweetmeats, pictures, &c.'[75] Eventually, the girls' mothers discovered what had happened to their daughters and reported the man to the police, who, faced with medical evidence, had little choice but to take the matter to court. For the defence, Advocate Falla argued that the porter should not be subjected to a severe sentence since he had never used any violence 'and that what had happened

---

[72] See, for instance, VD checks on thirteen-year-old Amelia Farley in 1853; fifteen-year-old Eliza Murphy in 1863; Mary Bond and Bridget Quin, both fourteen, in 1869 and 1882 (29.10.1853, IA, DC/HX 130-04; 21.4.1863, 3.6.1869, IA, DC/HX 127-01; 10.6.1882, IA, DC/HX 130-03).
[73] Jackson, *Child Sexual Abuse*, pp. 83–9.
[74] 15.9.1871, 16.9.1871, 14.10.1871, IA, AQ 0992/03. By 'unlawful carnal knowledge' was understood intercourse with a minor which could not be characterised as forcible rape.
[75] *Star*, 14.10.1871. My italics.

had been *with the children's consent.*⁷⁶ On the instructions of the Bailiff, Sir Peter Stafford Carey, the case was 'reduced to one of indecency' and the porter was sentenced to eight weeks' imprisonment.⁷⁷

From a modern perspective, it seems shocking that little girls of eight and ten could be thought capable of 'consenting' to the acts which their abuser performed, but Victorian Guernsey had no statutory age of consent. In this respect, the situation in Guernsey was very different from that in England and Wales, where the carnal knowledge of girls aged less than twelve had been made a statutory crime as early as 1275.⁷⁸ Guernsey's deficiencies in this area had been discussed in 1846 when Royal Commissioners came to the island to enquire into state of the criminal law. An exchange which took place between the Commissioners and HM Procureur Charles De Jersey is particularly eloquent of Guernsey's old-fashioned attitudes to these matters and worth reproduction here. Commenting on the island's lack of a statutory age of consent, the Commissioners asked 'You would probably take the age [of a child victim] as a matter of want of consent?' De Jersey replied that this had been 'tried' in the case of William Laurens in 1818. Ostensibly taking Laurens' part, De Jersey continued, 'The child consented; but they punished the man nevertheless.' 'What was the age of the child?', the Commissioners asked. 'From ten to eleven years old,' De Jersey replied, explaining again that Laurens had suffered eight weeks' imprisonment even though 'the girl in question belonged to a family whose sisters were not very well behaved; and there is no doubt but that the child was consenting.'⁷⁹

In England and Wales, the statutory age of consent had gradually risen through a series of statutes to reach sixteen in 1885.⁸⁰ This milestone was achieved by the 1885 Criminal Law Amendment Act, which also applied to Scotland and Ireland and made carnal knowledge of girls aged between

---

⁷⁶ *Star*, 14.10.1871. My italics.
⁷⁷ Carey was himself the father of seven girls. One wonders what his attitude would have been if any of his daughters had been exploited in the way experienced by these unfortunate girls.
⁷⁸ Jackson, *Child Sexual Abuse*, pp. 13, 159. In France, the age of consent was statutorily set at eleven in 1832 and raised to thirteen in 1863 (J.M. Donovan, *Juries and the Transformation of Criminal Justice in France in the Nineteenth and Twentieth Centuries* (Chapel Hill, 2010), p. 101).
⁷⁹ *Second Report of the Commissioners*, p. 276.
⁸⁰ Jackson, *Child Sexual Abuse*, p. 13.

thirteen and sixteen punishable by up to two years' imprisonment, and carnal knowledge of girls under thirteen liable to a maximum of imprisonment for life.[81] The 1885 Criminal Law Amendment Act was largely the product of a vociferous campaign by social purity lobbyists who hoped that raising the age limit for carnal knowledge prosecutions would help curb juvenile prostitution.[82] For much the same reasons, Jersey passed its own version of the Criminal Law Amendment Act in 1895 which also set the age of consent at sixteen.[83]

While Guernsey also had an active social purity lobby, it was unable to persuade the States to pass similar legislation until the Edwardian period. There are a number of complex reasons for this which will be explored in the next chapter. Ultimately, however, the States did pass a law akin to the 1885 Criminal Law Amendment Act in 1907.[84] Like its Westminster predecessor, *la Loi relative à la Protection des Femmes et Filles Mineures* was primarily concerned with deterring the recruitment of young girls to prostitution, and criminalised various types of abduction, detention, intimidation and false representation. Its most socially significant effect was, however, to set the female age of consent at sixteen. The law made carnal knowledge of girls between thirteen and sixteen (and 'female idiots and imbeciles' of any age) misdemeanours punishable by imprisonment for up to two years (unless the accused satisfied the court that he genuinely had reason to believe that a girl was over sixteen). The law also made carnal knowledge of girls aged under thirteen a felony with a maximum penalty of penal servitude at the discretion of the court, and attempted carnal knowledge of under-thirteens a misdemeanour subject to a maximum of two years' imprisonment.[85]

The most important innovation of this law was to introduce the concept of 'statutory rape', in which the question of consent was immaterial. Thus

---

[81] Jackson, *Child Sexual Abuse*, p. 13.
[82] Jackson, *Child Sexual Abuse*, p. 15. For more on the social purity movement, see n. 112, chapter 5.
[83] *Loi (1895) appliquant à cette Ile Certaines Provisions du Criminal Law Amendment Act*.
[84] O in C, 6.7.1907. The law had its origin in a petition submitted to the Bailiff by social purity campaigners in alliance with sympathetic States members (8.5.1906, GG, Royal Court Letter Book No. 18; *Billet*, 26.9.1906; *Star*, 25.9.1906).
[85] Note that 'imprisonment' was served in Guernsey's own prison, and 'penal servitude' in one of the English convict prisons.

when a thirty-year-old man was tried for violating an eleven-year-old at her parents' home in Mill Street in the autumn of 1910, the child's consent, or lack of it, was not even considered. HM Procureur reminded Jurats that the law under which the case was being tried was *la Loi relative à la Protection des Femmes et Filles Mineures* which criminalised all under-age sex irrespective of circumstances. The man was found guilty as charged and sentenced to seven years' penal servitude.[86]

The 1907 law was only in force for seven years. In 1914, it was repealed by a second law on this subject which re-enacted its provisions in more elaborate form.[87] Of interest to us are two particular changes. The first was to lay down that no prosecution in respect of offences against thirteen-to-sixteen-year-olds could be brought if the offence had taken place more than six months previously. The second was to institute lighter punishments for boys under sixteen convicted of carnal knowledge (or attempted carnal knowledge) of girls under thirteen, namely birching and/or reformatory school. The chief effect of these three alterations was to dilute the protections offered to females and increase those offered to males.

Between World War I and the end of our period, the *Filles Mineures* law underwent a number of further modifications, again intended to bring Guernsey more closely into line with the United Kingdom. A law of 1930 lengthened from six months to twelve the time limit within which prosecutions could be brought for offences against thirteen-to-sixteen-year-olds.[88] A law of 1950 restricted the 'reasonable cause to believe' defence to men of 23 and under who had never previously been charged with a sexual offence against a thirteen-to-sixteen-year-old (whilst however also making it available to men charged with indecent assault).[89] Finally, a law of 1956 further extended the 'reasonable cause to believe' defence to men of 23 and under who had previously been charged with a

---

[86] 31.10.1910, GG, *Livres en Crime*, vol. 54; 12.11.1910, *Livres en Crime*, vol. 55; *Gazette de Guernesey*, 19.11.1910.
[87] *Loi relative à la Protection des Femmes et Filles Mineures* (O in C, 16.7.1914). This law originated directly from the Law Officers during a period of legislative updating.
[88] *Loi relative à la Protection des Femmes et Filles Mineures (Amendement) 1930* (O in C, 27.10.1930). This law also made admissible the evidence of children too young to understand the nature of an oath, providing that the court was satisfied they were of sufficient intelligence and understood their duty to be truthful.
[89] Offences against Girls (Availability of Defences) Law 1950 (O in C, 21.7.1950).

sexual offence against a thirteen-to-sixteen-year-old, but had been acquitted.[90] Although these measures restored to females some of the ground lost to males in 1914, under-age girls were, on balance, left in a position less advantageous than between 1907 and World War I.

There is no doubt that the *Filles Mineures* laws contributed to an increase in the reporting and prosecution of sexual offences from the Edwardian period on. This effect moreover extended beyond carnal knowledge cases to encompass indecent assaults, notwithstanding that indecent assault *per se* was not dealt with by statute until considerably later.[91] Court registers from the first half of the twentieth century document gradually increasing numbers of prosecutions relating to sexual assaults on young girls. By the 1950s, these had risen to an average of just under ten per year. Many of these assaults were opportunistic in nature: carried out in urban alleys and stairways, in country lanes and fields, on beaches, inside parked vehicles, behind bushes in recreation areas (Beau Séjour and La Vallette were favoured St Peter Port locations). Others took the form of long-standing planned abuse, where a girl might be 'groomed' by an adult already known to her and exploited over several months or years. From time to time, a middle-class perpetrator might be brought to court, but prosecutions more usually concerned men from lower social strata: apprentices, farm labourers, greenhouse hands, hotel workers, and, before World War II, a noticeable number of garrison soldiers.

For all that, there seems to have remained a significant gulf between the incidence of child molestation and its prosecution. Many—perhaps most—affected families remained reluctant to report cases to the police. One major reason for this was the traumatic nature of the court process.[92] The Guernsey Rescue and Preventive Society, which supported families wishing to prosecute offenders, observed that the cross-examination of children in open court was a particular deterrent—'parents dread publicity and refuse to

---

[90] Offences against Girls (Availability of Defences) Law 1956 (O in C, 19.12.1956).

[91] The indecent assault of under-sixteens was made a statutory offence by the Protection of Children (Bailiwick of Guernsey) Law 1985, which prescribed maximum penalties of a £500 fine or five years' imprisonment.

[92] There was also a perception that incidents involving men of any standing were not worth reporting, since it was felt (not without reason) that the police and other bodies would find reasons not to pursue them.

prosecute'.[93] A further disincentive, even when victims did submit themselves to the ordeal of a public trial, was that the court seldom applied the maximum penalties available under the law. In all but the gravest offences, punishments of assaults on girls remained light throughout our period, consisting mainly of probation, bindings over, suspended sentences, and, at most, imprisonment for a month or two.

The lenience of these punishments becomes particularly apparent when they are compared with punishments for offences against boys. Louise Jackson has noted in her history of English child sexual abuse that, whereas the abuse of girls was generally not taken as seriously as it merited, there was always strong repugnance towards assaults on boys. This was perhaps inevitable, given that the police and judiciary were predominantly masculine institutions. According to Professor Jackson, boy victims were seldom attributed the sexual agency sometimes ascribed to girls, and they were most often posited as 'the defiled victims of disgustingly corrupt adult men'.[94] In the mid-1950s, two court cases took place in Guernsey which clearly illustrate disparities in the punishment of male-on-female assaults as compared with male-on-male ones. In March 1955, a 36-year-old man was found guilty of a sexual offence on a 14-year-old boy in an incident at a St Peter Port house which apparently involved no violence. He was sentenced to two years' hard labour.[95] Just a few months earlier, another 36-year-old man had assaulted a 15-year-old girl in a St Peters country lane after both had got off a late-night bus. Although the girl sustained a blow across the jaw, lost her shoes, and had 'her clothing, including her underclothing, badly torn', the defence counsel was reported to have argued 'that this was not such a grave offence as there was no intercourse'. Despite the obviously violent and traumatic nature of the incident, the girl's attacker was sentenced to only fifteen months.[96]

Discussion of these cases brings us to a necessary digression concerning male-on-male sexual offences. The next section will deal will assaults on boys, as also with the laws which were enacted to punish them. As this section

---

[93] 8.9.1927, IA, GW 01-02. A detailed account of the Guernsey Rescue and Preventive Society is provided in chapter 5.
[94] Jackson, *Child Sexual Abuse*, pp. 102-4. Sheila Jeffreys makes similar observations at pp. 55-8 of *The Spinster and her Enemies: Feminism and Sexuality, 1880-1930* (London, 1985).
[95] 19.3.1955, GG, *Livres en Crime*, vol. 72; *Star*, 21.3.1955.
[96] *Star*, 2.2.1953.

progresses, readers will note that this topic is not without relevance to the subject in hand, since—in Guernsey, at least—laws designed primarily to punish men were also used to punish women.

Sexual assaults on boys

In England and Wales, sodomy was first made a statutory offence in 1533.[97] In Jersey, it was made a statutory offence in 1800.[98] Victorian Guernsey had no equivalent statutes. Questioned on this matter by the 1846 Royal Commissioners, HM Procureur Charles De Jersey stated that sodomy could nevertheless be prosecuted under Guernsey's common law. He added, however, 'the Court are very unwilling to investigate such a case, and rather conceive that the investigation does more harm than the punishment would do good.'[99]

In England and Wales, the 1861 Offences against the Person Act extended the range of male-on-male sexual offences to encompass indecent assault as well as actual sodomy. In 1885, the Criminal Law Amendment Act went even further by making it a crime for any male person to 'engage in, procure, or attempt to procure the commission of any act of gross indecency' with another person of the male sex in a public or private place—a deliberately catch-all enactment which in effect criminalised all homosexual acts, whether they were consenting or not.[100]

Guernsey continued without a law on the subject for a further quarter of a century. In 1910, however, the island's Law Officers produced a *projet de loi* relating to sodomy which was approved by the States with little debate, and ratified by the Privy Council in 1911.[101] The *projet* does not seem to have been prompted by any external event, but seems rather to have been part of

---

[97] J.N. Katz, 'The age of sodomitical sin, 1607-1740', in J. Goldberg (ed.), *Reclaiming Sodom* (London, 1994), p. 47. Sodomy was also known as buggery and is usually interpreted as referring to anal intercourse between two males or a male and a female.
[98] *Loi (1800) sur le Crime de Sodomie.*
[99] *Second Report of the Commissioners*, p. 276.
[100] This statute applied throughout the United Kingdom.
[101] *Billet*, 7.12.1910; O in C, 25.5.1911.

the same exercise in legislative updating responsible for the second *Loi relative à la Protection des Femmes et Filles Mineures*.[102]

Surprisingly, the 1911 *Loi relative à la Sodomie* was not based on the 1885 Criminal Law Amendment Act, but on another statute which was by this time already fifty years old, namely the 1861 Offences against the Person Act, sections 61-3 of which it replicated almost verbatim. These specifically made the active participant in an act of anal intercourse with another male (or with a female or an animal) guilty of a felony under a maximum penalty of penal servitude for life, while also making attempted sodomy, and any male-on-male indecent assault, misdemeanours punishable by up to ten years' penal servitude.

Guernsey's sodomy law remained in this form for eighteen years. Ultimately, in 1929, the 1911 *Loi relative à la Sodomie* was repealed and replaced by a new law.[103] By this time, attitudes to homosexuality seem to have hardened, and the new law introduced some of the harsher provisions of the Criminal Law Amendment Act. While re-enacting the articles of the 1911 law relating to sodomy and indecent assault *per se*, the second *Loi relative à la Sodomie* also incorporated an article replicating word-for-word the section of the Criminal Law Amendment Act which dealt with 'gross indecency'.[104] Significantly, as we shall shortly see, the 1929 law was amended in 1948 to enable the prosecution of the passive as well as the active participant in an act of sodomy.[105]

In England and Wales, consensual homosexual acts performed in private by men over 21 were decriminalised by the 1967 Sexual Offences Act. Similar legislation followed in Scotland in 1980 and Northern Ireland in 1982. In Guernsey, the Sexual Offences (Bailiwick of Guernsey) Law 1983 brought Guernsey into line with the United Kingdom by also decriminalising homosexual acts within these parameters. This law was enacted on Home Office advice when it emerged (after a court case which had forced the change in Northern Ireland) that Guernsey's 1929 law was in breach of article 8 of

---

[102] See n. 87, above.
[103] *Loi relative à la Sodomie* (O in C, 7.5.1929).
[104] It further added a clause stipulating that consent was to be no defence when an indecent assault had been carried out on a child under sixteen.
[105] *Loi portant Amendement à la Loi de 1929 relative à la Sodomie* (O in C, 22.12.1948).

the European Convention which provided for the right to respect for private and family life.[106]

The amendment made to Guernsey's sodomy law in 1948 played a prominent part in a trial five years later, which saw a major prosecution for sodomy and one of the longest sentences ever received for this crime.[107] Ironically, the person who received the sentence was a woman. The act of sodomy (at night in a public park) was an act of prostitution, for which the woman was paid. The man who performed the act was sentenced to eighteen months' imprisonment. The woman, a divorcee with three children, was sentenced to four years' penal servitude in an English prison. A modern observer might wonder what public interest was served by the prosecution of this incident, and, in particular, by the disproportionate treatment meted out to the woman. The Bailiff, Sir Ambrose Sherwill, justified it by claiming that the act was due solely to her 'wanton incitement' of the man.[108] But the woman was well known to the authorities, and the sentence also removed a disruptive presence from the island. Whatever the case, the use of the sodomy law to punish this woman appears opportunistic, and her receipt of more than double the man's sentence also suggests a persistence of misogynistic bias among Guernsey's all-male courts.

Incest

Louise Jackson has described incest as historically the least reported and least prosecuted form of sexual abuse.[109] Her observation was made in the context of England and Wales, where (except for a brief period in Cromwellian times) incest was not a statutory crime in its own right until the early twentieth century.[110] In centuries prior to the twentieth, what was called 'incest' had been punishable only under Canon law. By this, however, was essentially meant marriage within the prohibited degrees, for which the worst penalty

---

[106] Correspondence between the Law Officers and Home Office on this matter is preserved in NA, HO 45/23231.
[107] 31.1.1953, GG, *Livres en Crime*, vol. 72; January 1953, IA, LO 056-11.
[108] *Star*, 2.2.1953.
[109] Jackson, *Child Sexual Abuse*, p. 46.
[110] Although rape could always be prosecuted as rape, whether it was perpetrated on a stranger or a daughter.

an ecclesiastical court could inflict was excommunication.[111] In Scotland, by contrast, incest had been punishable as a crime in the secular courts since 1567.[112]

The situation in England and Wales changed in 1908, when, following a long campaign by groups such as the NSPCC, the Punishment of Incest Act finally made sexual intercourse between close relatives a statutory crime. The law laid down that any male who had intercourse with a female he knew to be his mother, sister, daughter or grand-daughter was guilty of a misdemeanour and liable to a maximum of seven years' penal servitude. A female over sixteen was liable to the same penalty if she consented to such an act.

In Guernsey, as in pre-1908 England and Wales, incest had never been a statutory crime. In January 1909, however—just months after the English law had been passed—a particularly distressing case of familial sexual abuse came to the attention of Guernsey's authorities. The wife and teenage daughters of a 47-year-old father of six came forward with multiple allegations against him after one of the girls had become pregnant. According to the press report of the trial, HM Procureur drew Jurats' attention to the fact that, since incest was not a crime under Guernsey law and the girls were not under age, the man could only be tried only for rape.[113] There was, however, no obvious violence, and debate ensued as to whether rape necessarily involved force, and whether that force could be moral as well as physical.[114] The consensus appears to have been that it could, and the man was found guilty and sentenced to ten years' penal servitude.[115]

The trial came at an apposite time. Guernsey's Law Officers were already working on *la Loi relative au Mariage avec la Soeur d'une Femme Décédée*, which covered related subject-matter and was shortly due to come before the States.[116] They quickly produced another *projet* relating to incest proper and

---

[111] Jeffreys, *Spinster and her Enemies*, p. 76; Jackson, *Child Sexual Abuse*, pp. 13-14.

[112] J. Bourke, *Rape: A History from 1860 to the Present* (2007; London 2008 edn), p. 442.

[113] Note, however, that in the previous century the Royal Court had on occasion tried incest purely as incest notwithstanding the lack of a statute (*Second Report of the Commissioners*, p. 200).

[114] *Gazette de Guernesey*, 9.1.1909.

[115] 6.1.1909, GG, *Livres en Crime*, vol. 54.

[116] See section on Evolution of Guernsey marriage law, chapter 3.

submitted both *projets* to the States at the same time.[117] Both were approved, and in August 1909, *la Loi pour la Punition d'Inceste* was sanctioned by the Privy Council.[118] As was often the case with statutes of this nature, the new law was a word-for-word translation of the 1908 Punishment of Incest Act of England and Wales. Jersey, which did not experience this conjunction of events, never passed a statute regarding incest, and incest remains a common law offence there to this day.[119]

We have now run the full gamut of offences of which females could be said to be the chief victims. As we can see, such offences ranked low in the police and judiciary's scale of criminal priorities, and were only belatedly the subject of legislative enactments—usually as catch-up measures long after the United Kingdom had enacted the laws on which they were based. This is not entirely surprising given women's low civic status and—especially—men's monopoly of police, courts and legislature. In the next chapter, we will reverse the perspective and consider how Guernsey's authorities responded in cases where women themselves were the perpetrators of crime.

---

[117] *Gazette de Guernesey*, 24.4.1909.
[118] O in C, 3.8.1909.
[119] I thank Harry Stirk of Carey Olsen in Jersey for this information.

5

Female Criminality and Prostitution

Female criminality—an overview

We will begin this chapter by establishing the patterns underlying all criminality in late nineteenth- and early twentieth-century Guernsey, and attempting on this basis to evaluate women's position on the criminal spectrum relative to men. Before proceeding with our analysis, however, a few prefatory remarks are in order. As already noted in chapter 4, lesser criminal offences (as also most ordinance infractions) were tried summarily by the Police Court until 1925, after which they were tried in the newly created Magistrate's Court. Criminal offences of a more serious nature were tried on indictment by the Full Court. This section is based on the *Livres en Crime* and Magistrate's Court Books at Guernsey's Greffe and will include analysis of both summary offences and indictable offences.[1]

As also noted earlier, very few criminal offences were defined by statute during the period covered by this book. One of the only Guernsey statutes dealing with crime in the nineteenth century was the 1856 *Loi relative à l'Application des Peines tant au Criminel qu'en Police Correctionnelle*.[2] This defined a number of petty public order offences and prescribed penalties for them. The majority of more serious criminal offences were not dealt with

---

[1] Data provided hereunder are derived from an examination of *Livres en Crime* and Magistrate's Court Books in alternate years of alternate decades beginning in 1850 and ending in 1958.
[2] O in C, 24.6.1856.

statutorily until over a century later. In the absence of statutes, and because the *Coutume* had little relevance to modern crime, nineteenth- and early twentieth-century Royal Courts exercised a broad and somewhat arbitrary criminal jurisdiction. As the Royal Commissioners investigating Guernsey's criminal law in 1846 observed, the Court claimed the right to

> try and punish every offence against society; whatever, in point of fact, [is] malum in se ... [awarding] punishment in its discretion on every case.[3]

A full century later, matters had scarcely moved on: HM Comptroller W.P. Doyle made a virtually identical observation on the nature of Guernsey's court proceedings to the Privy Council committee enquiring into proposed reforms in the Channel Islands in 1946:

> as regards the bulk of the criminal law, I cannot find any principles upon which one can decide whether a man has committed a crime or not ... for the vast majority there is nothing to guide one ... you plead in an indictment in French the whole of the facts more or less in brief which constitute the crime, and they [the Royal Court] say that constitutes a crime or an offence which is "malum in se" and convict him.[4]

Given the lack of statutory definitions, I have used my own in categorising offences in the paragraphs which follow.

During the 1850s, about 240 individuals, male and female, were convicted of criminal offences in Guernsey each year. This equated to some eight convictions per thousand inhabitants, a lower rate than that of England and Wales for the same period, which was closer to fourteen per thousand.[5] The number of convictions rose slowly but consistently over ensuing decades and only once fell back to beneath their 1850s level: this was during the First World War decade, when convictions dropped to an average of 179 per year

---

[3] *Second Report of the Commissioners appointed to enquire into the State of the Criminal Law of the Channel Islands* (London, 1848), p. xv.
[4] *Evidence given before the Privy Council Committee on Proposed Reforms in the Channel Islands: Guernsey* (London, 1946), pp. 210, 212. Doyle was new to the island and somewhat taken aback at the differences between English and Guernsey criminal law.
[5] J.T. Hammick, 'On the judicial statistics of England and Wales, with special reference to the recent returns relating to crime', *Journal of the Statistical Society of London*, 30 (1867), p. 395.

(the most obvious reason for this was the absence of young men at the Front). By the final decade of our period, the 1950s, the number of convictions had risen to an average 630 a year. This equated to about fourteen per thousand inhabitants, which was again lower than the contemporary English rate of some eighteen per thousand.[6] More than a third of convictions in the 1950s were for motoring offences. This overlay of motoring convictions was essentially an artefact produced by modern lifestyles, and had already been of similar size in the 1930s. In order to make statistics properly comparable over time, motoring convictions have been excluded from our analysis from the 1930s onwards.

For most of our period, the vast bulk of convictions fell into three main categories: property crimes;[7] public order offences;[8] and offences involving inter-personal violence.[9] Analysis of court registers between the 1850s and 1950s shows that the balance between these three categories shifted substantially over time. In the 1850s, property crime accounted for 29 per cent of all convictions, while public order offences and inter-personal violence together accounted for 50 per cent. This situation continued broadly unaltered until the First World War decade, when both public order offences and offences involving inter-personal violence began perceptibly to decline.[10] The shift continued over ensuing years and by the 1950s had become quite pronounced, with property offences in this decade accounting for 40 per cent of convictions, and public order offences and inter-personal violence collectively accounting for just 27 per cent. This downward trend in crimes of violence and disorder closely mirrored the situation in other parts of Europe, where some scholars have explained it in terms of the population's increasing internalisation of a cultural model centred on self-control and respectability which was mediated by such institutions as schools, churches and youth clubs.[11]

---

[6] B.R. Mitchell, *British Historical Statistics* (Cambridge, 1988), pp. 13, 782.
[7] Thefts of all kinds as well as wilful damage done to property.
[8] Public drunkenness, vagrancy, begging, disturbances of the peace.
[9] Personal assaults of a physical, verbal or sexual nature.
[10] In this anomalous decade, infractions of ordinances constituted the largest single category at 28 per cent of all convictions. Property offences, public disorder offences and offences involving inter-personal violence were broadly level at about 18 per cent of convictions each.
[11] M. Eisner, 'Morality strikes back? A historical perspective on the latest increase in interpersonal violence', *International Journal of Conflict and Violence*, 2 (2008), p. 303.

We will now attempt to assess the specific contribution to this pattern made by females, but before we do so, we should first observe that, throughout our period, vastly larger numbers of males were convicted than of females. To emphasise this important point, figure 1 depicts the total number of male and female convictions recorded in the years analysed for this study.

Figure 1. Distribution of convictions by sex, selected decades, 1850s–1950s

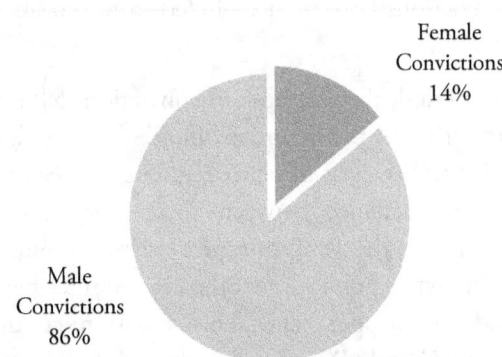

This is of course just a snapshot of aggregate totals and of necessity rather crude. If we refine the picture by breaking down the figures decade by decade, we find that the female proportion was not static, but gradually reduced over time.[12] In the 1850s, about 20 per cent of all convictions in Guernsey were of females, but by the 1950s this had dropped to 11 per cent. The declining trend in female convictions is broadly in line with a similar trend in England and Wales, where the proportion of female offenders appearing before magistrates' courts dropped from 21 per cent in 1860 to 10 per cent in 1950.[13]

As well as a large gap between the numbers of male and female offenders, there were distinct differences in the patterns of male and female offending. Figures 2 to 5 depict the differential distribution of convictions at the beginning and end of our period.

---

[12] Except for a short-lived upturn while the men were away during World War I.
[13] S. D'Cruze and L.A. Jackson, *Women, Crime and Justice in England since 1660* (Basingstoke, 2009), p. 18.

Figure 2. Distribution of male convictions, 1850s[14]

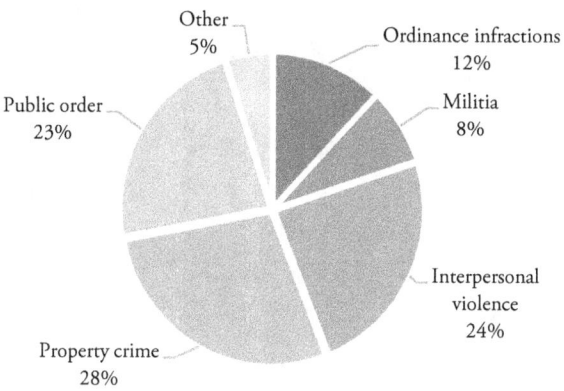

Figure 3. Distribution of male convictions, 1950s

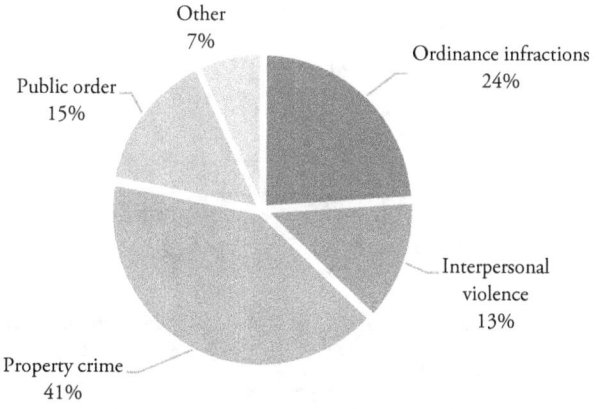

---

[14] Note the presence of militia-related offences in the male statistics for the 1850s but not the 1950s. These offences (failure to attend drill, insubordination, etc.), were usually punished with a small fine. The militia, which had always been subject to civil rather than military jurisdiction, ceased to exist in 1940.

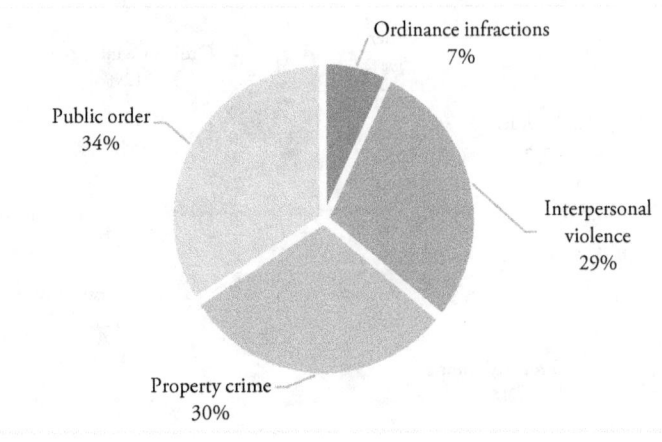

Figure 4. Distribution of female convictions, 1850s

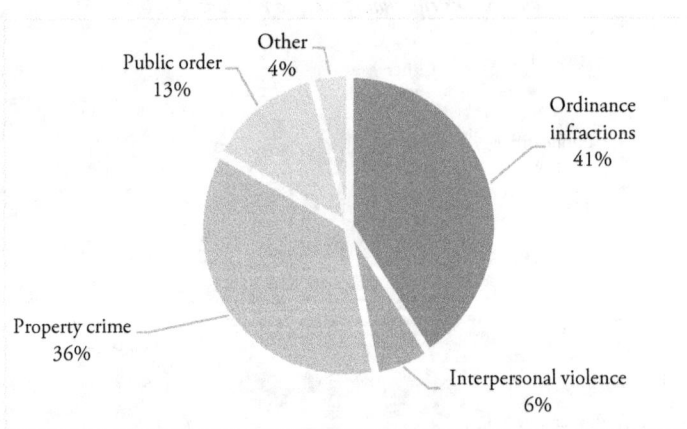

Figure 5. Distribution of female convictions, 1950s

Crime figures for both males and females repeat the same basic pattern identified in respect of all offending, namely a fall over time in public order offences and offences involving inter-personal violence, and a corresponding increase in convictions for property crime. It is notable that, as far as males were concerned, property crime already constituted the single largest category of convictions in the 1850s, albeit by a small margin. The situation with females was different: at more than a third of all female convictions in the 1850s, public order offences accounted for the largest share—a factor which helped tilt the overall balance against property crime. Public order offences continued to dominate female convictions until around the time of World War I. As the second half of this chapter will show, this situation was closely related to the prevalence of prostitution. After World War I, there was a noticeable drop in female convictions, not only for public order offences, but also for offences involving inter-personal violence. This decline was sustained over subsequent years, and by the 1950s, these two categories collectively accounted for less than a fifth of female convictions, with the most prevalent category of female offending now made up of relatively anodyne ordinance infractions.

Within the three categories themselves—property crime, public order and inter-personal violence—the specific types of offence for which women were prosecuted differed from those perpetrated by their male counterparts. As regarded property crime, theft which involved damage to property (such as housebreaking) or violence to persons (such as aggravated robbery) was largely the monopoly of men. Women were more typically prosecuted for opportunistic thefts of low-value domestic items. In the nineteenth century, such thefts were commonly of food, such as the ham, bread and butter stolen by Eliza Belford and Elizabeth Horley from the Reverend William Manning in September 1858.[15] They could also be of clothing or houseware, such as the flannel undervest and saucepan stolen by Marie Bichard from Susanne Simon in 1872.[16] Poverty was a common incentive for this type of theft. In the interests of repressing petty crime of this sort, Guernsey's nineteenth-century Police Court handed down deterrent sentences: Belford, Horley and Bichard were each sentenced to a month in prison. In the twentieth century, when poverty had diminished as a motivation for crime, a more typical female theft, though still opportunistic in nature, might involve the purloining of a desirable item from a workplace or employer. The theft of two skirts for which a woman shop assistant was fined in 1936 was fairly representative of female property crime after World War I.[17]

The kind of inter-personal violence perpetrated by women also differed from that engaged in by men. The infliction of serious injuries, in brawls or

---

[15] 4.9.1858, GG, *Livres en Crime*, vol. 35.
[16] 5.3.1872, GG, *Livres en Crime*, vol. 41.
[17] 25.11.1936, GG, *Livres en Crime*, vol. 64.

pre-planned attacks, was generally a men-only affair. Women were more usually prosecuted for noisy but fairly harmless quarrels, often with other women, which involved obscenities, hair-pulling, or missile-throwing. These spats were commoner in the nineteenth and early twentieth centuries than subsequently, and seem chiefly to have been associated with overcrowding in poor urban areas.

Sentencing was another area in which a gender disparity was discernible. In the early part of our period, imprisonment was the commonest form of punishment for both sexes, with more than half of all offenders convicted in the 1850s receiving prison sentences. Within these parameters, any female convicted of crime had a greater chance of being sent to prison than a male: some 61 per cent of females convicted in the 1850s received custodial sentences, compared with 54 per cent of males. Females were also less liable to receive very short sentences: some 35 per cent of females sent to jail in the 1850s were given terms longer than one week, as compared with only 29 per cent of males. A number of crime historians have noted a similar phenomenon in parts of England and Wales, and have suggested that the male judiciary might have come down harder upon females than males because their criminal behaviour was seen as transgressing gender norms.[18]

In the twentieth century, custodial sentences became less common as people became abler to pay fines, and courts gained access to new sentencing options such as probation. Thus only a fifth of Guernsey's convicted offenders received jail sentences in the 1950s. Significantly, the gender balance of those sentenced to prison also changed. Only 13 per cent of females convicted in the 1950s were given jail terms, as opposed to 21 per cent of males. There was also a difference in respect of fines. About a third of both males and females received their punishment in the form of fines in the 1950s, but, whereas 7 per cent of the males received fines of over £20, not one single female was fined over £20, and 93 per cent of females who received fines paid less than £10.[19]

The twentieth-century changes in sentencing policy occurred in tandem with the decline in female convictions mentioned earlier. In terms of raw

---

[18] L. Zedner, 'Women, crime, and penal responses: a historical account', *Crime and Justice*, 14 (1991), pp. 327–9.
[19] Figures are exclusive of fines incurred for motoring offences.

numbers, there were an average of forty-five female criminal convictions a year during the 1850s, but by the 1950s this had fallen to just twenty-five. Given that Guernsey's female population grew from 16,177 to 22,489 in the same period,[20] the drop in numbers represents a fall from a rate of three convictions per thousand females in the 1850s to a mere 0.1 convictions a century on. To what should we attribute this decrease? More than just the effect of a new cultural model, it was probably due to an abatement of raw poverty and exposure to harsh conditions. As the harshness of the poorest women's lives abated, so did their propensity not only to steal, but to drink, to engage in prostitution, and to brawl on the streets. In parallel with this, judicial attitudes towards them relaxed. The Jurats who judged these women in the 1850s were confronted by them daily on the streets, felt themselves at risk from their depredations, and were probably repelled by them. With a lessening of poverty as time went on, there was less to fear and be repelled by, and attitudes slowly became less punitive and more rehabilitative. In its early stages, this process was influenced by progressive notions emanating from England. From the 1920s, it was embedded by the appointment of an English barrister as magistrate. It was largely also to this that the twentieth-century changes in female sentencing were due.

Having now broadly placed females on Guernsey's criminal spectrum, we will turn to the specific types of offending which were peculiar to women. Of these, offences associated with infanticide, abortion and prostitution stand out as the most significant. We will devote the remainder of this chapter to a detailed exploration of each of these in turn.

Infanticide

Historically, the phenomenon of infanticide was closely related to the stigma attaching to single motherhood. A powerful taboo on female sexual activity outside marriage meant that anyone bearing an illegitimate child was exposed to a degree of public shame which is difficult to understand today. In a small island such as Guernsey, single motherhood would have been hard to conceal, and, given the austere Nonconformist Protestantism of many islanders,

---

[20] Figures from 1851 and 1951 censuses.

censure was perhaps all the harsher. If in employment, the woman concerned would have been likely to lose her situation. In extreme cases, she might have also been expelled from the family home and shunned by friends and relatives.

A woman in such a predicament had little hope of help from her parish. In most parishes it was a well-understood if unwritten rule that mothers of illegitimate children were ineligible for outdoor relief. In 1877, the St Peter Port Poor Law Board made this explicit by issuing a regulation specifying that 'the house' was to be the only option available to single mothers in need of relief.[21] Entering the Town Hospital as an unmarried mother was, however, a risky undertaking. In the 1820s, the Hospital instituted a scheme whereby single women giving birth in the institution were to be detained for five years in order to 'correct their morals'.[22] Although the five-year period was reduced to 'such time as the child require[d] its mother's care' in the 1840s,[23] this was enough to deter Guernsey's single mothers from resorting to the Hospital in any number throughout the nineteenth century.[24] Parochial authorities conceptualised this harsh treatment as a 'punishment' for immorality, and a disincentive to others who might be tempted down the same route. Such attitudes persisted well into the twentieth century and also informed the States' thinking when that body took over as chief provider of welfare assistance. The States introduced various means-tested assistance schemes from the 1920s onwards, but unmarried mothers were excluded from categories eligible for help until 1971.[25]

An unmarried mother's financial difficulties were further compounded by the fact that securing support from putative fathers was a difficult and time-consuming process. In the absence of a private agreement, this could only be done by launching an action for maintenance in the Ordinary Court,

---

[21] 9.4.1877, IA, DC/HX 054-06.
[22] 9.5.1826, IA, DC/HX 135-02.
[23] 4.5.1846, IA, DC/HX 130-01.
[24] R.-M. Crossan, *Poverty and Welfare in Guernsey, 1560–2015* (Woodbridge, 2015), pp. 142, 188.
[25] The Supplementary Benefit (Guernsey) Law 1971 (O in C, 5.4.1971) finally entitled unmarried mothers and pregnant women not living with a spouse or partner to claim means-tested benefits.

which in turn could only be enforced by execution and imprisonment.[26] In 1868, parameters for maintenance actions were set out in *la Loi relative à l'Entretien des Enfants Illégitimes*, which was based on the 1845 Bastardy Act of England and Wales.[27] This was however of more benefit to men than to women since its chief aim was to restrict the launching of actions to within a year of a child's birth, while doing nothing to expedite enforcement in cases of paternal recalcitrance.

This unsatisfactory situation endured for six decades. Only in 1927 did a second *Loi relative à l'Entretien des Enfants Illégitimes* supersede the 1868 law.[28] However, the new *Enfants Illégitimes* law, modelled on the English Bastardy Laws Amendment Acts of 1872 and 1873, was a distinct improvement on its predecessor. The law transferred responsibility for affiliation proceedings to Guernsey's new Magistrate's Court and empowered a mother to apply to the magistrate for a summons against the putative father. If the summons was granted, the man was compelled to appear in court, where the magistrate would determine paternity, and, where appropriate, order him to pay the mother a weekly maintenance allowance in respect of her child. Even more significantly, the 1927 law also established a mechanism for enforcement by making it possible to distrain a man's goods if he failed to pay.[29]

Despite all they had to contend with, a large number of Guernseywomen who found themselves unmarried and pregnant during our period carried their babies to term and acknowledged their maternity by registering their births. From the early 1900s, Guernsey's Medical Officers of Health monitored civil registers as part of their brief, and from time to time they published statistics on illegitimacy in their annual reports.[30] In comparison with those of England and Wales, Guernsey's illegitimacy rates in the first

---

[26] Here Guernseywomen nevertheless had an advantage over their French cousins, since in France paternity suits had been completely forbidden by the 1804 *Code Civil* and only became legally permissible after 1912 (J.F. McMillan, *France and Women, 1789-1914* (London, 2000), pp. 38-40, 187, 195).
[27] O in C, 29.2.1868.
[28] O in C, 13.5.1927.
[29] Orders made under this law between 1927 and 1976 are recorded at the Greffe in the register labelled *Enfants Illégitimes*.
[30] These were reproduced in *Billets d'Etat*.

half of the twentieth century seem high. Whereas the national illegitimacy rate of England and Wales usually varied between 4.2 and 4.8 per cent of live births between the 1900s and 1950s, in Guernsey it regularly exceeded 5 per cent.[31] During the German Occupation, the illegitimacy rate climbed even further, reaching as much as 18 per cent in 1942 and 21 per cent in 1945.[32]

While there are no statistics on babies whose lives ended before they reached the stage of registration, anyone browsing Guernsey newspapers from our period will be struck by the frequency of reports detailing the chance discovery of infant corpses—under hedges, down wells, in quarries, on beaches, floating in harbours, or, after World War II, deposited in German bunkers. These can be followed up in Police Occurrence Books or *Livres en Crime*, which contain a record of inquests. Most inquests on such infant corpses failed to identify a cause of death on account of decomposition. However, from time to time, clear evidence of foul play was noted. In 1856, an inquest on the body of a newborn boy found wrapped in a black skirt on an earth bank at Les Rocquettes in St Peter Port found that he had died of suffocation.[33] In 1877, an inquest on a female newborn discovered in Vauvert, St Peter Port found that she had died of strangulation.[34] In 1895, an inquest on another newborn girl washed up on the beach at Belgreve in St Sampsons found that her skull had been fractured by a blow.[35] There is nothing in Police Occurrence Books to suggest that much effort was made in such cases to track down whoever might have been responsible. As a correspondent to a local newspaper pointed out in 1880:

> cases of infanticide and deaths from neglect are, I fear, only too common here, but they are regarded as matters of course, and nobody takes any notice of them unless they are very glaring. Even then, unless suspicion points directly to anyone, the clue is not followed up, and the matter is after a time consigned to oblivion. It is nobody's business and ... people hate trouble.[36]

---

[31] L. Stone, *The Road to Divorce: England, 1530–1987* (1990; Oxford, 1995 edn), p. 445; *Billets*, 3.11.1919, 27.10.1926, 7.7.1939, 19.7.1950, 11.7.1951, 27.6.1956.
[32] *Billets*, 19.10.1945, 27.12.1946.
[33] 31.12.1856, 2.1.1857, IA, AQ 0991/03.
[34] 30.8.1877, IA, AQ 0992/04.
[35] *Star*, 21.12.1895, 24.12.1895.
[36] *Star*, 22.6.1880.

In England and Wales, infanticide first became a statutory offence under an Act of 1624.[37] This made the premeditated killing of a newborn a capital crime and established the legal presumption that, if an unmarried mother had concealed the death of her illegitimate child, she had probably killed it. The burden of proof in infanticide cases was thus—unusually—transferred from the prosecution to the defence. This situation lasted until the early nineteenth century when the 1803 Offences against the Person Act repealed the 1624 statute and laid down that newborn child murder was now to be tried in the same way as homicide. The 1803 Act thus relieved the defence of the need to prove innocence and placed an onus on the prosecution to provide evidence of guilt. However, the 1803 Act also made the mere concealment of a birth an offence in itself, punishable by up to two years' imprisonment. As infanticide *per se* still carried the death penalty, this led to a situation where cases of unexplained infant death occurring after 1803 were prosecuted more often as concealments than infanticides.

Although there were no more executions for infanticide in Britain after 1849, the death penalty was theoretically still available as a punishment until the 1920s. In England and Wales, it was effectively abolished by the Infanticide Act of 1922, which (elaborated by another Act of 1938) made it possible for a woman to claim as a defence for up to a year after childbirth that the balance of her mind was disturbed by parturition or lactation—a defence, which, if accepted, meant that she would be convicted not of murder, but of the lesser offence of manslaughter.[38]

---

[37] In Scotland, infanticide became a statutory offence in 1690. For an account of laws in respect of infanticide throughout the United Kingdom, see A.-M. Kilday, *A History of Infanticide in Britain, c.1600 to the Present* (Basingstoke, 2013), pp. 17–22, 114–18.

[38] France followed a similar trajectory. Under the 1810 *Code Pénal*, infanticide was subject to the death penalty. As juries grew progressively disinclined to inflict it, the lesser offence of concealment was introduced in 1863 and came to be the most common charge in cases of unexplained infant death. The death penalty for infanticide *per se* was abolished in 1901, and in subsequent decades prosecutions for both concealment and infanticide grew rarer as psychological explanations gained ground (J.M. Donovan, *Juries and the Transformation of Criminal Justice in France in the Nineteenth and Twentieth Centuries* (Chapel Hill, 2010), p. 131).

Guernsey, for its part, has never had a law relating specifically to infanticide.³⁹ Consequently, most neonaticides which reached Guernsey's Royal Court in the period covered by this book were tried under the common law. However, partly because of the reluctance to follow up suspicious deaths and partly because successfully accomplished concealment/neonaticide left no traces, trials for newborn child murder were relatively rare. To assess how the few cases of newborn child murder which did come to light were dealt with by Guernsey's judiciary, we will now examine a selection of such trials.

A particularly notorious case came up before the Royal Court in 1830. Although this trial took place two decades before the beginning of our period, we will briefly detail it here because it was the last such case for which the perpetrator suffered the death penalty.⁴⁰ Paradoxically (and exceptionally) the person executed in 1830 was a man, François Béasse. Béasse, a young Frenchman of independent means, had impregnated his servant, Sarah Elliott, and killed their baby shortly after birth.⁴¹ But while Béasse was convicted of murder and hanged, Elliott herself was convicted only of concealment and banished from Guernsey.⁴² No statutory offence of concealment existed locally, but the Royal Court were aware of its existence in England, and, as with many other crimes, they adapted their own practice to take account of this.

More typical of infanticide trials later on in the century was that of Sarah Morris in 1867, which is also worth describing in detail. Morris, aged 24,

---

³⁹ The subject was however addressed tangentially in the 1910 *Loi sur l'Avortement* (O in C, 7.11.1910) and 1917 *Loi ayant rapport à la Protection des Enfants et des Jeunes Personnes* (O in C, 24.1.1917), which, respectively, made it an offence to dispose of the body of a dead infant with the intention of concealing its birth, as also to abandon or expose an infant so as to endanger its life or health. These two provisions were copies of sections 27 and 60 of Westminster's 1861 Offences against the Person Act.
⁴⁰ The death penalty was applied in several instances of newborn child murder in the eighteenth century: see the cases of Jeanne Langley, Marie Rose, Catherine Deslandes *et al* in GG, *Préjugés en Crime*; see also J.M.Y. Trotter, 'The cost of an execution', *Quarterly Review of the Guernsey Society*, 15 (1959), pp. 73–5.
⁴¹ *Star*, 25.10.1830; *Comet*, 25.10.1830. See also NA, HO 17/26/132. The man's full name was Marie Joseph François Béasse.
⁴² Prior to being banished, Sarah Elliott was also required to perform public penance, which involved kneeling barefoot at the bar of the court, dressed in a white shift and carrying a candle. Elliott is the last woman known to have been subjected to this procedure. For more detail, see *Gazette de Guernesey*, 6.11.1830.

unmarried, and from Devon, was employed as a maid in a large house in Queen's Road, St Peter Port. Perhaps unaware of her pregnancy, she had carried her baby to term without telling anyone of her condition. Morris shared a bedroom with the middle-aged cook of the household. On Boxing Night 1867, the cook had noticed her companion getting in and out of bed and appearing to retch. The following morning, Sarah Morris remained in bed for an hour or so after the cook had risen, saying that she was unwell. The cook's suspicions were aroused, and she returned to the room once Morris had eventually left it. Opening the box where the maid kept her belongings, she found in it a dead baby wrapped in an article of Morris's clothing. An autopsy on the baby concluded that it had been born full-term and healthy but had died not long after birth from 'pressure on the windpipe' and a skull fracture, perhaps 'inflicted by a heavy instrument'.[43] Sarah Morris admitted concealing her baby's birth but denied killing it. Counsel for the defence argued that the baby's injuries might have been 'inflicted unknowingly' in the aftermath of birth, 'when the mother, as might well be supposed, was in the agony of mind and body inseparable from her situation.' The Jurats were divided in their view of the evidence. Two thought Morris innocent of any wrongdoing and voted for acquittal. Three considered that she had actively and knowingly killed her child and was hence guilty of murder. The remaining four felt that, although her actions had caused the baby's death, there had been no malice aforethought; they consequently advocated leniency. These four constituting a majority, Morris was found guilty of killing her infant, but without premeditation. She was sentenced to three months' imprisonment, to be followed by banishment. One of the newspapers reporting the trial deplored the court's verdict:

> this judgment has the effect of proclaiming that infanticide—a crime which is fearfully on the increase—involves no other punishment than three months' imprisonment, for in few cases of this nature can premeditation be proved, and the judgment seems to set aside the rule of law that intention is to be inferred from the act.[44]

---

[43] The trial was reported in detail in *Star*, 5.2.1867. See also 2.2.1867, GG, *Livres en Crime*, vol. 39, and Note 5, p. xiii, above.
[44] *Star*, 5.2.1867.

This was at a time when the British press was in the grip of a moral panic about newborn child murder, and the writer of the article was following a well-known trope.[45] Whatever the grounds for his fears, the 'leniency' nevertheless continued, since, after this date, most cases of unexplained neonatal death which came before the Royal Court were, as in England and Wales, dealt with not as neonaticides but concealments. The typical punishment for these, again as in England and Wales, was between one and three weeks' imprisonment.[46]

The case of a second Englishwoman, which occurred a few years after that of Sarah Morris, may stand as representative of late nineteenth-century and early twentieth-century practice. The woman, a domestic servant from Hertfordshire, was apprehended boarding the steamer to England after the discovery of her infant's corpse in a St Peter Port watercourse in 1871. Notwithstanding her suspicious behaviour and informants' suggestions of foul play, this young woman was tried only for having concealed the baby's birth and was sentenced to just two weeks imprisonment.[47]

Following the passage of the 1922 and 1938 English Infanticide Acts, modern psychological understandings of neonaticide also made their way to Guernsey, and progressively fewer prosecutions, even for concealment, were brought before the court. Thus, in the case of infanticide, social and legal attitudes can be seen to have undergone a distinct relaxation over time. In the case of our next subject—perhaps surprisingly—the situation was reversed. We shall now look at the evolution of attitudes to abortion.

Abortion

The contraceptive options of nineteenth- and early twentieth-century couples in both Guernsey and Great Britain were limited. Despite the fact that sheaths had existed since the mid-1700s and diaphragms and sponges were available from the late 1800s, public knowledge of these devices was

---

[45] Kilday, *History of Infanticide*, p. 119.
[46] D'Cruze and Jackson, *Women, Crime and Justice*, p. 80.
[47] 10.8.1871, 12.8.1871, GG, *Livres en Crime*, vol. 4; *Star*, 3.8.1871, 12.8.1871.

deliberately suppressed in the belief that they were immoral.[48] For this reason, it is generally held that the only contraceptive methods in common use at this time were abstinence and *coitus interruptus*.[49]

In the United Kingdom, knowledge of artificial contraceptive devices began slowly to spread after Marie Stopes and other family planning pioneers opened birth control clinics in the 1920s. In the 1930s, these private clinics were joined by a small number of local authority clinics after the passage of the 1929 Local Government Act.[50] Guernsey, for its part, had no proper family planning clinic until the States opened one in partnership with the Family Planning Association in 1970.[51]

In the absence of effective contraception, birth control in the nineteenth and early twentieth centuries was essentially reactive. Every culture in the world had its nostrums for an unwanted pregnancy. These could be as crude as taking a hot bath or jumping from a height, ingesting herbs such as pennyroyal and tansy, or douching with noxious substances such as turpentine and washing soda.[52] In late nineteenth-century Britain, patent abortifacients (pills which supposedly 'removed obstructions' and 'restored regularity') were particularly popular.[53] A report written in 1914 claimed that about eight in ten working-class English women regularly resorted to such pills.[54] These abortifacients were also available in Guernsey, the bulk of them probably through mail order. From the 1880s until the late 1920s, advertisements regularly appeared in Guernsey's newspapers for abortifacient pills. These advertisements never referred directly to pregnancy, but many emphasised that the pills should not be taken if the woman was pregnant, which was a convenient way of advertising their properties. Among them

---

[48] B. Brookes, *Abortion in England, 1900-1967* (1988; Abingdon, 2013 edn), p. 137.
[49] E.M. Roberts, *A Woman's Place: An Oral History of Working-Class Women, 1890-1940* (Oxford, 1984), p. 95.
[50] M. Spring Rice, *Working-Class Wives* (1939; London, 1981 edn), p. x; Brookes, *Abortion in England*, pp. 113, 128. This was considerably in advance of France, where municipal family planning clinics were permitted only from the 1960s (S.K. Foley, *Women in France since 1789* (Basingstoke, 2004), p. 256).
[51] *Billet*, 26.2.1969; *Guernsey Evening Press*, 28.7.1970.
[52] P. Knight, 'Women and abortion in Victorian and Edwardian England', *History Workshop Journal*, 4 (1977), pp. 57-68.
[53] Brookes, *Abortion in England*, pp. 3-5, 117-18.
[54] Report on the English Birth Rate, cited in Brookes, *Abortion in England*, p. 5.

(reproduced below) were Dr Rock's Female Pills—'no obstruction stands against them';[55] Ottey's Unlabelled Strong Female Pills—'always remove all obstructions ... invaluable to married women';[56] Towles' Pills—'immediately any irregularity occurs, take Towle's Pills ... woman's unfailing friend';[57] Martin's Apiol and Steel Pills—'a French remedy for all irregularities ... always keep a box in the house';[58] Le Brasseur's Pills—'Ladies, directly you notice any irregularity, take Le Brasseur's Pills'.[59]

Figure 6. Advertisements for abortifacients, Guernsey newspapers, 1888–1920

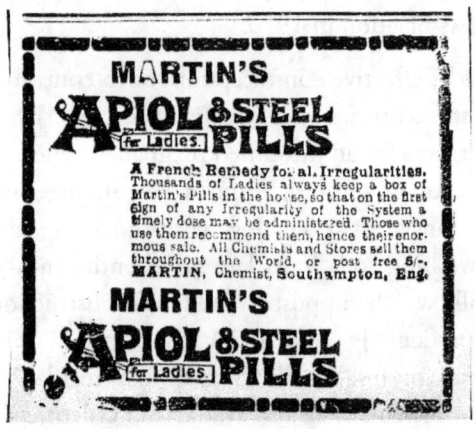

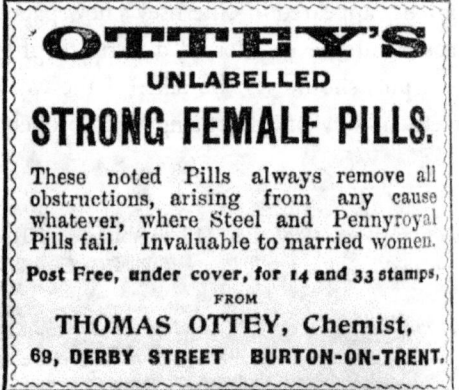

[55] *Star*, 28.7.1888.
[56] *Star*, 24.10.1895.
[57] *Star*, 20.3.1906.
[58] *Star*, 21.10.1916.
[59] *Star*, 31.7.1920.

Figure 6. Advertisements for abortifacients, Guernsey newspapers, 1888–1920 (continued)

Dr ROCK'S FEMALE PILLS

STEEL, PENNYROYAL, ALOES & BITTER APPLE.

THE MOST EFFECTUAL

NO OBSTRUCTION STANDS AGAINST THEM.

COATED, TASTELESS, and quite harmless to the most delicate constitution, but MARRIED LADIES should adhere strictly to the directions. 1/1½, 2/9, and 4/6 per box. By post, under cover, 1d. extra. Of all chemists, or direct from the UNIVERSAL DRUG CO., 19 and 21, QUEEN VICTORIA STREET, E.C.

INVALUABLE TO LADIES.

PENNYROYAL & STEEL

TOWLE'S PILLS

There is Nothing to Equal Them.

The oldest & only Reliable Remedy

will quickly correct all irregularities, remove all obstructions, and relieve all distressing symptoms.

Immediately any irregularity occurs, take Towle's Pills. The World knows no such preparation for Ladies as this invaluable specific, justly called

WOMAN'S UNFAILING FRIEND.

75 years' reputation.

No other female medicine in the world has received such widespread and unqualified endorsement.

In Boxes, 1/1½, 2/9, & 4/6 (the 2/9 boxes contain three times quantity of 1/1½ size). Of all Chemists, or Post Free for P.O. 1/3 or 2/10, or from Sole Proprietors: E. T. TOWLE & CO., Ltd., Manufacturing Chemists, NOTTINGHAM.

MISCELLANEOUS.

LE BRASSEUR'S PILLS. Ladies, directly you notice any irregularity of the system take Le Brasseur's Pills, they will speedily alleviate all suffering. Sample free or Boxes 3s., 5s., and 12s., sent anywhere on receipt of P.O. Write for a copy of the "Manual of Wisdom," containing most invaluable information to women. Sent post free.—The Manageress, Le Brasseur Surgical Co., Ltd. (Dept. M7), 90 and 92, Worcester Street, Birmingham.

These advertisements disappeared from Guernsey's newspapers after 1928 when the Advertising Association issued a circular to every newspaper in Britain urging the papers' advertising departments to stop accepting them. This was largely due to the campaign waged by Marie Stopes and her supporters, who objected to these pills on the grounds that they were essentially quack remedies predicated on women's ignorance.

While abortifacients were never illegal, instrumental abortion had been illegal in England and Wales for over a century. It was first made a criminal offence in England and Wales by the 1803 Offences against the Person Act (which, as noted earlier, also criminalised the concealment of births). Under sections 1 and 2 of the Act, which were intended to protect women from unscrupulous practitioners, the procurement of an abortion was a crime only in the person performing the procedure; the recipients were not themselves criminalised. Over subsequent decades, attitudes towards abortion tightened, and when the matter was addressed again in the 1861 Offences against the Person Act, both patients and practitioners were made liable to punishment, which was set at a maximum of life imprisonment for both.[60] One scholar has described the 1861 statute (parts of which remain in force at the time of writing) as embodying 'the most restrictive abortion legislation in Europe'.[61]

The first prosecution I have found for the performance of an abortion in Guernsey dates from 1899. The defendants in the trial were a married couple, both natives of France.[62] The husband, originally from Amiens, had previously worked as a druggist in Jersey. In March 1899 he appeared before the Royal Court for having aborted the pregnancies of six women (married and unmarried) in Guernsey. His wife was charged with aborting a further three.[63] The couple's activities only came to light because one of their patients had become so ill following a procedure that she had to be admitted to hospital. Acknowledging at the trial that Guernsey lacked any statutes regarding abortion, HM Procureur suggested that the Royal Court could

---

[60] For a summary of English abortion legislation, see Brookes, *Abortion in England*, pp. 24–6.
[61] M. Boyle, *Re-thinking Abortion: Psychology, Gender and the Law* (Hove, 1997), p. 13.
[62] The account which follows is synthesised from 11.3.1899, IA, AQ 0994/03; 11.3.1899, GG, *Livres en Crime*, vol. 51; *Gazette de Guernesey*, 18.3.1899.
[63] In France, although abortion was also illegal, it was nevertheless openly performed by practitioners such as druggists and midwives (A. McLaren, 'Abortion in France: women and the regulation of family size, 1800–1914', *French Historical Studies*, 3 (1978), pp. 472–3).

nevertheless 'create a precedent'. He then proposed that the man be sentenced to a year's imprisonment and ten years' banishment, and his wife to three months' imprisonment and ten years' banishment. The Court agreed (though not unanimously) and the couple were sentenced as above. None of their patients were prosecuted.

For more than a decade, Guernsey's authorities were content to let matters rest here. It was only during the Edwardian phase of legislative catch-up that the possibility of a written abortion law was addressed. Law Officers selected the 1861 Offences against the Person Act as a model and drafted a *projet de loi* that was little more than a translation into French of sections 58–60 of the Act. The *projet* was nodded through by the States and, duly ratified by Privy Council, became the 1910 *Loi sur l'Avortement*.[64] As per its 1861 model, the new law criminalised patients as well as practitioners, with a maximum penalty of life imprisonment for both parties.

Westminster's 1861 Offences against the Person Act is known not to have prevented backstreet abortions in England, and Guernsey's *Loi sur l'Avortement* was no different. However, as in the case detailed above, prosecutions only occurred when operations went wrong. One of Guernsey's most prolific twentieth-century abortionists was an Englishman who practised as a chiropractor in St Peter Port and went under the title of 'Doctor'. This man, who had been deported from the USA in 1939 for practising medicine without a licence, was twice prosecuted under the 1910 law. In 1943, Guernsey's Royal Court sentenced him to three years' imprisonment when a girl died from peritonitis after he had terminated her pregnancy. In 1950, he was sentenced to five years' penal servitude after another woman on whom he had operated required hospital treatment.[65] This individual's fee for performing abortions was substantial—£50 for the procedure for which he was prosecuted in 1950. Clearly, in this case and in others, the profit to be made from this trade outweighed any deterrent effect the 1910 law might have had.

By 1966, illegal abortion had become the chief cause of avoidable maternal death in England and Wales, and it was recognised that the *status quo* could not continue. David Steel's 1967 Abortion Act, although not

---

[64] O in C, 7.11.1910.
[65] 29.4.1950, GG, *Livres en Crime*, vol. 72; 4.4.1950, IA, LO 054-05; *Star*, 1.5.1950.

repealing the provisions of the 1861 Offences Against the Person Act, finally set out the parameters within which medical termination of pregnancy could be permitted, and it henceforth became possible to perform (or undergo) the procedure without fear of prosecution if two doctors agreed that a woman's physical or mental health would be made worse by continuation of pregnancy.[66] With abortion now legally available in England, it became common for Guernseywomen seeking terminations to have the operation performed across the Channel, and demand for local backstreet abortions died out. After a further three decades, abortion was eventually made legal in Guernsey itself by the Abortion (Guernsey) Law 1997, whose provisions were based on Westminster's 1967 Act.[67] Ironically, the three intervening decades had seen quantum advances in contraception, so that the need for safe abortion was no longer nearly so widespread as it had been when abortion was first made a crime.

Prostitution

The incidence and causes of prostitution in Guernsey

Although mainstream Victorian morality forbade women from engaging in sexual relations outside marriage, it was considerably more tolerant of this behaviour in men, and this created a demand for prostitution.[68] The demand was well catered for, not least because of restricted female work opportunities and the poverty faced by single women in lower social strata.

In Victorian and Edwardian St Peter Port, prostitutes were very much in evidence, as they were in towns all over Europe. A correspondent to the *Star* in 1868 complained that they could be 'counted by the score,

---

[66] Brookes, *Abortion in England*, pp. 133, 154-5. The 1967 Act applied to all parts of the United Kingdom save Northern Ireland.
[67] Abortion was also made legal in Jersey in the same year. In France, it had been formally legalised by *la Loi Veil* of 1975.
[68] For a seminal discussion of differential sexual morality, see K. Thomas, 'The double standard', *Journal of the History of Ideas*, 20 (1959), pp. 195-216.

half-intoxicated, lounging about the streets night after night'.[69] Thirty years later, St Peter Port's Constables estimated that the town hosted fifty full-time prostitutes, 'besides possibly double that number who are living in concubinage or adultery and receive visits from others than their paramours.'[70]

Studies of Victorian prostitution in England have shown that prostitutes were at their most numerous in port towns and military towns.[71] St Peter Port was both, which guaranteed a consistent supply of work. The trade did not however come solely from sojourning soldiers and sailors, since locals undoubtedly used prostitutes' services too. According to contemporary sources, native clients encompassed the entire social spectrum, from common labourers to 'wealthy, influential, powerful men'.[72]

Many of Guernsey's Victorian and Edwardian prostitutes worked from brothels, of which there were perhaps ten or twelve in St Peter Port.[73] At various times, there were brothels in Pedvin Street, Back Street, the Pollet and the South Esplanade. However, most late nineteenth- and early twentieth-century brothels were located in run-down tenement houses in Cornet Street and Rosemary Lane, which were on the main route into town from the garrison at Fort George. Plate 23 (overleaf) depicts a pair of young soldiers stationed at the Fort in the early twentieth century. Plate 24 (on the following page) shows the condition of Cornet Street and some of its female inhabitants at around the same period.

---

[69] *Star*, 5.7.1868.
[70] St Peter Port Constables to HM Procureur, 4.12.1894, IA, AQ 0982/02.
[71] D'Cruze and Jackson, *Women, Crime and Justice*, p. 68. Prostitutes were at their fewest in manufacturing towns where factory jobs were available to working-class women.
[72] Memorandum dated November 1895, LSE WL, 3HJW/F/06.
[73] No precise figures are available, but there are hints in Police Occurrence Books. In 1891 it was noted that eight of the town's brothel-keepers had been fined for illicitly selling alcohol (29.10.1891, IA, AQ 0994/01).

Plate 23. British soldiers at Fort George, 1904
© The Priaulx Library, Guernsey

Plate 24. Cornet Street, early twentieth century
Guernsey Museums & Galleries (States of Guernsey) 2018

Prostitution fell into three distinct phases during the period covered by this book. In the first, between the 1850s and 1880s, both brothel-keepers and prostitutes seem largely to have been natives of St Peter Port itself, with one or two from the country parishes and the occasional incomer from England, Jersey or France. In the second phase, between 1880 and World War I, prostitution was substantially taken over by the French.[74] A growing number of French brothel-keepers set up businesses in Guernsey from the 1870s, and, by the 1890s, virtually all employers in the trade were French.[75] This also transformed the make-up of the workforce, since brothel proprietors preferred to recruit staff in their home country.[76] The end of French domination and beginning of the third phase came with the Great War. French prostitutes first began to leave the island when the British garrison was withdrawn for overseas service in 1914.[77] When the conscription of locals began two years later, their rate of departure increased, so that, by the time of the armistice, only five remained.[78] The brothel-keepers left the island in tandem with their staff. This slowly unfolding exodus of both workers and employers marked the demise of organised prostitution in Guernsey and the end of the brothel system. Thereafter, and until the end of our period (with the exception of the German Occupation), most of Guernsey's prostitutes were local freelancers, operating casually and in isolation.

The factors which motivated women into taking up prostitution seem to have differed according to their origin, although poverty is a persistent theme. The French women who dominated the trade between the 1880s and 1918 may have been victims of the agricultural depression affecting north-western France during this period. French historian Gabriel Désert has found that many rural women were forced into prostitution in cities such as Caen, Cherbourg, Brest and St Malo by their inability to find employment in their

---

[74] Although locals participated to a reduced extent.
[75] All eight brothel-keepers fined for selling alcohol in 1891 had French names (see n. 73, above).
[76] Some contemporaries even hinted at a 'white slave trade' in French girls. In 1900, the *Star* featured a 'shocking' account of four French girls who found themselves in a Cornet Street brothel after having been enticed to Guernsey on a promise of jobs in domestic service (*Star*, 17.5.1900).
[77] The declining number of French prostitutes can be charted in IA, AQ 0975-05.
[78] St Peter Port Constables to Poor Law Board President, 9.9.1918, IA, DC/HX 253-01.

traditional roles in the countryside.[79] Once in these cities, they would have formed a pool of recruits on which Guernsey's French brothel-keepers could draw.

Native prostitutes were probably motivated by more general factors. Frances Finnegan, in her study of Victorian prostitutes in York, found that some of her subjects entered the trade after having suffered sexual abuse, or after having been seduced and abandoned early in life; others resorted to it after fleeing chaotic homes or escaping from poor law care; a third group had a mental impairment and were being exploited; another group were following mothers and sisters into a family occupation.[80] Almost all of Dr Finnegan's subjects were from very poor backgrounds, had little education, limited support networks and scant prospects of respectable employment. Hard evidence on the backgrounds of native Guernsey prostitutes is scarce, but, from the little that survives, it seems likely that they were also driven into the trade by factors of this kind.

Whether French or local, a prostitute's life was a hard one. Earnings were not high, and many prostitutes lived on the edge of destitution. Sarah Cook, a 23-year-old prostitute admitted homeless to the Town Hospital in 1871, was not atypical: found 'crawling with vermin' on arrival, her clothes were incinerated and her hair shaved off before she was allowed on to the wards.[81] A large number of prostitutes were also hardened drinkers if not alcoholics. Many were regularly arrested by the police for public drunkenness. One mid-nineteenth-century prostitute, Augustine Du Coispel, stands out for the frequency with which she was detained for drink-related incidents. A few hours after the last in a long series of arrests, she died in her prison cell, succumbing to what appears to have been alcoholic poisoning.[82] Vulnerability to casual violence was a further occupational hazard of prostitution. Girls were at risk of ill-treatment not only from clients, but

---

[79] G. Désert, 'Prostitution et prostituées à Caen pendant la seconde moitié du XIXe siècle, 1863-1914', *Les Archives Hospitalières. Cahier des Annales de Normandie*, 10 (1977), pp. 192, 204.
[80] F. Finnegan, *Poverty and Prostitution: A Study of Victorian Prostitutes in York* (1976; Cambridge, 2006 edn), pp. 7, 21.
[81] 10.2.1871, IA, DC/HX 059-01.
[82] The police identified her cause of death as 'excessive drunkenness' (5.10.1858, 7.10.1858, IA, AQ 0991/03).

also from pimps and brothel-keepers, who sometimes used violence to enforce control. In 1899, a 33-year-old French prostitute died from a blood clot on the brain a week after a beating from her pimp, who had forced her to continue working even after the beating, notwithstanding that she was clearly unwell.[83]

Feminist historian Judith Walkowitz has questioned the idea of the prostitute as victim in her studies of prostitution in England, suggesting that many working-class women resorted to it temporarily as a rational strategy over which they were able to exert considerable control. She has also refuted the idea that prostitutes were social outcasts, positing a relaxed working-class attitude towards female chastity, which allowed women to drop in and out of prostitution, moving seamlessly back into mainstream life once their careers were over.[84] I have not found any evidence to justify such a view in my study of Guernsey. Reversion to the mainstream was hardly an option when most local prostitutes, in the earlier part of our period at least, seem to have come from the margins of society to begin with. Moreover, those whose lives were not curtailed by drink, violence or illness seem largely to have ended their careers penniless in St Peter Port's workhouse.[85] Outcomes as regards the later French prostitutes are unknown, since these usually returned to France on quitting Cornet Street. However, according to Gabriel Désert, much prostitution associated with the French agricultural slump was only temporary, and—for a French girl—reversion to the mainstream after

---

[83] The pimp was ultimately found guilty of the prostitute's manslaughter and sentenced to twenty years' penal servitude (IA, LG 23-03 (01); *Gazette de Guernesey*, 25.3.1899).

[84] J.R. Walkowitz and D.J. Walkowitz, '"We are not the beasts of the field": prostitution and the poor in Plymouth and Southampton under the Contagious Diseases Acts', *Feminist Studies*, 1 (1973), pp. 73-106; J.R. Walkowitz, *Prostitution and Victorian Society: Women, Class, and the State* (Cambridge, 1980); J.R. Walkowitz, 'Male vice and feminist virtue: feminism and the politics of prostitution in nineteenth-century Britain', *History Workshop Journal*, 13 (1982), pp. 79-93.

[85] A small minority of prostitutes who entered the Town Hospital early in their careers were despatched to 'female penitentiaries' in Jersey or England where they were provided with domestic training and, eventually, respectable situations in places where their antecedents were unknown. These may have joined mainstream society, but since they were sent away from the island, it is not possible to assess whether rehabilitation was successful (Crossan, *Poverty and Welfare*, pp. 198-200).

working in Guernsey would not have been too difficult, given that the intervening distance ensured a clean slate.[86]

The management of prostitution

Managing prostitutes formed a significant part of the work of St Peter Port's Victorian and Edwardian police. They kept close tabs on individual women and adopted various tactics to get noisy and drunken ones off the streets. A common method of curtailing prostitutes' activities was to arrest them at night and release them early next morning. Between 1853 and 1859, about sixty individual women were subjected to overnight detention in St Peter Port, some on as many as eight occasions.[87] This was done *ad hoc* and required no judicial input. For the most troublesome prostitutes, the police had recourse to the courts. As in England and Wales, prostitution itself was never illegal in Guernsey, but a law of 1856 made prostitutes who behaved turbulently or indecently in public liable to up to eight days' imprisonment. It also made them liable to a 5s fine if they molested passers-by in a public place.[88] If the troublesome prostitute happened to be a non-native however, the police had an even more expeditious remedy: they could summarily eject her from the island. Under an ordinance of 1821, parish Constables had the power to expel without reference to the court any non-native they might consider to be 'of disreputable life, without means, unable to give a good account of themselves, or without employment'.[89] This power of summary expulsion, confirmed in later laws, was available for use with prostitutes up to World War II.[90]

In addition to the above, St Peter Port's constables also periodically summoned prostitutes to the Town Hospital for examination by the institution's medical officer. Any found suffering from sexually transmitted

---

[86] Désert, 'Prostitution et prostituées', p. 193.
[87] IA, AQ 0991/02, AQ 0991/03, AQ 0991/04.
[88] *Loi relative à l'Application des Peines tant au Criminel qu'en Police Correctionnelle* (O in C, 24.6.1856). This law was in place for over 120 years, only finally being repealed by the Summary Offences (Bailiwick of Guernsey) Law 1982 which *inter alia* made it an offence to loiter or solicit for the purposes of prostitution.
[89] Ord, 30.4.1821.
[90] Crossan, *Poverty and Welfare*, pp. 65-7.

diseases were then confined in the Hospital while they underwent a course of treatment. In a typical instance on 11 May 1855, nineteen prostitutes were called in for examination, fourteen of whom were subsequently detained.[91] Once in the Hospital, prostitutes were segregated in a ward of their own, initially known as the Magdalen Ward and later as the Lock Ward, where they were not allowed visitors.[92]

Although St Peter Port's system of compulsory examination and treatment was without any foundation in law, it bore strong similarities to legally instituted systems for the regulation of prostitution in force throughout Europe.[93] The British government also operated a regulatory regime. Initially, this was restricted to parts of the Empire where the health of British troops was thought to be particularly at risk.[94] However, between the 1860s and 1880s, the government extended its system of supervision and regulation to home soil. The regulatory system was implemented in a lengthening list of named military and naval towns by three successive statutes known as the Contagious Diseases Acts (CD Acts), passed in 1864, 1866 and 1869. These Acts empowered police in the named towns to arrest any woman thought to be a prostitute and submit her to medical examination. If found to have a sexually transmitted disease, she could then be detained for up to three months to undergo treatment. The names of all women who had been detained were recorded in a register and they were periodically re-called for examination thereafter.[95]

Almost as soon as Britain's CD Acts were passed, a vigorous campaign began for their abolition. This campaign, supported by feminists as well as religious objectors, was to have implications for later events in Guernsey, so we will pause to describe it in detail. One of the best-known of the feminist abolitionists was Josephine Butler, who in 1869 founded the Ladies' National Association for the Repeal of the Contagious Diseases Acts and in 1875 became the honorary secretary of the British, Continental and General

---

[91] 11.5.1855, IA, AQ 0991/02.
[92] Crossan, *Poverty and Welfare*, p. 198.
[93] For the regulatory regime in France, see A. Corbin, *Women for Hire: Prostitution and Sexuality in France after 1850* (London, 1990).
[94] India, Jamaica, Hong Kong, the Ionian islands, Malta, and parts of Australia (S. Steinbach, *Women in England, 1760-1914: A Social History* (London, 2004), pp. 199, 256).
[95] D'Cruze and Jackson, *Women, Crime and Justice*, p. 72.

Federation for the Abolition of the State Regulation of Vice.[96] Feminist abolitionists took particular issue with the gender bias of the Acts. Not only did they object to the Acts' implied recognition of a male right to paid sex, they found it profoundly unjust that women could be subjected to intrusive examination purely on suspicion, while no action whatever was mandated in respect of men. This, they felt, was symptomatic of all women's lack of equal rights. When Mrs Butler suggested to the Royal Commission on the CD Acts that men who frequented prostitutes should also be compulsorily examined, the Home Secretary Henry Bruce unconsciously summed up the essence of Victorian sexual hypocrisy, when he claimed

> there is no comparison to be made between prostitutes and the men who consort with them; with the one sex, the offence is committed as a matter of gain; with the other it is an irregular indulgence of a natural impulse.[97]

In 1871, the Ladies' National Association for the Repeal of the Contagious Diseases Acts presented Parliament with a petition for repeal signed by 250,000 women. Initially this had little effect, since the government was entrenched in its view that the Acts were vital to military health. This did not however deter the abolitionists. They recruited more activists, organised more public meetings, and continuously churned out anti-CD Act propaganda, with which they bombarded MPs. The pressure was kept up for more than a decade, with the eventual result that, in the spring of 1883, Parliament voted to suspend the operation of the CD Acts. After three years in abeyance, the Acts were completely repealed in 1886.

Credit for the final repeal of the CD Acts is usually given to the journalist W.T. Stead who, in the summer of 1885, published a series of articles on child prostitution in London. The public outrage stimulated by Stead's *exposé*, which culminated in an account of the procurement of a thirteen-year-old girl in a West End brothel, not only helped secure repeal of the CD Acts, but also facilitated the passage of the 1885 Criminal Law

---

[96] The range of feminist causes in which Mrs Butler took an interest extended well beyond the CD Acts. Most notably, she also helped found the Women's Franchise League and served as President of the North of England Council for the Higher Education of Women. For an informative biography, see J. Jordan, *Josephine Butler* (London, 2001).
[97] *Report of the Royal Commission into the Administration and Operation of the Contagious Diseases Acts* (London, 1871), p. 17.

Amendment Act.⁹⁸ With the passage of this Act, Westminster veered decisively away from regulation and towards suppression as a means of dealing with prostitution. To this end, the Act contained provisions which criminalised a range of sexually exploitative activities from brothel-keeping to the abuse of juveniles and obscene publications.⁹⁹

As historians have observed, the Contagious Diseases Acts were more successful at controlling women than disease.¹⁰⁰ No cure existed for either syphilis or gonorrhoea at the time the Acts were in force, and 'treatment' most commonly consisted of the topical application of mercury, whose only effect was to clear up lesions.¹⁰¹ The causative organism of gonorrhoea was only identified in 1879 and that of syphilis not until 1905. Syphilis remained incurable until the introduction of Salvarsan in 1910 and gonorrhoea until the sulphonamide drugs were developed in the mid-1930s.¹⁰²

Back in Victorian Guernsey, the St Peter Port police had continued to round up prostitutes for examination and treatment throughout the duration of the CD Acts and beyond. For most of this time, the military (for whose benefit the CD Acts had been enacted in England) had seemed satisfied with the local *ad hoc* system. In the mid-1890s, however, the confidence of the garrison authorities was shaken by a sharp rise in the virulence of sexually transmitted diseases among their troops. This they attributed to infection brought from France by prostitutes who had previously worked in the major French naval ports.¹⁰³ At the end of 1894, the garrison authorities urged the town Constables to take decisive action on French prostitutes and suggested that they apply to the Royal Court for legislation to regulate them.¹⁰⁴ This the Constables duly did,¹⁰⁵ and at the end of January 1895 the Court approved *l'Ordonnance Provisoire relative aux Maisons de Prostitution et aux*

---

[98] P. Bartley, *Prostitution: Prevention and Reform in England, 1860-1914* (London, 2000), p. 88.
[99] D'Cruze and Jackson, *Women, Crime and Justice*, p. 73.
[100] P. McHugh, *Prostitution and Victorian Social Reform* (London, 1980), p. 261; L. Abrams, *The Making of Modern Woman: Europe, 1789-1918* (Harlow, 2002), p. 155.
[101] F.B. Smith, *The People's Health, 1830-1910* (1979; London, 1990 edn), p. 294.
[102] A. Hardy, *Health and Medicine in Britain since 1860* (Basingstoke, 2001), pp. 69-70.
[103] De Vic Carey to Home Office, 9.11.1896, NA, HO 45/10142/B17748.
[104] *Comet*, 20.2.1895; *Star*, 21.2.1895.
[105] St Peter Port Constables to HM Procureur, 14.12.1894, IA, AQ 0982/02.

Prostituées.[106] This ordinance was mild in tenor. Its purpose was to keep prostitutes off the streets and men from congregating in brothels late at night. Laying down that any prostitute found on the streets after pub closing time could be fined up to £3, it also prohibited men from gathering in brothels after the pubs had closed, and brothel-keepers from allowing men to gather. What was more significant than the ordinance itself was the fact that, at the same time as they passed it, the Royal Court also approved a *projet de loi* on *maladies secrètes* (secret diseases) which was to be submitted to the States at their next meeting in February. This draft law was much more draconian than the ordinance and included provisions analogous to those of the CD Acts for the compulsory examination and detention of women thought to be engaged in prostitution. Evidence suggests that its text was dictated by the military.[107]

When knowledge of the proposed new law emerged, it provoked an explosive reaction from Guernsey's Methodist community. Taking their lead from the anti-CD Act movement in the United Kingdom, they swiftly mounted a campaign to oppose the state regulation of prostitution in Guernsey.[108] The campaign's chief instigator seems to have been Alfred Le Cheminant, the 34-year-old principal of the Guernsey High School for Boys and a prominent Wesleyan lay preacher. In one of his many letters on the subject to the *Star*, Le Cheminant, who advocated 'an equal standard of morality for both sexes', called upon the States to target clients as well as prostitutes, since 'the frequenters of these houses are as guilty and as worthy of reproach'.[109] Soon after the beginning of the Guernsey campaign, Alfred Le Cheminant wrote to the English anti-regulationist MP Henry Wilson, urgently appealing for the assistance of like-minded people in the United

---

[106] Ord, 21.1.1895.
[107] A letter from Albert Le Messurier to Henry Wilson (for more on whom, see n. 110, below) stated that the military were 'responsible for the proposed legislation, the Constables having in hand a letter from the Officer Commanding the Royal Fusiliers' (31.12.1895, LSE WL, 3HJW/F/06).
[108] Wesleyan Methodists, represented by the Wesleyan Society for the Repeal of the Contagious Diseases Acts, had been particularly energetic in the British anti-CD Act campaign (McHugh, *Prostitution and Victorian Social Reform*, pp. 194-5).
[109] *Star*, 3.1.1895.

Kingdom.[110] Wilson, a meticulous record-keeper, kept all the ensuing correspondence, so that a detailed account of the events which followed survives in his archive at the London School of Economics.[111]

At their first public meeting, Guernsey's anti-regulationists formed the 'Friends of the Social Purity Movement in Guernsey'.[112] A committee was elected, and Alfred Le Cheminant was appointed its secretary, with the assistance of another prominent Methodist, Albert Le Messurier. Following the meeting, many Anglican clergymen also joined the campaign, and several more public meetings were organised in the run-up to the States' debate on the proposed *maladies secrètes* law.[113] Attendees at these meetings were read a letter of support from Josephine Butler, and addressed in person by two prominent British anti-regulationists who had braved the winter storms to be present, the Reverend John Hunt Lynn and Mrs Laura Ormiston Chant.[114] By her own account—and despite a cold caught on the boat—the latter seems to have entered the fray with vigour, giving rousing speeches at the meetings, ghost-writing letters to the local press, and initiating a petition.[115]

---

[110] Henry Wilson (1833-1914) was a Nonconformist Sheffield industrialist who had become secretary to the Northern Counties Electoral League for the Repeal of the Contagious Diseases Acts in 1872 and corresponding secretary to the British, Continental and General Federation for the Abolition of the State Regulation of Vice in 1875. Between 1885 and 1912 he was also Liberal MP for Holmfirth.

[111] LSE WL, 3HJW/F/06.

[112] The Social Purity movement had sprung up in Britain after the passage of the 1885 Criminal Law Amendment Act, and included such groups as the National Vigilance Association, the Social Purity Alliance and the Moral Reform Union. Their chief aim was to hold men to the same moral standards as women by taking action to enforce the provisions of the Criminal Law Amendment Act (Bartley, *Prostitution: Prevention and Reform*, p. 155).

[113] *Star*, 12.2.1895, 14.2.1895, 19.2.1895.

[114] The Reverend Lynn was a Baptist minister who had worked for the National Association for the Repeal of the CD Acts from 1874 to 1886, and was now serving as secretary of the British, Continental and General Federation for the Abolition of the State Regulation of Vice. Mrs Chant was a feminist author and campaigner active in the Women's Liberal Federation, the British Women's Temperance Association and the Women Guardians' Society. She was also a founder member of the National Vigilance Association.

[115] L.O. Chant to W.S.B. McLaren, 18.2.1895, LSE WL, 3HJW/F/06.

Female Criminality and Prostitution 173

Plate 25. Laura Ormiston Chant
digitalcollections.nypl

The stated aim of Guernsey's Friends of Social Purity was to halt the progress of the draft *maladies secrètes* law and have it replaced with alternative legislation which replicated the provisions of the Criminal Law Amendment Act. In addition to their mass meetings, campaigners distributed pamphlets to all members of the States of Election,[116] and presented the Bailiff with a petition signed by 738 women.[117] Although the Friends' committee was entirely male, many women and girls were involved in canvassing, leafleting and signature collection. Mrs Angel, secretary of the local branch of the British Women's Temperance Association, and Captain Tunstall, a female Salvation Army Officer, performed particularly important roles as organisers.[118]

In the short term, at least, the activities of the Friends paid off. Rather than give the new law their immediate approval, the States resolved to postpone consideration of the *projet* until a specially appointed committee had examined the matter further. Among the States members appointed to the committee were two Anglican clergymen (rectors G.E. Lee and H.W. Brock), and two retired Generals (Jurats d.V. Carey and F.B. Mainguy).[119]

---

[116] A copy of the Friends' pamphlet survives in LSE WL, 3HJW/F/06. For the States of Election, see chapter 1, n. 2.
[117] *Comet*, 20.2.1895.
[118] L.O. Chant to W.S.B. McLaren, 18.2.1895, LSE WL, 3HJW/F/06.
[119] *Star*, 21.2.1895.

The *maladies secrètes* committee published their report nine months later. On the advice of local doctors Ernest Robinson and Octave Constantin, they gave their full and unreserved endorsement to all the measures set out in the original *projet*. The debate on the *projet* was then re-scheduled for the end of November.[120] Guernsey's Friends of Social Purity reacted to this news by re-launching their campaign. They began by circulating States members with their own counter-report, and, as the date of the November debate approached, held a second round of public meetings.[121]

This time, the meetings were addressed by a sizeable delegation of VIPs from the British, Continental and General Federation for the Abolition of the State Regulation of Vice. These included Henry Wilson and his wife Charlotte, Dr John Birkbeck Nevins,[122] Mrs Sarah Amos,[123] Mr William Coote,[124] the Reverend Allen Lees,[125] Brigadier-Surgeon Robert Pringle,[126] and Miss C.M. Whitehead.[127] The delegation was in Guernsey between 13 and 24 November 1895, and as well as addressing public meetings, also took part in canvassing, and conducted interviews with the Bailiff, Law Officers, rectors, Jurats and parish officials.[128] Josephine Butler, now aged 67, monitored proceedings from a distance. A few days before the States meeting, she sent Charlotte Wilson a letter of support for the Guernsey campaign in which she commented 'I do not see how poor little Guernsey can possibly stand against Mr Wilson's powerful guns and your own voice of persuasion.'[129]

---

[120] *Billet*, 29.11.1895.
[121] *Star*, 12.11.1895, 14.11.1895, 16.11.1895; *Comet*, 20.11.1895.
[122] Dr Nevins (1818–1903) was a Liverpool physician who founded the National Medical Association for the Repeal of the CD Acts in 1874 and was president of the British, Continental and General Federation for the Abolition of the State Regulation of Vice until 1896.
[123] Sarah Amos (*née* Bunting) was a prominent suffragist and women's rights activist.
[124] William Coote was secretary of the National Vigilance Association.
[125] Reverend Lees was a member of the Wesleyan Social Purity Committee.
[126] Brigadier-Surgeon Pringle was a workhouse guardian and well-known medical anti-regulationist.
[127] Miss Whitehead was a member of the British Committee of the British, Continental and General Federation for the Abolition of the State Regulation of Vice.
[128] Memorandum dated 25.11.1895, LSE WL, 3HJW/F/06.
[129] Josephine Butler to Charlotte Wilson, 21.11.1895, LSE WL, 3HJW/F/06. Mrs Butler made the Guernsey campaign the sole subject of the April 1896 issue of *The Dawn*, an abolitionist journal she edited herself (copy in 3HJW/F/06).

Female Criminality and Prostitution 175

Plate 26. Henry Wilson, MP
Sheffield Libraries and Archives (2018)

Plate 27. Josephine Butler
digitalcollections.nypl

Mrs Butler was wrong. On the second day of the November States meeting, having cleared the public gallery of women, Guernsey's Bailiff Thomas Godfrey Carey set the tenor of the *maladies secrètes* debate by putting his own weight squarely behind regulation. He contended that the proposed law was not punitive but 'curative', and that by identifying and treating 'women who were dangerous' it 'would protect generations of children yet unborn'.¹³⁰ HM Procureur Edward Chepmell Ozanne agreed that the law was not punitive, asserting instead that it was 'repressive', and adding that, since it was 'impossible to repress men, they must begin with women, for they were immoral; men did not walk about acting as the women did.' St Peter Port rector George Lee also spoke in favour of the proposed law, insisting that he saw 'no degradation in the examination, for if a good woman had sometimes to submit to it for good reasons, why should a bad woman object to it?' In his report to Henry Wilson, Albert Le Messurier commented that the Reverend Lee 'was surprisingly unsympathetic to the women but appeared to have great sympathy for the men.'¹³¹ In the event, the *projet*, slightly amended to allow women a right of appeal to the Royal Court, was approved by eighteen votes to sixteen.¹³²

Plate 28. Thomas Godfrey Carey¹³³
Guernsey Museums & Galleries (States of Guernsey) 2018

---

¹³⁰ This account of the debate is taken from a letter by Friends secretary Albert Le Messurier to Henry Wilson, (31.12.1895, LSE WL, 3HJW/F/06) which may not be entirely impartial.
¹³¹ We should note that, whereas Nonconformists in the United Kingdom had been universally opposed to the British CD Acts, Anglicans, who had closer links to government, were consistently more equivocal (McHugh, *Prostitution and Victorian Social Reform*, pp. 188, 193).
¹³² *Star*, 3.12.1895, 7.12.1895; *Billet*, 6.12.1895.
¹³³ Carey was knighted in 1900.

This, however, was not the end of the anti-regulationists' efforts. Since the law had to be ratified by the Privy Council before it could come into force, Guernsey's Friends of Social Purity petitioned the Council to withhold their sanction. This time the petition was signed by 2,436 women and 1,452 men, including three rectors, twenty-three Douzeniers and five Constables.[134] The British, Continental and General Federation for the Abolition of the State Regulation of Vice also petitioned the Privy Council, and there were in addition fifty-three other petitions, some from Guernsey, but most from United Kingdom bodies such as the National Vigilance Association, Moral Reform Union, Personal Rights Association, Social Purity Alliance and Women's Liberal Federation.[135]

This barrage of petitions prompted the Privy Council to seek clarification from the States. Thomas Godfrey Carey duly sent a letter of explanation outlining the reasons for the proposed law and recounting the vicissitudes of its passage. This did not however quite satisfy the Privy Council and they took the unusual step of submitting the matter to the Cabinet.[136] The Cabinet having expressed no objections, the *projet* was finally approved on 15 January 1897. After all the months of conflict and wrangling, the resulting *Loi relative aux Maladies Secrètes* was only two paragraphs long. It took the form of a simple permissive measure authorising the Royal Court to pass ordinances as and when necessary to curb the introduction of sexually transmitted diseases into Guernsey by ordering the compulsory examination and treatment of prostitutes, and by deporting any foreign prostitutes deemed dangerous to public health (both with a right of appeal to the Royal Court).

Although this undoubtedly represented a victory for Guernsey's establishment, it seems surprising that they persisted so doggedly in this course when they were aware that the CD Acts had been abolished in the United Kingdom, and that prostitution in Britain was now dealt with under

---

[134] *Star*, 19.12.1895. The 3,888 signatories equated to over 11 per cent of Guernsey's 1891 population.
[135] LSE WL, 3HJW/F/06.
[136] NA, HO45/10142/B17748, PC 8/472.

the Criminal Law Amendment Act.[137] Perhaps the reason for their persistence lay in the fact that Guernsey had already been dealing with prostitution in this way for well over a century.

Whatever the case, the Royal Court did not avail themselves of the faculty to make ordinances under the *Maladies Secrètes* Law for a full fifteen years. In a letter to Henry Wilson, Albert Le Messurier said that this was because they 'had not <u>dared</u> to do so'.[138] Ironically, however, the examination and treatment of prostitutes continued in precisely the same way as it had done before. Just six months after the Order in Council was issued and in the absence of any ordinance to this effect, St Peter Port's Constables reported to the military authorities:

> twenty-two women, eighteen of them foreign, were submitted to examination, with the result that twelve were found affected with venereal disease. The prostitutes of foreign nationality have been sent away and the British subjects detained in Hospital until such time as they may be pronounced cured.[139]

A record of the monthly examinations of St Peter Port prostitutes between 1908 and 1921 survives in two parochial registers.[140] The registers show that examinations took place in the Town Hospital at the beginning of every month, and any woman found to be infected with a sexually transmitted disease was consigned to the Lock Ward for a course of medication. Registers also show that women whose symptoms had cleared up after treatment were issued with pre-printed slips signed by one of the Hospital's doctors, which certified them free of disease. Under an agreement dating from the 1890s, the States paid the Hospital 1s 6d per day for each prostitute undergoing treatment, together with one-third of the costs of the medicines used.[141]

---

[137] They would also have known that Jersey, which faced similar problems in the 1890s, had followed the United Kingdom's lead by enacting their own *Loi (1895) appliquant à cette Ile Certaines Provisions du Criminal Law Amendment Act*, which *inter alia* prohibited brothel-keeping on pain of a fine or imprisonment.
[138] Le Messurier to Wilson, 17.1.1901, LSE WL, 3HJW/F/12. Le Messurier's underlining.
[139] St Peter Port Constables to Government Secretary, 1.6.1897, IA, AQ 0982/03.
[140] IA, AQ 0987-02 and AQ 0975-05.
[141] 9.1.1911, IA, DC/HX 046-01; 2.8.1918, IA, BF 018-13.

Some years after the first entries in St Peter Port's examination registers, an ordinance was finally enacted under the *Maladies Secrètes* law. This seems to have been made possible by the lapse of time since the 1895 furore and was prompted by the military authorities' desire for a uniform all-island system. Worried about a new upsurge in infections, the Deputy Assistant Adjutant General of the Guernsey and Alderney District requested in 1911 that measures be enacted under the *Maladies Secrètes* Law in order to institute a more consistent system. 'The arrangements for this at present are purely parochial,' he observed. 'It would appear desirable that the parochial system should be replaced by that of the States, in order that steps taken throughout the Island may be on more uniform lines.'[142] Thus, early in 1912, the Royal Court passed an ordinance which brought into force all the provisions available under the 1897 Order in Council.[143] After nearly 170 years during which the compulsory examination and treatment of prostitutes had been carried out informally, both were at last mandated by law.

As we saw earlier, the nature of prostitution in Guernsey changed after World War I. From being brothel-based and organised, it became casual and freelance. This lessened the effectiveness of the 1912 ordinance, as those engaging in the trade no longer formed a discrete and identifiable group. The number of women examined at the Town Hospital declined sharply after 1914, and the last of the regular sessions took place in October 1920.[144] Thereafter, sexually transmitted diseases were left to spread virtually unchecked. In the mid-1930s, the Sherwood Foresters, recently arrived to man the garrison, expressed alarm at rates of gonorrhoeal infection 'four times as high as the rate of infection of soldiers in England'.[145] Signalling the existence of a substantial pool of disease in the insular population, this prompted a request for appropriate action. The Royal Court responded by passing a second *Maladies Secrètes* ordinance which was much more wide-ranging than the first. The Court's 1936 *Ordonnance supplémentaire ayant rapport aux Maladies Secrètes* empowered Guernsey's Police Inspector

---

[142] Lt Col F.J. Ryder to Maj. Gen. Sir E. Hamilton, 10.10.1911, GG, Royal Court Letter Book No. 20.
[143] Ord, 22.1.1912.
[144] IA, AQ 0975-05.
[145] 4.1.1937, 13.1.1937, IA, LO 078-10. The Guernsey rate was 39 per 1,000 as compared with 9.8 per 1,000 in England.

(subject to the sanction of a Law Officer) to order the medical examination and detention in hospital of any woman against whom a complaint had been made that she had communicated, or was suspected of having communicated, a sexually transmitted disease to a male person.[146] Thus any woman in Guernsey was now liable to compulsory examination on the complaint of any man. This profoundly unequal piece of legislation can be said to have marked the high tide of Victorian double standards in Guernsey.

In the United Kingdom, a more enlightened approach towards the management of sexually transmitted diseases had by now been established. Pushed by wartime exigencies, the British government had passed the Venereal Diseases Act in 1917, which made free and confidential treatment available to both sexes at local authority clinics. Jersey had enacted a similar law in 1919.[147] Ever since the passage of the Venereal Diseases Act, Guernsey's Medical Officer of Health had been calling for the island to follow suit; however, the authorities had persistently demurred on grounds of cost.[148]

Dissatisfied with the 1936 *Maladies Secrètes* ordinance, the Sherwood Foresters exerted pressure on Guernsey's authorities to adopt the free treatment policy instituted in the United Kingdom and Jersey. After a further few months of resistance, the authorities finally succumbed. Setting aside cost objections, the Royal Court enacted a measure analogous to Westminster's Venereal Diseases Act in November 1937. Under this measure—*l'Ordonnance relative aux Maladies Secrètes*—a States-funded Venereal Diseases clinic was set up at the Town Hospital which offered free and confidential treatment to both males and females.[149] The new clinic clearly met a large and hitherto unfulfilled demand: in 1939, it provided courses of treatment to 759 individuals, just under half of whom were men.[150]

By the following year, however, everything had changed. Guernsey was occupied by German forces at the end of June 1940, and acquired a different

---

[146] Ord, 17.10.1936.
[147] *Loi (1919) sur le Traitement des Maladies Vénériennes*.
[148] 26.7.1918, 24.8.1918, 13.1.1919, 13.3.1919, IA, BF 018-13. See also NA, HO 45/12251.
[149] Ord, 27.11.1937.
[150] *Billet*, 17.4.1940.

set of military authorities to deal with. Unlike the British, the German military authorities set up brothels of their own. These brothels were staffed by a mixture of French and local women, the former predominating. A number of female Organisation Todt workers also provided paid sexual services.[151] The States' VD Clinic became busier than ever. On German orders, and at German expense, the Clinic conducted twice-weekly examinations of brothel workers and once-weekly examinations of OT workers.[152] To begin with, any prostitutes requiring treatment were admitted to the Town Hospital. In 1943, when the Hospital ran out of space for them, a special 'Hostel for Sick Women' was opened. This was situated at Hauteville, St Peter Port and was administered by the States' Board of Health.[153]

Just as the British military authorities had instigated earlier *Maladies Secrètes* ordinances, so the last in this series was passed at German military behest.[154] Born of concern at the number of soldiers contracting infections from civilians, the fourth *Ordonnance ayant rapport aux Maladies Secrètes* was passed in 1942.[155] Ironically, this was the most egalitarian of any of these ordinances. Acknowledging the obvious fact that men as well as women transmitted disease, it required 'any person, whether male or female' to seek medical treatment when suffering from a sexually transmitted disease, failing which the Medical Officer of Health could request a Law Officer to order compulsory examination and treatment. The ordinance was renewed annually until made permanent by article 70 of the Reform (Guernsey) Law 1948. The last order I have found for an examination under this law was dated January 1951. The recipient was a woman.[156]

---

[151] The Organisation Todt (OT) was responsible for the construction of fortifications.
[152] Rittmeister Fürst von Oettingen to Dr Symons, 30.3.1942, IA, CC 04-06.
[153] 21.4.1943, AS/MB 065-05.
[154] Dr Revell to Dr Symons, 30.6.1942, IA, LO 078-10; Feldkommandant Knackfuss to Dr Cambridge, 20.9.1942, IA, LO 078-10.
[155] Ord, 7.11.1942.
[156] IA, LO 078-10.

Rescue work and the Guernsey Rescue and Preventive Society

As we approach the conclusion of this chapter, it seems appropriate to add a short account of 'rescue work' in Guernsey, since this had an effect on many disadvantaged women's lives, not least prostitutes. Linked to a sense that better-off women had a responsibility for the morals of their less fortunate sisters, rescue work had been going on unsystematically throughout the nineteenth century, as charitably-disposed ladies participated in social missions run by their churches, subscribed to institutions such as Guernsey's Industrial Home for Girls, or funded the despatch of women to female penitentiaries.[157]

Shani D'Cruze and Louise Jackson have observed that rescue work in England acquired a more formal structure in the 1880s and 1890s, when a large number of dedicated rescue organisations were set up in the wake of the Criminal Law Amendment Act.[158] Rescue work also became more structured in Guernsey at around this time, though for reasons specific to the island. In 1895, at the height of the *maladies secrètes* controversy, Guernsey's Friends of Social Purity were criticised for not offering any practical help to prostitutes and others in similar situations. As a result, this group announced that it would give financial support to 'a Committee of Ladies who will undertake Rescue Work in Guernsey'.[159] These ladies set up an association which was officially launched in 1896 as the Guernsey Rescue and Preventive Society.[160]

Alfred Le Cheminant, who had instigated the campaign against the *maladies secrètes* law, was heavily involved in the Rescue and Preventive Society during its formative years. We know that, in 1901, he was serving as its secretary, and may have been doing so since its foundation.[161] In 1906, he helped the Society organise the petition which resulted in the passage of *la Loi relative à la Protection des Femmes et Filles Mineures*.[162] Unfortunately, Le

---

[157] For the Guernsey Industrial Home for Girls, see Crossan, *Poverty and Welfare*, p. 108. For female penitentiaries, see n. 85, above.
[158] D'Cruze and Jackson, *Women, Crime and Justice*, p. 110.
[159] *Star*, 23.2.1895.
[160] D. Langlois, 'The Guernsey Welfare Service, past, present and future', in M.E. Ogier (ed.), *Soroptimist Women International of Guernsey: Women in Guernsey at the Turn of the Millennium* (Guernsey, 1999), p. 25.
[161] A. Le Messurier to H. Wilson, 17.1.1901, LSE WL, 3HJW/F/12.
[162] *Star*, 25.9.1906. See also n. 84, chapter 4.

Cheminant died in 1907 at the age of 46. The untimely death of this energetic 'Christian socialist'[163] was undoubtedly a serious blow to the organisation, which was still in its infancy.[164] After Le Cheminant's death, Florence Ozanne took over as secretary and treasurer of the Society, a post she occupied until her own death in 1937. Mrs Ozanne, who appears to have been more conventional in her philanthropy, may have steered the Society along quieter lines than would have Le Cheminant had he survived.[165]

The Rescue and Preventive Society was an exclusively Protestant venture, but included Anglicans as well as Nonconformists.[166] Subscribing members, generally well-heeled, comprised both men and women. The Nonconformist and Anglican branches of the Society each had their own committees, but both sent representatives to a joint Executive Committee which ran the Society on a day-to-day basis. The latter was composed entirely of women.

The Society financed itself through fund-raising events as well as regular subscriptions and donations. In the early days, the local branch of the British Women's Temperance Association was its most important donor. In 1924, the Society entered into an association with the Winchester Diocesan Union for Preventive and Rescue Work, to which it henceforth submitted short annual reports.[167] From 1933, it received an annual grant from the Winchester Diocesan Union. In 1938, the Society changed its name to the Guernsey Social Welfare Mission. It did not however operate long under this title, since it was forced to cease its activities at the beginning of the German

---

[163] *Gazette de Guernesey*, 1.6.1907.
[164] The tragic circumstances of Le Cheminant's death are worth recounting. A temperance activist as well as a social purity campaigner, he had in 1906 lost a libel action filed against him by the tenant of the Imperial Hotel, whom he had publicly criticised following the death of a man after a drinking session at the hotel. The loss of this action appears to have triggered an episode of depression in Le Cheminant, a widower, and in May 1907 he took his own life (*Gazette de Guernesey*, 18.5.1907).
[165] *Née* Brock, Florence Ozanne was a founding member of the Rescue and Preventive Society and the wife of Jurat Edward Charles Ozanne. For a photograph of Mrs Ozanne see plate 18, p. 48, above.
[166] The account of the Society which follows is based on its minute books and case registers which are held at the Island Archives. For a full list of references, see under Primary Sources in Bibliography.
[167] The Society's annual reports from 1924 onwards can be found in Hampshire Record Office, 100M97/C1/1.

Occupation. It was refounded two years after the war as the Guernsey Moral Welfare Association.

In its mature years, the Society's main focus was on unmarried mothers, but it also dealt with neglected and abused children, teenage delinquents, and older women who had been in prison or had alcohol problems. Operating through a succession of salaried social workers, the Society offered women in all but the first category a variety of on-island assistance. This ranged from finding accommodation and arranging jobs to helping with the prosecution of sexual abuse. For unmarried mothers, however, the Society's usual policy—in line with the ethos of the times—consisted of despatch to specialist institutions outside the island. Thus many of the unmarried mothers who came to the Society's notice in the first half of the twentieth century found themselves sent off to Salvation Army Homes, Magdalen Homes, Rescue Homes and Training Homes all over southern England. Once the young women had served their term in these Homes and their babies had been adopted, many of them were moved on to jobs in England, where the Society endeavoured to keep up with them through letters and visits.

Until the 1950s, the Society had a semi-official role in local life, serving as an informal social work department. Records show that its Committee maintained close ties with parish poor law officers and, later, the States' Public Assistance Authority. When Probation Officers were first instituted in Guernsey in 1929, the Society's social worker was appointed Probation Officer for Girls, a post her successors were to hold until 1962.[168] When the Society was refounded after World War II, the States funded part of its social worker's salary. Between 1949 and 1953, the Society ran a Hostel for Girls in which young women convicted of minor offences were placed by the magistrate for set terms, under the care of the house-mother.

Although the Guernsey Rescue and Preventive Society undoubtedly did much good, it could also be high-handed, especially in the way it dealt with single mothers. As social attitudes relaxed and female job opportunities multiplied in the 1950s, unmarried mothers became better placed to resist interventions of this kind. Observing in 1955 that its Training Homes were

---

[168] Two local Probation Officers were instituted by the 1929 *Loi relative à la Probation des Délinquants* which was based on the 1907 English Probation of Offenders Act.

becoming progressively emptier, the Winchester Diocesan Council lamented 'they need moral and spiritual help, but—since they are economically secure—they will not accept it.'[169]

A decade on from the 1950s, Guernsey's Moral Welfare Society became concerned about its public profile. Wishing to shed its 'censorious' image, it re-branded itself as the 'Guernsey Welfare Service' in 1968.[170] This marked the end of its historical focus on marginal females. The Service continues to exist at the time of writing, but it now provides welfare support to a variety of clients of both sexes.

As we close this section, we should observe that rescue and preventive work was not the only option for socially conscious Guernseywomen in the early twentieth century. An alternative (and sometimes complementary) outlet was just opening in the form of service on parochial poor law boards. This proved to be among women's first steps towards full participation in civic life, which will form the subject of our next and final chapter.

---

[169] Winchester Diocesan Council for Moral Welfare 1955 Annual Report, Hampshire Record Office, 100M97/C1/1.
[170] *Guernsey Evening Press*, 3.11.1967.

6

Public Office, the Vote and States Membership

The reform process

As we saw in chapter 1, Guernsey's government fell into three tiers: the parishes, the Royal Court and the States. For most of the first fifty years covered by this book, women were excluded from all three. At parish level, only adult male ratepayers had the right to vote and stand for office. In the Royal Court, only men could stand as Jurats, and their electorate was exclusively male. In the States, too, only men could sit. Of the thirty-seven States members, twenty-two, or 60 per cent, sat *ex officio* and were voted in by no-one. The other fifteen were delegates sent by their parochial Douzaines, who were ultimately elected by male ratepayers.

Female participation in nineteenth-century English local government was considerably ahead of that in Guernsey. Here, the Municipal Franchise Act of 1869 had given unmarried female ratepayers the vote in municipal elections and permitted them to stand for election as poor law guardians (and later as members of the School Boards set up by the 1870 Forster Education Act).[1] Building on this, the Local Government Act of 1888 gave unmarried female ratepayers a vote in county council elections, and, six years later, the Local Government Act of 1894 swept away the strictures regarding marriage, and permitted all female ratepayers, whatever their marital status, to vote and

---

[1] Note that the legal personality of a married woman was seen as subsumed into that of her spouse, which at this time disentitled her to a vote in her own right.

stand in urban district, rural district, and parish council elections. Thirteen years on, the 1907 Qualification of Women Act further extended this principle by permitting married or unmarried female ratepayers to vote and stand in borough and county council elections, including for the office of mayor. This last statute put male and female ratepayers on an equal footing as far as English and Welsh local government was concerned.[2]

As we shall see, Guernsey was to take many decades longer to reach this position. Here, for the first intimations of change, we must revert to the late nineteenth century. The onset of this change was stimulated by a very particular conjunction of events, which we will briefly summarise. The late 1880s and early 1890s saw a serious dispute between the States and the ratepayers of St Peter Port, in which the main point at issue was the apportionment of education costs between States and parish.[3] It was essentially a flare-up of town ratepayers' long-standing grievances over what they saw as their inadequate representation in the States. Mounting discontent in the parish led in October 1891 to the ratepayers' appointment of a committee to press for States reform.[4] It also seems to have led—more significantly for our purposes—to the submission to the Bailiff of a petition signed by sixty-one ratepaying spinsters and widows of St Peter Port.[5] The signatories (all of them patrician ladies) complained that, although they contributed to parochial taxes, they were denied the 'right'—which they suggested such contributions conferred—of speaking and voting at parish meetings. The ladies accordingly requested that this injustice be remedied forthwith.

The ladies' petition seems to have been part of a concerted action planned in advance. A month earlier, a letter from someone calling themselves 'CONSTITUTIONALIST' had appeared in the *Star* claiming that there was no written law prohibiting women from voting at parochial level, and that 'a

---

[2] I. Machin, *The Rise of Democracy in Britain, 1830–1918* (Basingstoke, 2001), pp. 75, 107–8.
[3] On the dispute, see R. Hocart, *An Island Assembly: The Development of the States of Guernsey, 1700–1949* (Guernsey, 1988), pp. 64–7; D. Mulkerrin, 'The development of elementary education in the island of Guernsey 1893-1935', (unpub. MA dissertation, University of London, 1981), pp. 16–33.
[4] Hocart, *Island Assembly*, p. 71.
[5] 5.10.1891, GG, *Requêtes*, Vol. 3. I am grateful to Vikki Ellis of the Island Archives for drawing my attention to this petition.

widow or spinster who is a householder and pays her taxes most certainly ought to have a vote ... in the disposal of monies.'[6] The principle of female parochial enfranchisement was approved by the Royal Court almost as soon as the petition was received, and HM Procureur produced a *projet* he had already prepared.[7] This campaign seems to have had little to do with a wish for female enfranchisement *per se*. Rather, it appears to have been prompted by these ladies' desire to contribute to the dispute between town and States— education was, after all, a traditionally female sphere. The lack of a link with general suffrage issues seems to be borne out by the fact that, while schools and States reform were discussed *ad infinitum* in press letters columns at this time, correspondence on female enfranchisement was conspicuous by its near-complete absence.

When the *projet* on female parochial enfranchisement was submitted to the States for their approval, disagreement arose as to whether women should be allowed to serve in parish office as well as vote at parish meetings. The *projet* itself included an article explicitly debarring women from office, but other influential bodies, including Guernsey's Chamber of Commerce, expressed the view that conferral of voting rights should be coupled with imposition of a duty to serve.[8] This view was shared by Jurat Frederick Jeremie, who brought an amendment which sought to make women eligible for election to parochial poor law boards and education committees, as they were in England.[9] A majority of States members thought it simpler to debar women from office entirely than to make exceptions for specific roles, and rejected Jeremie's amendment.[10] The *projet* was then passed in its original form. *La Loi donnant aux Femmes Droit de Voter dans les Assemblées Paroissiales* received Privy Council approval in February 1892.[11] As well as prohibiting women from serving in parochial office, it restricted the female right to speak and vote at parish meetings to ratepaying spinsters, widows and judicially separated married women who paid rates in the parish in question.

---

[6] *Star*, 1.9.1891.
[7] *Star*, 6.10.1891.
[8] 30.11.1891, IA, AQ 044-05; see also *Star*, 3.11.1891.
[9] Jeremie was a 78-year-old retired Anglican clergyman (see obituary in *Star*, 23.2.1895).
[10] *Star*, 5.12.1891.
[11] O in C, 6.2.1892.

The dispute over education was resolved in the mid-1890s, but the campaign for reform of the States continued for the rest of the century.[12] After debating and rejecting a series of possible reforms, the States finally passed *la Loi relative à la Réforme des Etats de Délibération* in June 1899.[13] Essentially a compromise, this law increased parochial representation in the States by adding to the existing Douzaine delegates nine new States Deputies, who were to be elected on an all-island basis by the combined parochial electorates. As well as adult male ratepayers, these also included the small number of female ratepayers who had been enfranchised at parish level in 1892.[14] Only men were however permitted to stand as candidates. The first Deputies' election under the new law was held on 30 January 1900.[15]

The 1899 Reform Law improved the democratic balance in the States by reducing to 50 per cent the proportion of members sitting *ex officio* and increasing to 49 per cent the proportion who owed their seats to ratepayers' votes. However, this was hardly popular democracy: owing to the relatively high property qualification for acceptance as a ratepayer, the electorate for States Deputies represented at best about 25 per cent of Guernsey's adult male population, and perhaps as little as 2 per cent of its adult female population.[16] This democratic deficit remained a major source of dissatisfaction for reform-minded islanders, and a new pressure group calling itself the Guernsey Reform Association sprang up to agitate for a lowering of ratepayers' property qualifications. The Reform Association's vigorous

---

[12] The education dispute was resolved by the passage of the 1893 *Loi sur l'Instruction Publique* which imposed a fifty-fifty division of education costs between St Peter Port and the States (R.-M. Crossan, *The States and Secondary Education, 1560–1970* (Guernsey, 2016), pp. 28–9).

[13] O in C, 8.8.1899.

[14] Lest this should seem a particularly precocious instance of female enfranchisement in what amounted to a national legislature, we should note that a much larger proportion of women were enfranchised at national level in the Isle of Man in 1881, in New Zealand in 1893, in Australia in 1902 and in the Grand Duchy of Finland in 1906 (P. Bartley, *Votes for Women* (London, 2007), p. 8; M.E. Wiesner-Hanks, *Gender in History: Global Perspectives* (2001; Oxford, 2011 edn), p. 157).

[15] Deputies' elections were held in the winter months from their inception until 1955, when they were moved to the spring.

[16] For a discussion of ratepayer numbers, see R.-M. Crossan, *Guernsey, 1814–1914: Migration and Modernisation* (Woodbridge, 2007), pp. 151–5.

campaign prompted the States to appoint a Suffrage Committee to investigate further reforms of the franchise in 1905.[17]

Three years later, the Suffrage Committee submitted a report to the States recommending that the franchise for Deputies' elections be extended to all adult men and adult single women.[18] The States received the report favourably but requested the Committee to expand on its recommendations in a second report.[19] After a further five years of deliberation, the Committee came back to the States in 1913 with detailed proposals in respect of both parochial and Deputies' elections. Somewhat surprisingly, they recommended on this occasion that the States introduce universal, non-property-based suffrage for both types of election, and that this be extended to women as well as men.[20] The reason why this was surprising lay in the fact that, in the United Kingdom at this time, only two-thirds of adult men had a vote in parliamentary elections, and no women had a vote in them at all.[21]

The Bailiff, William Carey, seems to have disapproved of both universal male suffrage and votes for women. When the Committee's proposals were debated in the States in October 1913, he called for outright rejection, reminding members that Westminster had not yet adopted universal male franchise and that the British Prime Minister Herbert Asquith was implacably opposed to female suffrage. Interestingly, he also remarked that, although certain women did have the States franchise in Guernsey, 'very few' of them made use of it.[22] The Suffrage Committee's proposals were rejected by

---

[17] Hocart, *Island Assembly*, pp. 73-4; R.-M. Crossan, *Poverty and Welfare in Guernsey, 1560–2015* (Woodbridge, 2015), p. 80.
[18] The minutes of the States' Suffrage Committee for the period 1905-13 survive in IA, AS/MB 023-04.
[19] Hocart, *Island Assembly*, p. 74.
[20] 19.3.1913, 7.5.1913, 21.8.1913, IA, AS/MB 023-04; *Billet*, 29.10.1913.
[21] During the nineteenth century, parliamentary suffrage had gradually been extended through the Representation of the People Acts of 1832, 1867 and 1884 while remaining exclusively male and property-based. The qualification established by the latest of these was household occupancy or rental of unfurnished lodgings to the value of £10 a year in England and Wales, to which in Scotland was added personal payment of rates (Machin, *Rise of Democracy*, p. 101).
[22] For an account of the debate and the Bailiff's contribution to it, see *Gazette de Guernesey*, 8.11.1913.

thirty-seven votes to six. Following this resounding defeat, the Committee was disbanded, and the suffrage issue was shelved for several years.

At this stage, it may be useful to summarise the history of the campaign for female parliamentary suffrage in the United Kingdom. The beginnings of an organised campaign can be dated to the passage of the Contagious Diseases Acts in the 1860s.[23] Anti-CD Act campaigners saw votes for women both as a recognition of women's rights to equal citizenship and as a necessary means of effecting practical change. The matter was brought before the House of Commons during debates over the 1867 Representation of the People Act. As the Act was being discussed, the philosopher, feminist and Liberal MP John Stuart Mill presented a petition to Parliament calling for women's suffrage.[24] Mill then followed this up by tabling an amendment to the Act seeking the extension of the franchise to adult females. Unsurprisingly, neither of these initiatives bore fruit. However, they did galvanise supporters of female suffrage into founding the National Society for Women's Suffrage in 1868, which in turn prompted the formation of other suffrage groups. Over the next three decades, women's suffrage groups multiplied and became increasingly uncoordinated. In 1897, in the hope of achieving greater focus, some of these groups came together under the leadership of Millicent Fawcett as the National Union of Women's Suffrage Societies (NUWSS). The NUWSS was committed to working through existing legal and parliamentary channels, and several years passed with no noticeable sign of progress. In 1903, frustrated by the NUWSS's apparent ineffectiveness, Emmeline Pankhurst and her daughters formed the Women's Social and Political Union (WSPU) which resolved to use more radical methods. The *Daily Mail* later coined the term 'suffragettes' for WSPU members, both as a derogatory label, and to distinguish them from the 'suffragists' of the NUWSS. Regarding it as a badge of honour, WSPU members quickly adopted the name for themselves. In 1905, the WSPU embarked on a campaign of civil disobedience. Beginning with passive defiance, this campaign escalated into

---

[23] M. Walters, *Feminism: A Very Short Introduction* (Oxford, 2005), p. 68. For more on these Acts, see section on the Management of prostitution, chapter 5.
[24] This was in fact the second time that women's suffrage was brought before the House. In the debates which had preceded the first Representation of the People Act more than thirty years earlier, the radical MP Henry Hunt had, like Mill, presented a petition requesting the extension of the franchise to women. The petition was dismissed as an irrelevance and consigned to parliamentary oblivion.

violent acts such as window-breaking, sabotage and arson. In the eight years between 1906 and 1914, more than a thousand suffragettes were arrested and imprisoned for criminal acts. Many were force-fed when they went on hunger-strike in protest against imprisonment.[25]

In Guernsey, there was no mirroring of such activities. The island had no tradition of violent protest, and its small size precluded the formation of a critical mass of women sufficiently dedicated to the local suffrage cause to undertake action.[26] It is difficult to gauge the reactions of Guernsey people to the activities of suffragettes in the United Kingdom, but some documents survive which suggest they could be hostile, especially among men (this would tally with the situation in Britain, where historians have noted a generally negative attitude among men of all classes).[27] One of these Guernsey documents is a short essay dating from 1909 entitled 'The Militant Suffragette' which is held by the Island Archives. The essay lambasted the 'men-women' or 'women-men' whose 'foolish movements express a stubborn resistance to the laws of nature and the will of God'. Arguing that their 'ludicrous' behaviour has lost them the respect and sympathy of men, the essay concludes 'if such outbreaks are the expression of women's rights, it would be better and more womanly to sit at home with their wrongs.'[28]

---

[25] S. D'Cruze and L.A. Jackson, *Women, Crime and Justice in England since 1660* (Basingstoke, 2009), pp. 93-4.

[26] The island did nevertheless have links with the British suffragette movement which are worth a brief footnote. A woman called Nellie Martel took a prominent part in WSPU organisation and campaigning between 1905 and 1908. English-born, she had emigrated to Australia, where in 1885 she had married expatriate Guernseyman Charles Martel, a photographer. In 1904, the couple left Australia for England after Mrs Martel failed in a bid for election to the New South Wales Senate. Mrs Martel resigned from the WSPU in 1908 on account of the escalating violence, but she remained active in feminist campaigns until her death in 1940. Somewhat less significant though still of interest is the fact that Christabel Pankhurst and fellow WSPU activist Annie Kenney spent some time in Guernsey in the spring of 1910 to recuperate from campaigning activities. They did not draw attention to their presence by making any public appearances, and local newspapers appear to have been oblivious to their visit. For more on both of these connections, see M. Pugh, *The Pankhursts* (2001; London, 2002 edn), p. 209, 124-5, 136.

[27] Bartley, *Votes for Women*, p. 132.

[28] IA, AQ 1129/08-002. The essay is initialled 'H.A.T.'; I am informed by Nathan Coyde of the Island Archives that the writer was Harold Augustus Tooley, who perished in World War I. What makes his views particularly interesting is that he was married to Zélie Tooley (*née* Hocart) who was one of the first women to stand for election to Guernsey's States.

Another instance (undated, but from the same period) survives at the Priaulx Library in the form of a satirical skit by William Vaudin, a local grower. Entitled 'A Peep in the Future, or The Royal Court in the Year 2000: The Suffragettes in Power', the skit depicts a Court composed entirely of comical female figures adjudicating on a number of stereotypically feminine issues in a stereotypically feminine way: punishing a wife-beater, rejecting an application for an alcohol licence, decreeing the abolition of school homework, and awarding assistance, rather than punishment, to two jobless men who have stolen to feed their families. The skit invites us to judge their actions as silly and illogical.

Whatever the case, the advent of World War I brought about significant changes, both in the United Kingdom and in Guernsey. Shortly after war was declared in August 1914, both suffragists and suffragettes abandoned their crusade for votes in favour of supporting the war effort. In particular, they organised campaigns encouraging women to serve as nurses, munitions workers and Land Army volunteers. The patriotism shown by feminists during the war helped confer respectability on the suffrage cause. This was compounded by a feeling that the wartime efforts of ordinary womenfolk merited due recognition and reward. Thus when the matter of the suffrage was again addressed by Parliament in 1918, the claims of women were considered alongside those of men. It was felt that full adult male suffrage was unavoidable since no government could withhold the vote from men who had risked their lives for their country. Many politicians also believed that adding females to the mix would moderate the effect of enfranchising a large number of lower-class males. They did not, however, wish to see female voters outnumber males (as demography would ensure) so a 30-year age limit for women was inserted into the parliamentary Bill.[29] A new Representation of the People Act was passed in February 1918. Men over 21 were given the vote purely as individuals, provided they could meet a residence requirement of six months in the constituency where they were to vote. For women the conditions were more stringent. Not only had they to have passed the age of 30, but they had also to fulfil one or more additional requirements, *viz.* that they be householders or married to householders, occupy property worth at

---

[29] Bartley, *Votes for Women*, pp. 145-6, 150, 152.

least £5 a year, or hold a university degree. These strictures left more than a third of adult women unenfranchised.[30]

As we saw in chapter 2, Guernseywomen mobilised themselves for the war effort in much the same ways as their contemporaries across the Channel: they served as nurses and auxiliaries at the Front; they travelled to England to work as munitionettes; and they replaced men in essential occupations at home. Most significantly for current purposes, the war years also saw the first Guernseywomen co-opted to serve on States committees: a Mrs Priaulx and a Miss Clothier, appointed to the States Food Control Committee (set up to control wartime rationing) in August 1917.[31] The contribution of these ladies (and others who ran Guernsey's many wartime charities) stimulated a desire in some quarters to see women play more of a role on public bodies. As the war came to a close, the Bailiff received a petition signed by twenty-one States members and others (all men) stating that 'the highest public interest' now demanded that women be permitted to serve in parochial office.[32] The States greeted the proposal with some enthusiasm and approved the measure in principle by twenty-nine votes to ten.[33] A law followed in October 1919 which enabled female ratepayers to serve in parochial public office, with the now familiar proviso that they be unmarried, widowed or legally separated from their husbands.[34] The law also stipulated that any woman so elected by her fellow ratepayers should not be compelled to take up the office to which they had elected her. This was born of a concern that women might be unequal to the tasks demanded by certain parochial offices, such as that of Constable, which in some country parishes still included public order duties.[35] In January 1920, the parish of St Peter Port acquired its first lady Overseers of the Poor: Miss Louisa Collings and Mrs C.J. Gardner.[36] Miss Marie Randall followed a year later.

---

[30] Machin, *Rise of Democracy*, pp. 143–4.
[31] Hocart, *Island Assembly*, p. 90. For a photograph of Miss Clothier, see plate 18, p. 48.
[32] *Billet*, 26.3.1919.
[33] *Star*, 27.3.1919.
[34] *Loi relative à l'Eligibilité des Femmes aux Charges Paroissiales* (O in C, 9.10.1919).
[35] *Star*, 15.5.1919. In retrospect, this concern seems misplaced: not only were Constables shortly to be relieved of public order duties by the inception of the Island Police, no woman was actually elected to the office of Constable until 1975 (*Guernsey Evening Press*, 11.12.1975).
[36] 6.1.1920, IA, DC/HX 052-01.

While these changes were occurring at parish level, other changes were afoot in the States. The same forces which had compelled the United Kingdom and other European countries to widen the parliamentary franchise after World War I also pertained in Guernsey where, notwithstanding the wartime sacrifices of ordinary men and women, only just over a quarter of the post-war adult population had a vote in States elections.[37] In October 1918, seven months after the passage of Westminster's Representation of the People Act, Guernsey's Bailiff was presented with three petitions for the reform of the States.[38] Two of these petitions, echoing the Suffrage Committee in 1913, proposed *inter alia* to extend the franchise in Deputies' elections to all adult males and females. The States responded by appointing a Reform Committee to weigh up the merits of each of the three petitions and draft their own consolidated set of recommendations. After several months of deliberations, the Reform Committee submitted their proposals to the States early in 1920.[39] The Committee's recommendation as regarded the suffrage was to abolish the ratepayer franchise in Deputies' elections and introduce modified universal adult franchise, proposing that all men over 20 and women over 30 should be given the vote, as in Westminster's 1918 Representation of the People Act.[40] In the course of the States debate on the reform proposals, Deputy Frederick Luff (who had earlier been involved with the Guernsey Reform Association) tabled an amendment to equalise the voting age for both men and women at 20.[41] Perhaps predictably, given the 1913 precedent, this was rejected by a large majority who felt that it was not advisable to 'take a step in advance of England.'[42] In the end, the States approved the Reform Committee's original proposal for modified universal suffrage, and also voted to continue the franchise for the small number of women between 20 and 30 who already enjoyed it by virtue of being

---

[37] In 1919, with insular ratepayers numbering 6,787 and the total adult population c.24,500, the precise proportion was 27.7 per cent (*Census 1921: Jersey, Guernsey and Adjacent Islands* (London, 1924); *Billet*, 19.2.1919).
[38] The text of the three petitions is in *Billet*, 19.2.1919.
[39] In the meantime, Jersey had passed its own *Loi sur les Droits Electoraux* in May 1919 which gave the vote in States elections – subject to certain conditions – to men over 20 and women over 30 (20 was the age of majority in all Channel Islands).
[40] *Billet*, 28.1.1920. The proposal however differed from Westminster's 1918 arrangement in that it required no property qualifications for women in addition to age.
[41] *Star*, 28.1.1920.
[42] *Star*, 29.1.1920.

ratepayers.⁴³ The reforms were embodied in *la Loi supplémentaire à la Loi relative à la Réforme des Etats de Délibération*, which was sanctioned by the Privy Council in October 1920.⁴⁴ In addition to extending the franchise, the law also doubled the number of States Deputies from nine to eighteen, and divided the island into five electoral districts.⁴⁵ Finally, and perhaps most significantly, the law also permitted women over 30 to stand for election as Deputies. In this respect, Guernsey was in advance of Jersey, where women were not permitted to stand for the States until 1924,⁴⁶ but behind the United Kingdom, where the Parliament (Qualification of Women) Act had had permitted women to stand for Parliament in 1918.

The first Deputies' election under the new arrangements took place on 28 December 1920. There were forty-one candidates for the eighteen Deputies' seats, only two of whom were women.⁴⁷ These women, Louisa Collings and Edith Carey, were both standing in St Peter Port, where twenty candidates were contesting eight seats. Both of them were unmarried, both of patrician origin, and both conservative in their opinions. Louisa Collings was the same woman who had been elected a St Peter Port Overseer the previous year. Edith Carey, then aged 56, was a well-known local historian. Preoccupied with the past, Miss Carey appears to have been less than forward-looking in her views. According to a press report, she expressed the opinion that Guernsey's schoolgirls should be 'taught to look after a home instead of being instructed in ... subjects of no use to them in after life.' She also expressed her distrust of 'that spirit of Bolshevism ... working everywhere by stealth', and her strong opposition to the introduction of old age pensions.⁴⁸ 'People will no doubt say I am hard,' Miss Carey told the paper, 'but I do not see why a

---

⁴³ The lower limit of 20 was an innovation, since the 1892 law which enfranchised female ratepayers at parish level made no reference to age.
⁴⁴ O in C, 13.10.1920.
⁴⁵ The electoral districts were as follows: No. 1 - St Peter Port (eight Deputies); No. 2 - St Sampsons and the Vale (five Deputies); No. 3 - Castel, St Saviours and the Forest (two Deputies); No. 4 - St Martins and St Andrews (two Deputies); No. 5 - St Peters and Torteval (one Deputy).
⁴⁶ Jersey's *Ajoutement à la Loi (1856) sur l'Augmentation du Nombre des Membres des Etats* of March 1924 empowered women over 30 to stand for election as States Deputies.
⁴⁷ *Star*, 13.12.1920.
⁴⁸ Old age pensions, eventually introduced in 1926, were a hot topic in early 1920s elections (Crossan, *Poverty and Welfare*, p. 245-6).

man who has done nothing for himself, or a woman who has wasted money that she might have saved, should be supported at the expense of others.'[49]

Perhaps surprisingly, neither Miss Carey nor Miss Collings appear to have taken a stand on women's issues. They may possibly have calculated that this would draw attention to their femininity and put them at a disadvantage; or they may have had no strong views. The most prominent proponent of women's issues at the 1920 election was, paradoxically, a man—the 30-year-old lawyer Ambrose Sherwill, who, among other things, expressed an interest in introducing a married women's property law and reforming the inheritance law.[50] Only 3,027 islanders turned out to vote in 1920, but Sherwill's youth, articulacy and intelligence clearly appealed to those who did, and he topped the poll.[51] For their part, neither Miss Carey nor Miss Collings were elected. A *Star* editorial expressed surprise at their failure. Estimating that one-third of voters in the election had been female, it opined:

> had the women electors polled solidly for Miss Carey and Miss Collings, they would have been returned very near the head of the poll, even without the support of the votes of the sterner sex ... Evidently, the lady voters are lacking faith as to the abilities of the candidates of their own sex, or can it be (as one lady voter confided to me) that they object to "petticoat government"?[52]

At all events, Guernsey did not have to wait much longer for its first female States Deputy. The second election under the new system took place on 31 January 1924. This time there were four women among the forty-three candidates: Marie Randall, Marie Naftel, Adele Dorey and Patricia Ozanne. The first three were standing in St Peter Port, and the fourth in St Peters and Torteval. Marie Randall was the 42-year-old unmarried daughter of a respected local brewer and already serving as a St Peter Port Overseer. Marie Naftel was the widow of *Ecrivain* Joseph Naftel and well-known for her charity work.[53] Adele Dorey was the wife of serving States Deputy Philemon Dorey, and Patricia Ozanne was married to the rector of St Peters. Unlike

---

[49] *Star*, 21.12.1920.
[50] For Sherwill's views, see *Star*, 22.12.1920. For his achievements, see chapter 3.
[51] The 3,027 voters represented only about 12 per cent of the potential electorate created by the recent franchise extension (*Star*, 29.12.1920).
[52] *Star*, 30.12.1920.
[53] *Ecrivains* were law agents without legal qualifications who specialised in the drafting of deeds, wills and other legal instruments.

their 1920 predecessors, these women were not only vocal but progressive on women's issues, espousing equality of voting age, the introduction of a married women's property law, and inheritance law reform.[54] They were also all in favour of introducing old age pensions, improving conditions in the schools, and tackling local housing problems. The one policy which divided them was that of 'Local Option'. A hot topic in the 1920s and much advocated by temperance organisations, this was a form of local prohibition. Marie Naftel and Adele Dorey were strongly in favour of Local Option, but the other two female candidates opposed it.

Some 4,347 voters turned out for the 1924 election, which was better than the 3,027 who turned out in 1920 but still represented only a small fraction of the adult population.[55] Adele Dorey, Marie Naftel and Patricia Ozanne all failed in their election bids, but Marie Randall garnered the second largest number of votes in St Peter Port and, with it, the first female seat in the States.[56] Given that the Westminster parliament had admitted its first female member only five years earlier, Miss Randall's election was a considerable achievement.[57]

To what did Marie Randall owe her success? Undoubtedly, many factors were involved, but one of the most significant must have been her popularity among St Peter Port's business community. Firstly, she came from a highly respected commercial family, which gave her ready-made standing in the business sector. Secondly, the local Chamber of Commerce had formally endorsed her candidature.[58] Thirdly, unlike both of her female adversaries in St Peter Port, she was forthrightly opposed to Local Option, and this would strongly have commended her to the town's many hoteliers, publicans, and wine and spirits merchants.[59] Finally, the business community was a predominantly masculine sphere, and the 'breath of virility' which a local

---

[54] The women's manifestos are to be found in *Star*, 16.1.1924, 19.1.1924, 26.1.1924.
[55] *Star*, 1.2.1924.
[56] *Star*, 2.2.1924.
[57] Jersey did not return a female States Deputy until the election of Ivy Forster in 1948 (M. Syvret and J. Stevens (eds), *Balleine's History of Jersey* (1950; Andover, 1998 edn), p. 265).
[58] 9.1.1924, IA, AQ 40/08. The Chamber had itself only started admitting female members in 1918 (13.3.1918, IA, AQ 40/06).
[59] *Star*, 19.1.1924, 26.1.1924.

newspaper detected in Marie Randall could only have enhanced her appeal.[60] The fact that she belonged to the female sex therefore appears to have been neither an asset nor a liability in her electoral performance.

Plate 29. Marie Randall
Island Archives Service, Guernsey

Four years after Miss Randall's election, the saga of female suffrage at Westminster underwent a further evolution in the form of the 1928 Equal Franchise Act.[61] This statute, the last and arguably the most significant of the series begun in 1918, abolished the age limit and property qualifications for female parliamentary voters and finally gave women the vote on exactly the same terms as men. Two years later, Jersey equalised the male and female voting age in States elections, while nevertheless retaining property

---

[60] *Guernsey Evening Press*, 26.1.1924.
[61] Its full title was the Representation of the People (Equal Franchise) Act 1928.

qualifications.[62] After the equalisation of voting ages in Jersey, letters began to appear in Guernsey's newspapers advocating a similar measure in Guernsey. One such letter, published in the *Star* in December 1932, was signed by 'A Woman Under 30' and sardonically looked forward to turning

> that marvellous age when, it would seem, the women of Guernsey suddenly become endowed with the brains which they lacked before and with an equally sudden power of being able to discern men of sound character and clear vision.[63]

It was not until late in 1933 that the matter of the female voting age was finally taken up in the States. This was prompted by a petition from fourteen Deputies and others calling for the equalisation of the voting age at 20.[64] Marie Randall (still a Deputy) was among the signatories, though not at the top of the list. The measure was debated in the States, but, despite Jersey's example, many members felt that the time was not ripe for such a move in Guernsey, and the States rejected it by thirty-one votes to eighteen.[65] Some of the thirty-one States members who voted against the measure may well have had views similar to that of another newspaper correspondent—'Une Femme'—who had declared in the run-up to the debate:

> women have no more right to equal voting powers than they have to places in industrial offices ... Their place is in the home, and when they are there, they should be fully occupied with domestic matters and not politics ... I fail to see why they should have a vote at all—let alone on equal terms with men![66]

After this failure, the issue was left in abeyance for five years. However, in 1938, Marie Randall took it upon herself to bring the matter back to the

---

[62] *La Loi sur les Droits Electoraux*, passed by Jersey's States in July 1930, repealed the 1919 law of the same name and, while still subjecting eligibility to vote in States elections to a number of conditions, allowed suitably qualified members of both sexes to vote at 21. That Jersey reached this milestone comparatively quickly may have been due in part to the activities of the Women's Jersey Political Union which had been founded in 1923 specifically to campaign for women's rights (C. Platt, *A Concise History of Jersey: A New Perspective* (Jersey, 2009), p. 107).
[63] *Star*, 7.12.1932. It is interesting that the writer still thought in terms of discriminating between *men* of sound character and clear vision.
[64] *Billet*, 11.10.1933.
[65] *Star*, 12.10.1933.
[66] *Star*, 3.10.1933.

States. By this time, Guernsey had a new Bailiff in the person of Victor Carey, and the general election of 1935 had brought in a number of progressive Deputies. Virtually the same petition was submitted in 1938 as in 1933, with the sole difference that a female voting age of 25 was now requested.[67] The matter was debated inconclusively at two successive States meetings. The request for a voting age of 25 had effectively muddied the waters, since the question was no longer one of straightforward gender equality.[68] Finally, the Bailiff himself settled the issue by reinstating sexual parity as the crux of the matter. He put a proposal of his own to the States and asked them simply to accept or decline it. The proposal was to place women on exactly the same footing as men by reducing to 20 both the female voting age and the age at which females could stand as Deputies—without property qualifications in either case.[69] In support of his proposal, Carey declared:

> I can see no reason why women should not be accorded equal rights with men on both these matters. Furthermore, I would gladly welcome a greater number of women members in the States as I am of opinion that their views on many matters ... and especially on such questions as Public Assistance, Hospitals, Sanitation and Education, would be of great value.[70]

Taking their lead from the Bailiff, the States voted *nem. con.* to reduce the female voting age to 20, and by twenty-nine votes to seven to reduce to 20 the age at which females could stand for election as Deputies. One of the seven who voted against, the rector of St Andrews, was disturbed at the thought of a house 'full of young men and women'—after all, he grumbled, the States 'was not a cocktail party ...'[71]

The law finally enacting universal adult suffrage in elections to Guernsey's States was sanctioned by the Privy Council in June 1939.[72] Less than three months later, World War II broke out. Unfortunately, this precluded the

---

[67] *Billet*, 7.10.1938.
[68] *Star*, 7.10.1938, 1.12.1938.
[69] Victor Carey, appointed Bailiff in 1935 and now aged 64, had in his early days been something of a moderniser (Crossan, *Guernsey, 1814–1914*, p. 273).
[70] *Billet*, 21.12.1938.
[71] *Star*, 21.12.1938.
[72] *La Loi relative à la Réforme des Etats* (O in C, 23.6.1939).

holding of any elections for the duration of the war, which delayed yet further the implementation of universal adult suffrage.[73]

More than six years after the Reform Law was passed, a States election on the basis of universal adult suffrage finally took place on 27 December 1945. This milestone had been passed more than sixteen years earlier in the United Kingdom, where the first general election on universal adult franchise was held in May 1929. In Jersey and France, however, the watershed was reached at much the same time as in Guernsey. Jersey held its first States election on the basis of universal adult franchise on 5 December 1945.[74] The women of France, who had had no electoral voice at all prior to World War II, first exercised suffrage on equal terms with men in the municipal elections of April 1945 and the national elections of October 1945.[75]

The Second World War also heralded another watershed for Guernsey. Just weeks after the island was liberated, a group of Deputies petitioned the Bailiff to investigate the full democratisation of the States, which still contained unelected rectors and Jurats. Another Reform Committee was set up, and the long process of formulating and agreeing constitutional changes began. After three years of proposals and counter-proposals (and the contribution of a Committee of the Privy Council), the States finally passed a new reform law in 1948.[76] This law embodied the most fundamental restructuring of Guernsey's legislature to date. All the rectors and Jurats who sat *ex officio* were removed; the number of Douzaine representatives was reduced to ten; twelve indirectly-elected Conseillers were introduced;[77] and—most important of all—the number of directly-elected Deputies was

---

[73] By-elections in which women could have voted on equal terms with men were scheduled in District No. 1 on 17.7.1940 and District No. 4 on 21.8.1940, but neither was actually held (17.5.1940, 26.3.1941, IA, BA 56-11).

[74] The Franchise (Jersey) Law was passed by Jersey's States in September 1945. This repealed the 1930 *Loi sur Les Droits Electoraux* and allowed men and women over 21 to vote in both parish and States elections purely as individuals (R.G. Le Herissier, *The Development of the Government of Jersey, 1771–1972* (Jersey, 1973), p. 117).

[75] S.K. Foley, *Women in France since 1789* (Basingstoke, 2004), pp. 232, 239. Universal manhood suffrage had been introduced to France after the revolution of 1848.

[76] The Reform (Guernsey) Law 1948 (O in C, 5.8.1948). For an account of the law's genesis, see Hocart, *Island Assembly*, pp. 124-32.

[77] Conseillers were to be elected by the States of Election and fulfil a quasi-senatorial role. For details on the States of Election, see chapter 1, n. 2.

increased to thirty-three. This, for the first time in history, gave Deputies an overall majority in Guernsey's States.

The 1948 Reform Law also introduced a measure of change at parish level, extending a general right to vote and stand for office to those now eligible to vote and stand in States elections. However, on the principle that general legislation does not repeal special legislation, married women (as opposed to women who were single, separated or widowed) continued to be barred from voting and standing in parochial elections by virtue of the 1892 *Loi donnant aux Femmes Droit de Voter dans les Assemblées Paroissiales* and 1919 *Loi relative à l'Eligibilité des Femmes aux Charges Paroissiales*.[78] This anomaly was only removed by the Parochial Taxation and Voting Law 1963, which—finally and very belatedly—allowed all women to participate in parochial administration and government on a completely equal footing with men.[79]

Female States Deputies, 1920s–1950s

After Marie Randall was elected in 1924, there were ten further general elections of Deputies in the period covered by this book.[80] All were characterised by voter apathy. The average number of voters in general elections between 1924 and 1958 was 3,747. The lowest recorded turn-out was 1,511 in 1932, which equated to about 6 per cent of those potentially eligible. The highest turn-out was 7,279 in 1948, about 26 per cent of those eligible.[81] In the general election of 1958, the last in our period, turn-out was 5,216, and the proportion of those eligible taking part just 16 per cent.[82]

The average number of candidates in pre-war Deputies' elections was twenty-six, and the average number of women standing just two. In post-war elections, the average number of candidates rose to forty-nine, and the average number of female candidates to four. In 1930 and 1935, Marie Randall was the sole female candidate. In 1924, as noted above, she was

---

[78] *Billet*, 11.12.1957.
[79] O in C, 29.8.1963.
[80] These were held on 16.12.1926, 22.1.1930, 6.12.1932, 18.12.1935, 28.12.1938, 27.12.1945, 28.12.1948, 27.12.1951, 24.3.1955, 27.3.1958.
[81] *Star*, 7.12.1932, 28.12.1948, 29.12.1948.
[82] *Star*, 29.3.1958.

joined by Marie Naftel, Adele Dorey and Patricia Ozanne; in 1926, she was joined by Patricia Ozanne and Zélie Tooley; in 1932 she was joined by Vera Carey; in 1938 and 1945 she was joined by Nina Worley.[83] With the exceptions of Marie Randall and Vera Carey, all the women who stood in general elections up to and including that of 1945 were unsuccessful. Vera Carey however served only six months as a Deputy. She was elected at a by-election in May 1932 but lost her seat in the general election six months later.[84] This left Miss Randall to serve as Guernsey's solitary female Deputy for almost twenty-four years.

The reforms of 1948 marked a minor turning-point in the fortunes of female Deputies. In the election of December 1948 there were six women candidates.[85] Dorothy Higgs was standing in St Sampsons; Mabel Poat in St Martins; and Marie Randall in St Peter Port, where she was opposed by Marguerite Ross, Kathleen Robilliard and Nina Worley.[86] Two of the novice female candidates were successful, and Marie Randall found herself joined in the States by Marguerite Ross and Kathleen Robilliard.[87] Like Miss Randall, Miss Ross and Miss Robilliard retained their seats in subsequent elections, and the trio sat together as sole female Deputies until 1955, when Marie Randall retired at the age of 74. Marguerite Ross and Kathleen Robilliard are shown in plates 30 and 31 overleaf.

---

[83] *Star*, 2.12.1926, 16.1.1930, 2.12.1932, 5.12.1935, 10.12.1938, 18.12.1945.
[84] *Star*, 21.5.1932, 7.12.1932. Vera Carey was the niece of Edith Carey who had stood in the 1920 Deputies' election. She had a particular interest in history and conservation, and served as honorary secretary of *la Société Guernesiaise* (*Star*, 2.12.1932).
[85] *Star*, 20.12.1948.
[86] The 1948 Reform Law had replaced the five pre-war electoral districts with ten constituencies coterminous with the island's ten parishes.
[87] *Star*, 29.12.1948.

Plate 30. Marguerite Ross
Island Archives Service, Guernsey

Plate 31. Kathleen Robilliard
Courtesy of the Guernsey Press

The general election of 1955 was the first to take place in the spring and the first for thirty-one years in which Marie Randall had not stood. Marguerite Ross and Kathleen Robilliard were joined as candidates by two other women: Isabella Graesser, who was standing in St Martins, and Mona Stranger, standing in the Castel.[88] Of these four female candidates, three were successful: seasoned campaigners Ross and Robilliard, and newcomer Graesser.[89] Isabella Graesser was the first woman to be elected in a constituency outside St Peter Port. Misses Ross, Robilliard and Graesser were not to sit as a trio for very long, however, as the latter resigned in 1957. Nevertheless, Miss Graesser was replaced as the third female Deputy by Enid Fletcher, returned in a Vale by-election of March the same year.[90]

As noted earlier, the last election of our period took place in 1958. There were five female candidates: Enid Fletcher, Marguerite Ross and Kathleen Robilliard, plus newcomers Norah Wheadon and Emma Ferbrache, both of whom were standing in St Peter Port.[91] The success rate this time was 100 per cent, and all five of these women were returned.[92] Norah Wheadon, the first married female Deputy, was to serve in the States until 1970.[93] Emma Ferbrache served until 1973. The five-strong female contingent elected in 1958 represented the largest number of women Deputies ever to serve in the States at one time. Nevertheless, as just five out of fifty-five States members, they were as drops in an ocean of men.

Of the eight women elected to the States between 1924 and 1958, five served terms of ten years or more. Most female candidates who secured a seat went on to prove competent and popular Deputies. The chief reason for their limited numbers was not that women were shunned by the electorate but that so few women stood for election. For every female candidate who stood at an election between 1924 and 1958, there were on average twelve male candidates. The following paragraphs will explore reasons for the female electoral dearth.

---

[88] *Star*, 10.3.1955.
[89] *Star*, 25.3.1955.
[90] *Star*, 29.3.1957.
[91] *Star*, 12.3.1958.
[92] *Star*, 28.3.1958.
[93] Mrs Wheadon served her last two years as a Conseiller, the first woman elected to this role. See Appendix 3 for the terms served by female States Deputies between 1924 and 2016.

In May 1948, a short-lived left-wing newspaper, *Channel Island News and Views*, published an article headed 'Wake Up, Guernsey Housewives!'[94] The article contended:

> if our Deputies are to represent truly the people of Guernsey, there should be a more or less equal number of men and women in the States. But if these women are to represent the people of Guernsey, they must include women of the working class. We do not want women who have an income of £10 or more dictating to the working-class housewife how to spend her £4. We want to see working-class housewives in the States.

But no working-class housewife ever stood. Had any been so inclined, it would have been almost impossible for an ordinary married woman with domestic responsibilities to spare the time and energy to sustain a political career. With States duties impinging on home duties, she would have had to pay someone else to provide childcare and cleaning services, and her £4 per week would not have sufficed.[95] Further, it would have taken an unusual mid-twentieth-century husband to allow his wife even to consider standing as Deputy.

Thus it was a special type of woman who stood for the States between the 1920s and 1950s. Most were unmarried, middle-aged and middle-class. This rendered them free of male tutelage, free of child-rearing responsibilities, and wealthy enough to maintain themselves while performing States duties *gratis*. Essentially, they were much the type who would earlier have found fulfilment in voluntary charitable work. A brief look at the profiles of some prominent women Deputies will bear this out.[96]

Kathleen Robilliard, Norah Wheadon and Emma Ferbrache were all in their fifties when first elected Deputies. Marie Randall and Marguerite Ross were in their forties. All save Norah Wheadon were lifelong spinsters. All were comfortably off. Marie Randall, the daughter of a well-to-do brewer, was a

---

[94] A single copy survives in the Priaulx Library.
[95] States members were unpaid, although in 1951 a small allowance had been introduced to compensate employed members for working time lost while on States' business (*Star*, 16.3.1955).
[96] Unless otherwise stated, information in the following paragraphs is derived from *Star*, 26.1.1924, 11.12.1945, 18.12.1948, 23.12.1948, 17.12.1951, 18.3.1955, 8.4.1957, 22.3.1955, 13.3.1958, 15.3.1958; *Guernsey Evening Press*, 10.6.1954, 27.1.1965, 1.2.1968; *Guernsey Press*, 29.6.2001, 17.1.2014.

woman of private means. Kathleen Robilliard, the daughter of a timber merchant, owned a vinery. Norah Wheadon, the daughter of an army officer, was married to a successful grower. Marguerite Ross and Emma Ferbrache were the exceptions in having sustained professional careers in their own right (as a chiropodist and nurse respectively), but they appear to have retired from their professions before they took up politics.

All the female Deputies had long records of voluntary service before entering the States (and many maintained such activities while in the States). Marie Randall saw frontline service during World War I, when, already in her mid-thirties, she went to France as a member of a Voluntary Aid Detachment. She also worked for the YMCA, served as vice-president of the Guernsey Swimming Club and took a lifelong interest in the Girls' Friendly Society.[97] Like Miss Randall, Kathleen Robilliard worked as a nurse in World War I and in later years was active in the British Legion. Norah Wheadon had a particularly extensive portfolio of activities, serving *inter alia* as honorary secretary of the Soldiers', Sailors' and Airmen's Families Association, chair of the British Red Cross War Disabled Committee and president of the Ladies' College Guild. Marguerite Ross was also very active, serving as head of the Guernsey Women's Voluntary Service, vice-president of the women's section of the northern branch of the British Legion, vice-president of the Northern Nursing Division of the St John Ambulance Brigade, and island secretary of the Girl Guides Association.

Plate 32 (overleaf), which shows a group of retired and serving female Deputies in 1976, provides an interesting visual insight into the type of women who served as mid-twentieth-century States members. Standing, from left to right, are Marguerite Ross (1949-61), Jenny Cherry (1976-9), Valerie Renouf (1976-92), Ivy Blackwell (1967-70), Norah Wheadon (1958-70), Elizabeth Lincoln (1970-85) and Stella Ogier (1976-85). Seated are Iris Pouteaux (1964-76, 1979-85), Edith Albigès (1964-76) and Emma Ferbrache (1958-70). The photograph was taken to celebrate the retirement of Miss Albigès.

---

[97] The Girls' Friendly Society supported young working women by providing them with mentoring and practical help. The Guernsey branch (now defunct) was founded in 1891 (*Star*, 21.11.1891).

Plate 32. Retired and serving female Deputies, 1976
Courtesy of the *Guernsey Press*

Notwithstanding that most of the older women Deputies in this photograph were unmarried, they strike the modern observer as quintessentially maternal. They were, by their own account, primarily interested in the spheres of local government traditionally considered as 'feminine', i.e., welfare, health and education. Their male colleagues also viewed them in this way, and once inside the States, all of these women were channelled into such areas.[98] They seem to have welcomed these roles, and indeed to have seen them as a continuation, or intensification, of the voluntary work they performed outside.

On social and moral issues, the early generations of women Deputies were broadly conservative, as was consistent with their age and background. Marie Randall, for example, was resolutely opposed to divorce and repeatedly voted against its introduction when the matter was debated in the 1930s.[99] In the

---

[98] To take a few early examples: the two most important States committees on which Marie Randall saw service were the Education Council and Board of Health. She also served on the St Peter Port Poor Law Board, Public Assistance Authority and Town Hospital Board.
Norah Wheadon served for many years on the Education Council and Insurance Authority; Marguerite Ross on the Education Council and Children Board; Kathleen Robilliard on the Housing Authority; Emma Ferbrache on the Board of Health.
[99] *Star*, 13.7.1933, 27.3.1935.

1950s, she was against the introduction of a Social Insurance scheme and assisted a caucus of like-minded Deputies in delaying it by more than a decade.[100] Only with the election of much younger women such as Jenny Cherry in the 1970s was this conservative mould broken.

While serving as a Deputy, Jenny Cherry was notably active on women's issues, in particular the matters of equal pay and child guardianship, the latter of which featured on the States' agenda during her tenure.[101] A self-declared feminist, she was influenced by the late twentieth-century Women's Liberation movement. Her predecessors, for their part, were not greatly influenced by feminism of any sort, since they had all largely grown up during the long lull between feminism's first and second waves. The only exception to this was Marie Randall, who was a contemporary of Christabel Pankhurst and in her mid-twenties at the height of the suffragette campaign. I have not found any evidence to suggest that Miss Randall ever identified herself as a feminist; nevertheless—and in spite of her social conservatism—she stood out among her female colleagues in her outspoken support of women's issues. As much as anything else, this was because her tenure, a generation earlier than that of the others, coincided with the period when many of the worst disabilities affecting Guernseywomen came under States scrutiny. In the 1920s, Miss Randall strongly backed the introduction of a married women's property law; in the 1930s, she pressed actively for the equalisation of male and female voting ages; throughout her political career, she consistently advocated the equalisation of inheritance rights; and she also did her best (though unsuccessfully) to secure better pay and conditions for female States employees.[102]

It may perhaps be appropriate at this point to consider women who stood for election but were unsuccessful. Two in particular stand out: Patricia Ozanne, who stood in St Peters and Torteval in 1924 and 1926, and Nina Worley, who stood in St Peter Port in 1938, 1945 and 1948. These women had less conventional opinions than the women who did gain seats, and one wonders what impact they might have had on local politics had they been

---

[100] Kathleen Robilliard also belonged to this grouping. For more on the 1950s campaign against Social Insurance, see Crossan, *Poverty and Welfare*, pp. 250-4.
[101] Jenny Cherry's election manifesto is in *Guernsey Evening Press*, 16.3.1976. For more on child guardianship, see section on Guardianship and custody, chapter 3.
[102] See for instance *Guernsey Evening Press*, 24.1.1947.

returned. Mrs Ozanne, a vivacious Irishwoman, was strongly opposed to Guernsey's payment of the 'Imperial Contribution' (an annual contribution to the Imperial Exchequer requested by the British government to help with the costs of World War I). Mrs Ozanne advised against yielding to government pressure to provide regular payments on the grounds that this would compromise Guernsey's time-honoured immunity from United Kingdom taxation. At a meeting in 1924, she was reported to have urged islanders 'to value their freedom before it was torn from them', contrasting Guernsey, which 'had always been free' with her native Ireland, where 'freedom had been purchased with the tears of her women and the blood of her men.'[103] Notwithstanding that Mrs Ozanne's energy and eloquence went down well in some quarters, her electoral failure was made almost inevitable by the fact that she found herself pitted against Walter Sarre in both 1924 and 1926. Sarre was a respected Torteval farmer and grower who had served as a Douzenier and as Vice-President of the West United Agricultural and Horticultural Society.[104] His solid appeal to conservative rural ratepayers outweighed Mrs Ozanne's attractions, and he topped the poll on both occasions.

Nina Worley was an English-born hospital dispenser. A Quaker by creed, she defined herself as 'an internationalist and socialist'.[105] Before the Second World War, she ran the 'Guernsey League of Freedom' and, although she appears to have belonged to no party, she presented herself in elections as 'the workers' candidate'. Her views were decidedly unorthodox and anti-establishment. Aside from her staunch opposition to vivisection and compulsory vaccination, she also advocated (long before any of these policies were actually adopted) the removal of rectors from the States; the introduction of allowances to enable workers to serve as Deputies; the abolition of birching; the introduction of States pensions at 60 for both sexes; and the institution of shorter working hours and longer paid holidays for all employees.

---

[103] *Star*, 16.1.1924.
[104] *Star*, 19.1.1924.
[105] The information in this paragraph is culled from Miss Worley's election manifestos in *Star*, 12.12.1938, 15.12.1938, 24.12.1938, 18.12.1945, 24.12.1948, and from her testimony to the Privy Council in *Evidence given before the Privy Council Committee on Proposed Reforms in the Channel Islands: Guernsey* (London, 1946), pp. 231-3.

Plate 33. Nina Worley
Island Archives Service, Guernsey

For at least a partial explanation of Miss Worley's electoral failure, we need look no further than the nature of the electorate. We have seen that voter participation in mid-twentieth-century elections was low. This was because turn-out seems essentially to have been limited to the same core of ratepayers who had exercised the franchise when it was property-based. As a *Star* editorial noted after the first election on universal male franchise in 1920, it was the working classes who were most conspicuous by their absence.[106] The same dearth of working-class voters continued to be observed at ensuing elections. Some of the more left-wing witnesses who gave evidence to the 1946 Privy Council Committee on Proposed Reforms in the Channel Islands asserted that election candidates were well aware that this was the case, and consequently relied on being known in the right circles rather than making the effort to court popular votes through public meetings or canvassing.[107]

---

[106] *Star*, 29.12.1920, 30.12.1920.
[107] *Evidence given before the Privy Council Committee*, pp. 91, 92, 106. Indirect corroboration of this comes from the fact that Marie Randall held her seat in the 1938 general election despite being absent throughout the pre-electoral period on a planned tour of New Zealand (*Star*, 10.12.1938).

They also expressed the belief that the lack of working-class voters was due to the differential treatment of ratepayers and non-ratepayers in compiling the polling list, since ratepayers' names were simply carried over from parish rate lists, while non-ratepayers had to register in person.[108] An effort was made to remedy this situation in the 1948 Reform Law, which laid down that all adults on Guernsey's National Register would now have their names automatically inscribed on the electoral roll.[109] Nevertheless, when the elections of 1948 and 1951 were carried out on this system, it did not appreciably increase turn-out. The fact was that the unpropertied had never had a say in any of Guernsey's tiers of government until the reforms of 1919, and most seem to have continued to feel that it was not their affair. It is difficult to say whether this was from cynicism as to the possibility of change, from a sense that government was safe in the hands of those who had always monopolised it, or from sheer lack of interest.

At all events, if our equation of the minority who voted with the core of parochial ratepayers is correct, then their votes may be seen as motivated by a desire to protect their own position. Wary of any change to a *status quo* which had served them well, they tended to vote for candidates in their own image. This meant that unusual women such as Nina Worley—and anyone outside the mainstream—stood little chance of winning seats.

As the foregoing pages have shown, all the landmarks in female civic participation came later in Guernsey than in the United Kingdom—on average by two or three decades. We may attribute this tardiness to two main factors. The first lies in the enduringly conservative character of Guernsey's legislature, a conservatism which was also responsible for delaying many other improvements to women's lives. The second lies in the political indifference of women themselves. Changes may have come sooner if Guernsey had had a feminist movement to agitate for women's rights, but most working-class women did not concern themselves with such matters, and their social superiors appear to have been content with traditional ways. Thus the reforms, when they came, were largely initiated by men—and they were initiated as belated catch-up measures when advances in the United Kingdom made persistence in the old ways untenable. Ambrose Sherwill, who had

---

[108] *Evidence given before the Privy Council Committee*, pp. 91, 107, 108, 232.
[109] The National Register was a list of all persons in the Bailiwick kept by the States between 1945 and 1952.

himself initiated such measures amid female unconcern, vouched before the 1946 Privy Council Committee on Proposed Reforms in the Channel Islands that the average Guernseywoman had 'very little interest in public affairs'.[110] The regrettable conclusion we must therefore draw is that Guernseywomen's emancipation was not, indeed, self-won, but achieved on the shoulders of bolder and more enterprising women elsewhere.

---

[110] *Evidence given before the Privy Council Committee*, p. 159.

Conclusion

It is a truism that men and women cannot exist without one another. That said, they have rarely co-existed on equal terms. In most parts of the world and for most of time, the former have exercised dominance over the latter. Without entering into the complexities of evolutionary biology, the root of this dominance appears to lie in the compulsion felt by men (generically rather than individually) to manage their sexual, emotional and practical need of women by exerting control over them. In primitive times, control was facilitated by men's greater strength and their freedom from the burdens of parturition and lactation. As civilisation grew more sophisticated, control was reinforced and entrenched in the myriad anti-egalitarian cultural, religious and legal structures which gave human societies their shape.

The period covered by this work was chosen for its special significance to the history of western women. Its opening decades marked the first weakening of these anti-egalitarian structures and women's first steps towards emancipation. The process was by no means fully accomplished by the end of our period (and remains unaccomplished still), but the landmark changes on which further progress depended had largely been achieved.

In the first half of the nineteenth century, as from time immemorial, western society was run entirely by men in the interests of men. Government, the judiciary, public administration, the military, academia, finance and all other aspects of the social framework were male preserves from which females were excluded. Women had only one legitimate place, and that was in the home, under the protection of men, dependent upon men, serving the domestic and reproductive needs of men.

Any woman without male protection who was forced to earn her own living outside the home was at an immense disadvantage. Women's opportunities for work were limited to a handful of designated feminine occupations for which the remuneration was a fraction of that for men's work. The best that women from the lowest ranks could aspire to was domestic service, charring or other unskilled work. Women further up the scale might find employment as dressmakers, shop assistants or elementary schoolteachers. Even higher-class women were limited in their options. They could hire themselves out as governesses, seek to set up a school or try to earn a living by writing. The professions, however—law, medicine, accountancy, engineering, architecture—were entirely closed off to them. Not only were they debarred by convention, their inferior education left them unqualified.

Central to the exercise of male dominance was the institution of marriage. With scant prospect of living independently, marriage was for most women a practical necessity. However, the conjugal bargain was profoundly unequal. For a husband, the bargain began and ended with sustenance. If he fulfilled this obligation, his wife had no further claim on him. She, by contrast, became totally his: her possessions became his; her person became his; any children she bore were exclusively his.

Men were hardly likely to give up these advantages voluntarily, so how, we may legitimately ask, was it ever possible for women to bring about a change? The process was slow and incremental, and it proceeded at different paces in different countries. In Britain, it might be said to have got under way in the 1850s, when the first organised feminist groups were established. These groups typically consisted of urban upper- and middle-class women. One of the earliest was the circle around Barbara Smith (later Bodichon) in London.[1] Among the first preoccupations of these early activists was the education of upper- and middle-class girls. Barbara Bodichon founded her own progressive school, and joined fellow educational pioneers Frances Buss, Dorothea Beale and Emily Davies in a scheme to extend higher education to girls which culminated in the opening of Girton College in 1873.[2]

Progress occurred on many fronts, but, arguably, it was early feminist successes in the educational field which created the first serious cracks in the structures of male dominance. Advances in female education unleashed upon late Victorian society a cohort of knowledgeable, confident, capable women, some of whom went on to earn independent livings as professionals, and

---

[1] M. Walters, *Feminism: A Very Short Introduction* (Oxford, 2005), p. 49. Miss Smith and her friends were known as the Ladies of Langham Place after one of the venues for their meetings.

[2] J. Kamm, *How Different from Us: A Biography of Miss Buss and Miss Beale* (1958; Abingdon, 2012 edn), pp. 65, 93–6. For more on Misses Buss and Beale, see section on Education, chapter 2.

some of whom went on to occupy newly available seats on Boards of Guardians, School Boards and local councils.

In introducing to the public mind the idea that females might have a useful civic role to play, this opened a breach which later let more women into spheres from which they had hitherto been excluded. Moreover, these confident and assertive women provided a reservoir of organisers and activists for the major feminist campaigns initiated in the later nineteenth century. Under the leadership of such intellectually emancipated women, these campaigns gradually bore fruit, and within the space of a few decades, many of the linchpins of male dominance had been removed.

We might identify the following as the landmark achievements of the British feminist campaigns: the 1878 Matrimonial Causes Act which allowed battered wives to apply for summary separation orders with maintenance; the 1882 Married Women's Property Act which gave married women ownership and control of their property; the 1885 Criminal Law Amendment Act which set the statutory age of consent at sixteen; partial female parliamentary enfranchisement in 1918 followed by full enfranchisement in 1928; and the equalisation of male and female grounds for divorce in 1923.

What is notable for the purposes of the current study is that the achievement of all these milestones took considerably longer in Guernsey. The local variant of the 1878 Matrimonial Causes Act was enacted only in 1890; that of the 1882 Married Women's Property Act not until 1928; Guernsey had no statutory age of consent until 1907, no divorce until 1946, and men and women did not vote on equal terms in States elections until 1945.

In all of these respects, Guernsey was closer to France than to Britain. Here, it was not until the twentieth century that married women were granted full legal capacity, control over their property, or equal parental rights with their husbands; and universal adult franchise was implemented at much the same time as in Guernsey.[3] This may have been due to a degree of cultural affinity. In France, although a feminist movement had existed since the

---

[3] L. Abrams, *The Making of Modern Woman: Europe, 1789-1918* (Harlow, 2002), p. 274; S.K. Foley, *Women in France since 1789* (Basingstoke, 2004), p. 204; J.F. McMillan, *France and Women, 1789-1914* (London, 2000), p. 152.

1860s, it remained the preserve of an elite and never assumed a popular dimension. Few of the traditionally-minded inhabitants of rural or small-town France had any enthusiasm for social innovation, and, in the provinces, the cause of women's rights was viewed with indifference if not hostility.[4] We should not push the analogy too far, but this certainly had echoes in Guernsey, not only in the rural parishes but also in St Peter Port.

Whatever the case and despite the delays, much had been achieved in Guernsey by the 1950s, and there is no doubt that mid-twentieth-century Guernseywomen were legally and politically in a better position than their grandmothers a century earlier. What had not changed so radically were underlying attitudes. Men were still regarded as breadwinners, and women as home-makers and child-rearers. Such an outlook ensured that education continued to be organised along gender lines, and that women remained disproportionately concentrated in low-paid unskilled jobs.

In the 1950s, disparities such as these persisted all over the western world, and it took a second wave of feminism, which was instigated in America in the 1960s and spread to Britain in the 1970s, to bring about change at a more fundamental level. By this stage, Guernsey was fully open to external influences, and as powerfully affected by late twentieth- and early twenty-first-century equal opportunity reforms as anywhere else. These reforms benefited Guernseywomen in much the same ways as they did women elsewhere, and it is almost superfluous to observe that insular women currently have access to better civil rights, better legal protections, better educational provision, better career opportunities and greater financial independence than at any time in history.

Moreover, marriage is no longer the embodiment of sexual inequity it once was. Much of the historical unfairness in marriage arose not from the law of marriage itself but from deeply embedded traditional understandings of the conjugal bargain which found legal expression in such phenomena as the marital rape exemption, spousal rights of 'correction', actions for restitution of conjugal rights and compensatory damages in cases of adultery. With the abolition of all of these, marriage has lost many of its most atavistic features. Even more significantly, however, deep-rooted social changes have silently revolutionised cultural attitudes to marriage from within. Women's

---

[4] McMillan, *France and Women*, pp. 130–1, 218.

financial independence has removed the economic need to marry. Evolving moral attitudes have dispensed with marriage as a prerequisite for family formation. Whereas marriage in the past centred on procreation and succession, modern unions are much more about voluntary resource-pooling and companionship (especially in their recent same-sex incarnation). Guernsey's current marriage and divorce laws do not do justice to these profound attitudinal changes: nearly a century old, they remain imbued with the norms and values of the past. Since marriage has been so central to our study, we will close with the observation that if these laws are to have any relevance to contemporary realities, then the time has come, not just for a cosmetic update, but for a fundamental reconceptualisation of marriage itself.

Appendix 1

Distribution of female occupations, 1851 and 1951

Proportion of Bailiwick female workforce in various occupations, 1851

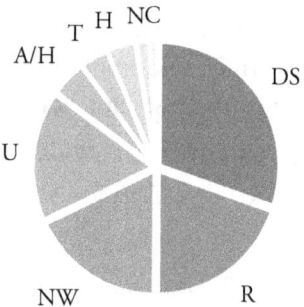

Proportion of Bailiwick female workforce in various occupations, 1951

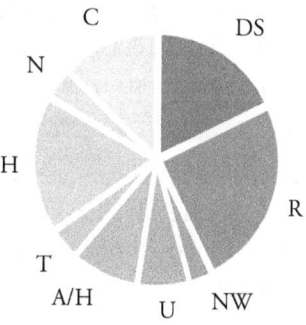

Key: DS: domestic service; T: teaching; R: retailing; H: hospitality (innkeeping, hotel-keeping, waiting, bar work, etc.); NW: needlework trades (dressmaking, shirt-making, tailoring, etc.); N: nursing and midwifery; U: unskilled (charwomen, laundresses, ironers, etc.); C: clerical (also including telegraphists and telephonists); A/H: agriculture and horticulture

Sources: PP 1852-3 LXXXVIII; *Census 1951: Report on Jersey, Guernsey and Adjacent Islands* (London, 1956)

Appendix 2

Guernsey Women's History Timeline

1840 *Loi sur les Successions* (O in C, 13.7.1840) removes some of the injustices suffered by women in inheritance matters

1840 Guernsey's first Marriage Law (O in C, 3.10.1840) introduces civil marriage and permits Nonconformist clergymen to conduct marriages in Nonconformist churches

1865 *Loi relative aux Preuves* (O in C, 29.6.1865) allows a wife to give evidence in court to prove ill-treatment of herself on the part of her husband

1868 *Loi relative à l'Entretien des Enfants Illégitimes* (O in C, 29.2.1868) sets out framework for obtaining maintenance orders from the Ordinary Court in cases of illegitimacy

1872 Ladies' College opens, offering middle-class girls an academic education

1890 *Loi relative à la Séparation de Mari et Femme en Police Correctionnelle* (O in C, 30.6.1890) allows wives to apply to the Police Court for separation with maintenance from abusive husbands

1892 *Loi donnant aux Femmes Droit de Voter dans les Assemblées Paroissiales* (O in C, 6.2.1892) allows rate-paying spinsters, widows and legally separated married women to speak and vote at parish meetings, but denies them public office

1895 Girls' Intermediate School opens

1899 *Loi relative à la Réforme des Etats de Délibération* (O in C, 8.8.1899) introduces nine Deputies to the States to be elected by all male ratepayers and female ratepayers who are spinsters, widows or legally separated from their husbands

1900 Mary Sinclair becomes the first female doctor to be licensed to practise in Guernsey

1907 Guernsey's first 'age of consent' law (*Loi relative à la Protection des Femmes et Filles Mineures*, O in C, 6.7.1907) criminalises sexual intercourse with girls under 16

1909 *Loi relative au Mariage avec la Soeur d'une Femme Décédée* (O in C, 3.7.1909) permits marriage between a man and his deceased wife's sister

1909 *Loi pour la Punition d'Inceste* (O in C, 3.8.1909) makes incest a criminal offence

1910 *Loi sur l'Avortement* (O in C, 7.11.1910) criminalises abortion

1917 Miss Priaulx and Mrs Clothier become the first women to sit on a States committee

1918 Guernsey's Chamber of Commerce admits its first female member

1919 Guernsey's second Marriage Law (*Loi ayant rapport aux Mariages célébrés dans l'île de Guernesey et dans les îles d'Aurgeny et de Serk*, O in C, 15.4.1919) permits weddings in private houses and subjects Roman Catholic weddings to statutory provisions

1919 *Loi relative à l'Eligibilité des Femmes aux Charges Paroissiales* (O in C, 9.10.1919) permits rate-paying unmarried women, widows, and women legally separated from their husbands to serve in parochial public office

1920 Miss Collings and Mrs Gardner are elected St Peter Port's first female Overseers of the Poor

1920 *Loi supplémentaire à la Loi relative à la Réforme des Etats de Délibération* (O in C, 13.10.1920) introduces universal male adult franchise in elections for States Deputies but limits the female franchise to women over 30 (plus rate-paying spinsters, widows or legally separated women over 20); the law also permits women over 30 to stand for election as States Deputies

1924 Marie Randall is elected Guernsey's first female States Deputy

1926 *Loi ayant rapport à l'Emploi de Femmes, de Jeunes Personnes et d'Enfants* (O in C, 5.11.1926) restricts the employment of women at night and in certain industries

1927 *Loi relative à l'Entretien des Enfants Illégitimes* (O in C, 13.5.1927) empowers the Magistrate to grant summary maintenance orders in cases of illegitimacy

1928 *Loi étendant les Droits de la Femme Mariée quant à la Propriété Mobilière et Immobilière* (O in C, 13.7.1928) gives married women the same property rights as men and unmarried women, allowing them to own and manage their own property, as well as to make and enter contracts on their own behalf

1930 second *Loi relative à la Séparation de Mari et Femme en Police Correctionnelle* (O in C, 28.7.1930) enhances Magistrate's Court's powers in respect of summary separation orders

1936 Midwives Ordinance (Ord, 1.2.1936) introduces registration for midwives and makes it obligatory for them to summon a doctor in cases of emergency

1939 *Loi relative à la Réforme des Etats* (O in C, 23.6.1939) reduces to 20 the age at which women may vote and stand in Deputies' elections, thereby instituting universal adult suffrage

1939 Matrimonial Causes Law (O in C, 3.7.1939) introduces divorce to Guernsey, but its implementation is delayed for seven years

1945 first Deputies' election under universal adult suffrage (27.12.1945)

1946 Ord, 31.8.1946 brings 1939 Matrimonial Causes Law into force

1946 first divorce to be granted in Guernsey (14.11.1946)

1950 Royal Court of Guernsey (Miscellaneous Reform Provisions) Law 1950 permits women to stand for election as Jurats

1954 the Law of Inheritance 1954 (O in C, 13.4.1954) equalises male and female inheritance rights

1957 Norah Wheadon is elected Guernsey's first female Douzenier

1963   Parochial Taxation and Voting Law (O in C, 29.8.1963) allows married women full rights to vote and stand for election at parish level

1968   Norah Wheadon is elected Guernsey's first female Conseiller

1971   Social Insurance (Overlapping Benefits) (Amendment) (Guernsey) Regulations 1971 and Social Insurance (Maternity Benefit) (Guernsey) Regulations 1971 introduce States' maternity benefit for working women

1971   Supplementary Benefit (Guernsey) Law 1971 (O in C, 5.4.1971) entitles single mothers to receive States' supplementary benefit

1973   Barbara Nicolle is elected Guernsey's first female parochial Procureur des Pauvres

1973   Rosalyn Brelsford becomes Guernsey's first female advocate

1975   Diana Meldrum is elected Guernsey's first female parish Constable

1975   Guernsey's first female police officers are appointed

1978   Law Reform (Age of Majority and Guardianship of Minors) (Guernsey) Law (O in C, 21.3.1978) equalises the rights of mothers and fathers over their children

1985   Dorothy Le Pelley is elected Guernsey's first female Jurat

1996   Jurat Eileen Glass is appointed Guernsey's first female Acting Magistrate

1997   the Abortion (Guernsey) Law 1997 legalises abortion

2004   Cherry McMillen is appointed Guernsey's first female Stipendiary Magistrate

2005   the Prevention of Discrimination (Enabling Provisions) (Bailiwick of Guernsey) Law 2004 and the Sex Discrimination (Employment) (Guernsey) Ordinance 2005 outlaw discrimination on the basis of sex

2012   Megan Pullum is appointed Guernsey's first female Law Officer (initially HM Comptroller, but becomes HM Procureur in 2016)

Appendix 3

Female States Deputies, February 1924–March 2016

Marie Randall	1924-55
Vera Carey	May-December 1932
Kathleen Robilliard	1949-66
Marguerite Ross	1949-61
Isabella Graesser	1955-7
Enid Fletcher	1957-61
Norah Wheadon	1958-61 (Conseiller 1968-70)
Emma Ferbrache	1958-70
Edith Albigès	1964-76
Iris Pouteaux	1964-76, 1979-85
Ivy Blackwell	1967-70
Elizabeth Lincoln	1970-85
Rosemary Morris	1970-3
Stella Ogier	1976-85
Barbara Nicolle	1976-88
Valerie Renouf	1976-92
Jennifer Cherry	1976-9
Patricia Lihou	1979-85 (Conseiller April–July 1985)
Joan Reddy	1982-5
Joyce Cook	1982-8
Jean Pritchard	1985-94 (Conseiller 1994-7) 1997-2008
Blanche Dorey	1985-97
Carol Fletcher (later Steere)	1985-97 (Conseiller 1997-2000) 2008-12
Patricia Mellor	1988-2004
Susan Plant	1985-94 (Conseiller 1994-8)
Patricia Robilliard	1991-2004
Janine Le Sauvage	1994-2008
Judith Beaugeard	1994-2004

Mary Lowe	1994–7 (Conseiller 1997–2000)
	2000–
Ann Robilliard	1998–2004
Claire Waite (later Le Pelley)	2000–8
Samantha Maindonald	2003–12
Carla McNulty Bauer	2004–12
Wendy Morgan	2004–8
Diane Lewis	2004–8
Jennifer Tasker	2005–12
Gloria Dudley-Owen	2008–12
Tania Stephens	2008–12
Yvonne Burford	2012–16
Sandra James	2012–16
Michelle Le Clerc	2012–
Heidi Soulsby	2012–

Source: https://www.gov.gg/history

Bibliography

Primary Sources

Greffe, St Peter Port, Guernsey
Acts of the Ecclesiastical Court
Contrats pour la Date
Livres en Crime
Magistrate's Court Books
Ordonnances
Plaids de Meubles
Préjugés en Crime
Requêtes
Royal Court Letter Books

Priaulx Library, St Peter Port, Guernsey
Anon. (ed.), *Approbation des Lois, Coutumes, et Usages de l'Ile de Guernesey ratifiée au Conseil Privé le 27 Octobre 1583* (Guernsey, 1822)
Billets d'Etat
Bowes, E.J. and Gregg, H.V., *A Short Survey of the Development of the Education System in the Island of Guernsey* (unpub. typescript, 1968)
Census Enumerators' Books, Guernsey, 1851–1901 (microfilm)
Census of Great Britain, 1851: Population Tables, Scotland and Islands in the British Seas (London, 1852)
Census of England and Wales, 1861: Population and Houses, England and Wales and Islands in the British Seas (London, 1862)
Census of England and Wales, 1871: Population and Houses, England and Wales and Islands in the British Seas (London, 1871)
Census 1881: Islands in the British Seas (London, 1883)
Census 1891: Islands in the British Seas (London, 1893)

Census 1901: Islands in the British Seas (London, 1903)
Census 1911: Islands in the British Seas (London, 1913)
Census 1921: Jersey, Guernsey and Adjacent Islands (London, 1924)
Census 1931: Jersey, Guernsey and Adjacent Islands (London, 1933)
Census 1951: Report on Jersey, Guernsey and Adjacent Islands (London, 1956)
Census 1961: Report on Jersey, Guernsey and Adjacent Islands (London, 1966)
Channel Islands News and Views (May, 1948)
De Gruchy, W.L. (ed.), *L'Ancienne Coutume de Normandie* (Jersey, 1881)
Everard, J.A. (ed.), *Le Grand Coutumier de Normandie* (Jersey, 2009)
Guernsey church and civil marriage registers (microfilm)
Orders in Council (published volumes)
Ordinances (published volumes)
Vaudin, W., *A Peep in the Future, or The Royal Court in the Year 2000: The Suffragettes in Power* (printed brochure, c.1910)
Walton, E., *Guernsey Women and the Great War* (unpub. typescript, 2011)

Island Archives, St Peter Port, Guernsey

AQ 0227/09 – St Martins Police Occurrence Book, 1909–11
AQ 0227/10 – St Martins Police Occurrence Book, 1911–15
AQ 0227/14 – St Martins Police Occurrence Book, 1915–19
AQ 0446/04 – St Peter Port District Nursing Association Committee Minutes, 1931–45
AQ 0507/02 – Vale Police Occurrence Book, 1894–9
AQ 0507/03 – Vale Police Occurrence Book, 1899–1902
AQ 0819/72 – Case Registers of Myra Pipe (midwife), 1923–37
AQ 0966/01 – St Peter Port Douzaine Deliberations, 1848–73
AQ 0975-05 – St Peter Port Venereal Disease Examination Register, 1913–21
AQ 0982/02 – St Peter Port Constables' Letter Book, 1891–6
AQ 0982/03 – St Peter Port Constables' Letter Book, 1896–1902
AQ 0987/02 – St Peter Port Venereal Disease Examination Register, 1908–13
AQ 0991/02 – St Peter Port Police Occurrence Book, 1853–6
AQ 0991/03 – St Peter Port Police Occurrence Book, 1856–9
AQ 0991/04 – St Peter Port Police Occurrence Book, 1859–61
AQ 0992/01 – St Peter Port Police Occurrence Book, 1861–6

AQ 0992/02 – St Peter Port Police Occurrence Book, 1866-9
AQ 0992/03 – St Peter Port Police Occurrence Book, 1870-3
AQ 0992/04 – St Peter Port Police Occurrence Book, 1873-8
AQ 0993/01 – St Peter Port Police Occurrence Book, 1878-83
AQ 0993/02 – St Peter Port Police Occurrence Book, 1883-9
AQ 0994/01 – St Peter Port Police Occurrence Book, 1889-93
AQ 0994/02 – St Peter Port Police Occurrence Book, 1893-7
AQ 0994/03 – St Peter Port Police Occurrence Book, 1897-1901
AQ 0994/04 – St Peter Port Police Occurrence Book, 1901-5
AQ 0995/01 – St Peter Port Police Occurrence Book, 1905-10
AQ 0995/02 – St Peter Port Police Occurrence Book, 1910-13
AQ 0995/03 – St Peter Port Police Occurrence Book, 1913-19
AQ 40/06 – Guernsey Chamber of Commerce Minutes, 1911-18
AQ 40/08 – Guernsey Chamber of Commerce Minutes, 1918-24
AQ 44/05 – Guernsey Chamber of Commerce Minutes, 1889-1902
AQ 1008/01 – St Peter Port Tax Book, 1894-1907
AQ 1044/01 – Ladies' College Minute Book, 1872-8
AQ 1129/08-002 – 'The Militant Suffragette' by Harold Tooley, 8.11.1909
AS/MB 023-04 – States Suffrage Committee Minutes, 1905-13
AS/MB 026-01 – States Matrimonial Causes Committee Minutes, 1935-7
AS/MB 065-05 – States Public Assistance Authority, Hospital Board Minutes, 1942-7
AS/MB 104-01 – States Intermediate Schools Committee Minutes, 1882-1913
AS/MB 104-09 – States Education Council, Miscellaneous Committee Minutes, 1927–53
AS/MB 105-02 – States Education Council Minutes, 1921-8
AS/MB 105-04 – States Education Council Minutes, 1938-47
AS/MB 105-05 – States Education Council Minutes, 1947-51
AS/MB 106-03 – States Education Council, Primary School Committee Minutes, 1939-51
BA 56-11 – States Supervisor's Election File, 1939-46
BF 018-13 – Bailiff's Office, Venereal Disease File, 1918-48
BF 026-17 – Bailiff's Office, Matrimonial Causes File, 1949-57
BF 096-15 – Guernsey Marriage Guidance Council, miscellaneous records, 1949-73
CC 04-06 – States Controlling Committee, Venereal Disease File, 1942-5

DC/HX 046-01 – St Peter Port Poor Law Board Minutes, 1907–15
DC/HX 052-01 – St Peter Port Poor Law Board Minutes, 1915–24
DC/HX 054-05 – St Peter Port Poor Law Board Minutes, 1852–73
DC/HX 054-06 – St Peter Port Poor Law Board Minutes, 1873–88
DC/HX 057-01 – Town Hospital House Committee Minutes, 1889–96
DC/HX 059-01 – Town Hospital House Committee Minutes, 1871–81
DC/HX 062-03 – St Peter Port Poor Law Board Vice-President's Letter Book, 1881–9
DC/HX 127-01 – Town Hospital House Committee Minutes, 1862–70
DC/HX 130-01 – Town Hospital Board of Directors' Minutes, 1842–9
DC/HX 130-03 – Town Hospital House Committee Minutes, 1882–9
DC/HX 130-04 – Town Hospital House Committee Minutes, 1853–61
DC/HX 135-02 – Town Hospital Board of Directors' Minutes, 1822–9
DC/HX 136-09 – Town Hospital House Committee Minutes, 1874–80
DC/HX 253-01 – St Peter Port Poor Law Board Correspondence, 1910–20
DC/HX 272-10 – States Central Poor Law Board Staff Handbook, 1930
EC 062-10 – States Education Council, Female School Leavers, 1954–76
EC 077-10 – States Education Council, Ladies' College, 1960–4
EC 145-05 – States Education Council, Ladies' College Scholarships, 1955–82
Evidence given before the Privy Council Committee on Proposed Reforms in the Channel Islands: Guernsey (London, 1946)
GW 01-01 – Guernsey Rescue and Preventive Society Minutes, 1923–32
GW 01-02 – Guernsey Rescue and Preventive Society Minutes, 1927–34
GW 01-03 – Guernsey Rescue and Preventive Society Minutes, 1934–9
GW 01-04 – Guernsey Rescue and Preventive Society Minutes, 1937–9
GW 01-05 – Guernsey Social Welfare Mission Minutes, 1939–40
GW 01-06 – Guernsey Moral Welfare Association Casebook, 1948–53
GW 01-13 – Guernsey Moral Welfare Association Legislation Sub-Committee Minutes, 1948–52
GW 02-05 – Guernsey Moral Welfare Association Minutes, 1957–62
LG 23-03 (01) – Lieutenant-Governor's Correspondence re. Françoise Conan
LO 023-08 – Law Officers' Divorce File, 1936–7
LO 027-22 – Law Officers' Midwives' Registration File, 1933–4
LO 031-02 – Law Officers' Offence Reports and Prosecutions, 1946–7
LO 038-03 – Law Officers' Offence Reports and Prosecutions, 1949
LO 042-11 – Law Officers' Letter Book, 1909–12

LO 054-05 – Law Officers' Offence Reports and Prosecutions, 1949–51
LO 056-11 – Law Officers' Offence Reports and Prosecutions, 1951–3
LO 078-10 – Law Officers' *Maladies Secrètes* File, 1936–51
PC 146-01 – Island Police Occurrence Book, November 1950–April 1951
PC 146-02 – Island Police Occurrence Book, April–September 1951
PC 146-03 – Island Police Occurrence Book, September 1951–April 1952
PC 146-04 – Island Police Occurrence Book, April–September 1952
PC 146-05 – Island Police Occurrence Book, September 1952–May 1953
PC 146-07 – Island Police Occurrence Book, December 1953–August 1954
PC 146-08 – Island Police Occurrence Book, August 1954–March 1955
PC 181-01 – Island Police Occurrence Book, January 1915–April 1917
PC 181-02 – Island Police Occurrence Book, April 1917–April 1919
PC 181-03 – Island Police Occurrence Book, May 1919–September 1920
PC 184-02 – Island Police Occurrence Book, December 1929–March 1930
PC 184-03 – Island Police Occurrence Book, March–July 1930
PC 184-04 – Island Police Occurrence Book, July–November 1930
PC 184-05 – Island Police Occurrence Book, November 1930–February 1931
PC 185-02 – Island Police Occurrence Book, November 1931–February 1932
PC 185-03 – Island Police Occurrence Book, February–May 1932
PC 185-04 – Island Police Occurrence Book, May–July 1932
PC 185-05 – Island Police Occurrence Book, July–September 1932
PC 185-06 – Island Police Occurrence Book, September–December 1932
PC 186-01 – Island Police Occurrence Book, December 1932–February 1933
PC 186-06 – Island Police Occurrence Book, December 1933–February 1934
PC 186-07 – Island Police Occurrence Book, February–May 1934
PC 187-01 – Island Police Occurrence Book, May–July 1934
PC 187-02 – Island Police Occurrence Book, July–September 1934
PC 187-03 – Island Police Occurrence Book, September–November 1934
PC 187-04 – Island Police Occurrence Book, November 1934–January 1935
PC 188-03 – Island Police Occurrence Book, November 1935–January 1936
PC 188-04 – Island Police Occurrence Book, January–March 1936
PC 188-05 – Island Police Occurrence Book, March–May 1936
PC 188-06 – Island Police Occurrence Book, May–July 1936
PC 189-01 – Island Police Occurrence Book, July–August 1936
PC 189-02 – Island Police Occurrence Book, August–October 1936
PC 189-03 – Island Police Occurrence Book, October–December 1936
PC 189-04 – Island Police Occurrence Book, December 1936–February 1937

PC 190-05 – Island Police Occurrence Book, December 1937–February 1938
PC 190-06 – Island Police Occurrence Book, February–April 1938
PC 191-01 – Island Police Occurrence Book, April–June 1938
PC 191-02 – Island Police Occurrence Book, June–July 1938
PC 191-03 – Island Police Occurrence Book, July–August 1938
PC 191-04 – Island Police Occurrence Book, August–October 1938
PC 191-05 – Island Police Occurrence Book, October–November 1938
PC 191-06 – Island Police Occurrence Book, November 1938–January 1939
PC 198-06 – Island Police Occurrence Book, November 1949–June 1950
PC 198-07 – Island Police Occurrence Book, June–November 1950
PC 199-02 – Island Police Occurrence Book, October 1955–May 1956
PC 199-03 – Island Police Occurrence Book, May–November 1956
PC 199-04 – Island Police Occurrence Book, November 1956–July 1957
PC 199-06 – Island Police Occurrence Book, December 1957–May 1958
PC 199-07 – Island Police Occurrence Book, May–September 1958
PC 199-08 – Island Police Occurrence Book, September 1958–March 1959

National Archives, Kew

HO 17/26/132 – Case of Marie Joseph François Béasse, 1830
HO 45/10142/B17748 – *Maladies Secrètes* Law, 1895-7
HO 45/12251 – Venereal Diseases (Channel Islands), 1918–26
HO 45/13835 – Guernsey Marital Separation Law, 1929–30
HO 45/21143 – Guernsey Matrimonial Causes Law, 1938–47
HO 45/23231 – Guernsey Sexual Offences Law, 1983
HO 45/233135 – Guernsey Sodomy Law, 1929–48
HO 45/24658 – Guernsey Stipendiary Magistrate, 1914–25
HO 98/88 – Guernsey Statistical Return, 1847
PC 8/472 – *Maladies Secrètes* Law, 1896

Hampshire Record Office

100M97/C1/1 – Annual Reports of the Winchester Diocesan Union for Preventive and Rescue Work, 1914–72

Women's Library, London School of Economics
3HJW/F/06 – Papers of H.J. Wilson, Guernsey File, 1895
3HJW/F/12 – Papers of H.J. Wilson, British Committee File, 1901

Parliamentary Papers
1819 IX (Digest of Parochial Returns made to the Select Committee on the Education of the Poor)
1833 XXXVII (1831 census analysis)
1844 XXVII (1841 census analysis)
1852–3 LXXXVIII (1851 census analysis)
1883 LXXX (1881 census analysis)
1893–4 CVII (1891 census analysis)
1903 LXXXIV (1901 census analysis)

Newspapers and magazines
Comet
Gazette de Guernesey
Gentleman's Magazine
Guernsey Evening Press
Guernsey Press
Guernsey Weekly Press
Jersey Independent and Daily Telegraph
Monthly Illustrated Journal
Star
The Guernsey and Jersey Magazine

Secondary Sources

Pre-1920 publications
Anon., *The Stranger's Guide to the Islands of Guernsey and Jersey* (Guernsey, 1833)

Anon., *A Short History of the Temperance Movement in Guernsey, 1566–1900* (Guernsey, 1900)

Anon. (ed.), *A Treatise on the History, Laws and Customs of the Island of Guernsey by Mr Warburton, a Herald and Celebrated Antiquary in Charles II's Reign* (Guernsey, 1822)

Ansted, D.T. and Latham, M.A., *The Channel Islands* (London, 1862)

Bear, W.E., 'Glimpses of farming in the Channel Islands', *Journal of the Royal Agricultural Society of England*, 24 (1888), pp. 365-97

Berry, W., *The History of the Island of Guernsey* (London, 1815)

Blackstone, W., *Commentaries on the Laws of England*, 4 vols (Oxford, 1765-9), 1

Boland, H., *Les Iles de la Manche* (Paris, 1904)

Caird, M., *The Morality of Marriage and Other Essays on the Status and Destiny of Woman* (London, 1897)

Carey, E.F. (ed.), *Guernsey Folk Lore from MSS by the Late Sir Edgar MacCulloch* (London, 1903)

Carey, L., *Essai sur les Institutions, Lois et Coutumes de l'Ile de Guernesey* (c.1750; Guernsey, 1889)

Clarke, L.L., *Redstone's Guernsey Guide* (Guernsey, 1841)

Dally, F.F., *A Guide to Jersey, Guernsey, Sark, Herm, Jethou, Alderney, etc.* (London, 1858)

Dally, F.F., *A Guide to Guernsey* (London, 1860)

Dally, F.F., *Agriculture of the Channel Islands* (Guernsey, 1860)

Davis, E.V., *Sarnia's Record in the Great War* (Guernsey, 1919)

Duncan, J., *The History of Guernsey* (London, 1841)

Durell, E. (ed.), *An Account of the Island of Jersey by the Rev. Philip Falle to which are added Notes and Illustrations* (Jersey, 1837)

Hale, M., *History of the Pleas of the Crown*, 2 vols (London, 1736), 1

Hammick, J.T., 'On the judicial statistics of England and Wales, with special reference to the recent returns relating to crime', *Journal of the Statistical Society of London*, 30 (1867), pp. 375-426

Inglis, H.D., *The Channel Islands*, 2 vols (London, 1834), 2

Jacob, J., *Annals of Some of the British Norman Isles Constituting the Bailiwick of Guernsey* (Paris, 1830)

Jeaffreson, J., *Brides and Bridals* (London, 1872)

Jeremie, J., *Historical Account of the Island of Guernsey* (Guernsey, 1821)

Jeremie, P., *On Parochial and States Taxation in Guernsey* (Guernsey, 1856)

Jeremie, P., *On the Law of Real Property in Guernsey* (1862; Guernsey, 1866 edn)
Le Cras, A.J., *The Laws, Customs, and Privileges, and their Administration, in the Island of Jersey* (London, 1839)
Le Marchant, T., *Remarques et Animadversions sur l'Approbation des Lois et Coustumier de Normandie usités ès Jurisdictions de Guernezé*, 2 vols (c.1660; Guernsey, 1826)
Llewelyn Davies, M. (ed.), *Maternity: Letters from Working Women Collected by the Women's Co-Operative Guild* (London, 1915)
Mill, J.S., *Dissertations and Discussions Political, Philosophical and Historical*, 2 vols (London, 1859), 1
Mill, J.S., *On the Subjection of Women* (1869; Oxford, 1991 edn)
Quayle, T., *A General View of the Agriculture and Present State of the Islands on the Coast of Normandy* (London, 1815)
Report of the Commissioners appointed to inquire into the Civil, Municipal and Ecclesiastical Laws of Jersey (London, 1860)
Report of the Royal Commission into the Administration and Operation of the Contagious Diseases Acts (London, 1871)
Second Report of the Commissioners appointed to enquire into the State of the Criminal Law of the Channel Islands (London, 1848)
Terrien, G., *Commentaires du Droict Civil tant Public que Privé Observé au Pays et Duché de Normandie* (1574; Rouen, 1654 edn)
Tupper, F.B., *The History of Guernsey and its Bailiwick* (Guernsey, 1854 and 1876 edns)
Walmesley, W.G. (ed. K.C. Renault), *A Pedestrian Tour through the Islands of Guernsey and Jersey* (1821; Chichester 1992 edn)

Post-1920 publications

Abrams, L., *The Making of Modern Woman: Europe, 1789–1918* (Harlow, 2002)
Anderson, N.F., 'The "Marriage with a Wife's Deceased Sister Bill" controversy: incest anxiety and the defence of family purity in Victorian England', *Journal of British Studies*, 21 (1982), pp. 67–86
Anderson, O., 'The incidence of civil marriage in Victorian England and Wales', *Past & Present*, 69 (1975), pp. 50–87

Anderson, O., 'Civil society and separation in Victorian marriage', *Past & Present*, 163 (1999), pp. 161–201

Anon., *Ecole Intermédiaire, 1895–1955: Souvenir* (Guernsey, 1955)

Arnot, M.L., 'Understanding women committing newborn child murder in Victorian England', in S. D'Cruze (ed.), *Everyday Violence in Britain, 1850-1950: Gender and Class* (Harlow, 2000)

Ashley, A., 'A note on the claims of spouses and children to a part of personal property as illustrated by the traditional systems of the Channel Islands and the Isle of Man respectively, and their position today there and in Scotland', *The International and Comparative Law Quarterly*, 2 (1953), pp. 274–87

Barclay, K., *Love, Intimacy and Power: Marriage and Patriarchy in Scotland, 1650-1850* (Manchester, 2011)

Bartley, P., *The Changing Role of Women, 1815-1914* (London, 1996)

Bartley, P., *Prostitution: Prevention and Reform in England, 1860-1914* (London, 2000)

Bartley, P., *Votes for Women* (London, 2007)

Behlmer, G., 'Summary justice and working-class marriage in England, 1870-1940', *Law and History Review*, 2 (1994), pp. 229–75

Bennett, J., 'Feminism and history', *Gender and History*, 3 (1989), pp. 251–72

Blakesley, C.L., 'Child custody and parental authority in France and Louisiana', *Boston College International and Comparative Law Review*, 4 (1981), pp. 283–359

Bland, L., '"Purifying the public world: feminist vigilantes in late Victorian England', *Women's History Review*, 3 (1992), pp. 397–412

Bléry, C., 'The evolution of the Norman matrimonial regime after 1789', in G. Dawes (ed.), *Commise 1204: Studies in the History and Law of Continental and Insular Normandy* (Guernsey, 2005)

Bourke, J., *Rape: A History from 1860 to the Present* (2007; London 2008 edn)

Boyle, M., *Re-thinking Abortion: Psychology, Gender and the Law* (Hove, 1997)

Breitenbach, E., Fleming, L., Kehoe, S.K. and Orr, L. (eds), *Scottish Women: A Documentary History, 1780-1914* (Edinburgh, 2013)

Brookes, B., *Abortion in England, 1900-1967* (1988; Abingdon, 2013 edn)

Bryant, M.E., *The Unexpected Revolution: A Study of the Education of Women and Girls in the Nineteenth Century* (London, 1979)

Bruley, S., *Women in Britain since 1900* (London, 1999)

Buckfield, J.E., *The History of the Guernsey Ladies' College, 1872–1963* (Guernsey, 1965)

Burnett, J., 'Exposing "the inner life": the Women's Co-Operative Guild's attitude to "cruelty"', in S. D'Cruze, (ed.), *Everyday Violence in Britain, 1850–1950: Gender and Class* (Harlow, 2000)

Carey, d.V., 'The abandonment of the grand principles of Norman custom in the law of succession of the Bailiwick of Guernsey', *Jersey & Guernsey Law Review* (February 2014)

Chamberlain, G., 'British maternal mortality in the 19th and early 20th centuries', *Journal of the Royal Society of Medicine*, 99 (2006), pp. 559–63

Chase, H.C. and Curran, E.W. (eds), *Infant and Perinatal Mortality in England and Wales* (Washington, 1968)

Clark, A., 'Domesticity and the problem of wifebeating in nineteenth-century Britain: working-class culture, law and politics', in S. D'Cruze (ed.), *Everyday Violence in Britain, 1850–1950: Gender and Class* (Harlow, 2000)

Conley, C.A., 'Rape and justice in Victorian England', *Victorian Studies*, 29 (1986), pp. 519–36

Coontz, S.J., *Marriage, A History* (New York, 2005)

Corbin, A. (tr. A. Sheridan), *Women for Hire: Prostitution and Sexuality in France after 1850* (London, 1990)

Crossan, R.-M., 'The retreat of French from Guernsey's public primary schools, 1800–1939', *TSG*, 25 (2005), pp. 851–88

Crossan, R.-M., *Guernsey, 1814–1914: Migration and Modernisation* (Woodbridge, 2007)

Crossan, R.-M., *Poverty and Welfare in Guernsey, 1560–2015* (Woodbridge, 2015)

Crossan, R.-M., *The States and Secondary Education, 1560–1970* (Guernsey, 2016)

David, M.E., 'Women and gender equality in higher education?', *Education Sciences*, 2 (2015), pp. 10–25

Davidoff, L., *Worlds Between: Historical Perspectives on Gender and Class* (London, 1995)

Dawes, G., *Laws of Guernsey* (Oxford, 2003)

Dawes, G. (ed.), *Commise 1204: Studies in the History and Law of Continental and Insular Normandy* (Guernsey, 2005)

Dawes, G., 'A brief history of Guernsey law', *The Jersey Law Review* (February 2006)

D'Cruze, S., 'Introduction', in S. D'Cruze (ed.), *Everyday Violence in Britain, 1850-1950: Gender and Class* (Harlow, 2000)

D'Cruze, S. (ed.), *Everyday Violence in Britain, 1850-1950: Gender and Class* (Harlow, 2000)

D'Cruze, S. and Jackson, L.A., *Women, Crime and Justice in England since 1660* (Basingstoke, 2009)

De Garis, M., 'The parish of St Pierre du Bois and some of its inhabitants in the eighteenth and early nineteenth centuries', *TSG*, 14 (1949), pp. 479–88

De Garis, M., *Folklore of Guernsey* (Guernsey, 1975)

Désert, G., 'Prostitution et prostituées à Caen pendant la seconde moitié du XIXe siècle, 1863-1914', *Les Archives Hospitalières. Cahier des Annales de Normandie*, 10 (1977), pp. 187–208

Doggett, M.E., *Marriage, Wife-Beating and the Law in Victorian England* (Columbia, 1993)

Donovan, J.M., *Juries and the Transformation of Criminal Justice in France in the Nineteenth and Twentieth Centuries* (Chapel Hill, 2010)

Dyhouse, C., 'Miss Buss and Miss Beale: gender and authority in the history of education', in F. Hunt (ed.), *Lessons for Life: The Schooling of Girls and Women, 1850–1950* (Oxford, 1987)

Eisner, M., 'Modernity strikes back? A historical perspective on the latest increase in interpersonal violence', *International Journal of Conflict and Violence*, 2 (2008), pp. 289–316

Emsley, C., *Crime and Society in England, 1750-1900* (1987; Harlow, 1996 edn)

Evans, K., *The Development and Structure of the English Educational System* (London, 1975)

Everard, J.A. and Holt, J.C., *Jersey 1204: The Forging of an Island Community* (London, 2004)

Feeley, M.M. and Little, D.L., 'The decline of women in the criminal process, 1687-1912', *Law & Society Review*, 25 (1991), pp. 719-58

Finnegan, F., *Poverty and Prostitution: A Study of Victorian Prostitutes in York* (Cambridge, 1979)

Foley, S.K., *Women in France since 1789* (Basingstoke, 2004)

Fuller, C., '"The irons of their fetters have eaten into their souls": nineteenth-century feminist strategies to get our bodies onto the political agenda', in S. D'Cruze (ed.), *Everyday Violence in Britain, 1850-1950: Gender and Class* (Harlow, 2000)

Gahan, F., 'The law of the Channel Islands, IV: criminal law in Guernsey', *The Solicitor Quarterly*, 2 (1963), pp. 148-160

Gallienne, W., 'La fauch'rie l'âne: a description of the last fauch'rie l'âne to be enacted in the island', *TSG*, 23 (1992), pp. 319-21

Gillis, J.R., *For Better for Worse: British Marriages, 1600 to the Present* (Oxford, 1985)

Girard, P.J., 'Development of the bulb and flower industry in Guernsey', *TSG*, 13 (1939), pp. 284–98

Girard, P.J., 'The Guernsey grape industry', *TSG*, 15 (1951), pp. 126–44

Girard, P.J., 'Country life and some insular enterprises of the late 19th century', *TSG*, 19 (1972), pp. 88–105

Goldberg, J. (ed.), *Reclaiming Sodom* (London, 1994)

Gordon, E., 'Irregular marriage: myth and reality', *Journal of Social History*, 47 (2013), pp. 507-25

Hall, L.A., 'Hauling down the double standard: feminism, social purity and sexual science in late nineteenth-century Britain', *Gender & History*, 16 (2004), pp. 36-56

Hammerton, A.J., *Cruelty and Companionship: Conflict in Nineteenth-Century Married Life* (London, 1992)

Hardy, A., *Health and Medicine in Britain since 1860* (Basingstoke, 2001)

Hatton, T.J. and Bailey, R.E., 'Women's work in census and survey, 1911-1931', *The Economic History Review*, 54 (2001), pp. 87-107

Hayes, A. and Urquhart, D. (eds), *The Irish Women's History Reader* (London, 2001)

Heaume, D.O., *Life in Guernsey, 1904-1914* (Guernsey, 1967)

Henderson, J. and Wall, R. (eds), *Poor Women and Children in the European Past* (London, 1994)

Henriques, U.R.Q., 'Bastardy and the New Poor Law', *Past & Present*, 37 (1967), pp. 103-29

Higgs, E., 'Occupations and work in the nineteenth-century censuses', *History Workshop Journal*, 23 (1987), pp. 59-80

Hocart, R., *An Island Assembly: The Development of the States of Guernsey, 1700–1949* (Guernsey, 1988)

Hocart, R., *The Country People of Guernsey and their Agriculture, 1640–1840* (Guernsey, 2016)

Horn, P., *The Rise and Fall of the Victorian Servant* (Thrupp, 1990)

Howarth, J., 'Public schools, safety-nets and educational ladders: the classification of girls' secondary schools, 1880–1914', *Oxford Review of Education*, 11 (1985), pp. 59–71

Hugo, G.W.J.L., *Guernsey as it Used to Be; Some Aspects of the Island in my Boyhood, Youth, and Early Manhood, with Allusions to Well-known Persons* (Guernsey, 1933)

Hunt, F., 'Introduction', in F. Hunt (ed.), *Lessons for Life: The Schooling of Girls and Women, 1850–1950* (Oxford, 1987)

Hunt, F., 'Divided aims: the educational implications of opposing ideologies in girls' secondary schooling, 1950–1940', in F. Hunt (ed.), *Lessons for Life: The Schooling of Girls and Women, 1850–1950* (Oxford, 1987)

Hunt, F. (ed.), *Lessons for Life: The Schooling of Girls and Women, 1850–1950* (Oxford, 1987)

Jackson, L.A., *Child Sexual Abuse in Victorian England* (London, 2000)

Jeffreys, S., *The Spinster and her Enemies: Feminism and Sexuality, 1880–1930* (London, 1985)

Jeffs, D.A. (ed.), *One Hundred Years of Health: The Changing Health of Guernsey, 1899–1999* (Guernsey, 1999)

Johnson, P. (ed.), *Twentieth-Century Britain: Economic, Social and Cultural Change* (Harlow, 1994)

Jones, A., 'The community nursing service', in D.A. Jeffs (ed.), *One Hundred Years of Health: The Changing Health of Guernsey, 1899–1999* (Guernsey, 1999)

Jordan, J., *Josephine Butler* (London, 2001)

Kamm, J., *How Different from Us: A Biography of Miss Buss and Miss Beale* (1958; Abingdon, 2012 edn)

Kamm, J., *Indicative Past: A Hundred Years of the Girls' Public Day School Trust* (1971; Abingdon, 2007 edn)

Katz, J.N., 'The age of sodomitical sin, 1607–1740', in J. Goldberg (ed.), *Reclaiming Sodom* (London, 1994)

Kelsey, J.C., *Changing the Rules: Women and Victorian Marriage* (Kibworth Beauchamp, 2016)

Kent, S.K., *Gender and Power in Britain, 1640-1990* (London, 1999)
Kilday, A.-M., *A History of Infanticide in Britain, c.1600 to the Present* (Basingstoke, 2013)
Knight, P., 'Women and abortion in Victorian and Edwardian England', *History Workshop Journal*, 4 (1977), pp. 57-68
Lacey, N., *Unspeakable Subjects: Feminist Essays in Legal and Social Theory* (Oxford, 1998)
Lane, J., *A Social History of Medicine: Health, Healing and Disease in England, 1750-1950* (London, 2001)
Langlois, D., 'The Guernsey Welfare Service, past, present and future', in M.E. Ogier (ed.), *Soroptimist Women International of Guernsey: Women in Guernsey at the Turn of the Millennium* (Guernsey, 1999)
Le Cornu, N., 'Brothels and houses of ill-fame in Jersey, 1790-1918', *Bulletin of the Jersey Society in London*, 7 (2001), pp. 9–11
Le Herissier, R.G., *The Development of the Government of Jersey, 1771-1972* (Jersey, 1973)
Levine, P., '"Walking the streets in a way no decent woman should": women police in World War I', *The Journal of Modern History*, 66 (1994), pp. 34-78
Lewis, H.D., 'The legal status of women in nineteenth-century France', *Journal of European Studies*, 10 (1980), pp. 178-88
Loudon, I., 'Obstetric care, social class, and maternal mortality', *British Medical Journal*, 293 (1986), pp. 606-8
Loudon, I., 'Puerperal fever, the streptococcus, and the sulphonamides, 1911-1945', *British Medical Journal*, 295 (1987), pp. 485-90
Loudon, I., 'The transformation of maternal mortality', *British Medical Journal*, 305 (1992), pp. 1556-60
Loudon, I., *Death in Childbirth: An International Study of Maternal Care and Maternal Mortality, 1800-1950* (Oxford, 1992)
Loveridge, J., *The Constitution and Law of Guernsey* (1975; Guernsey, 1997 edn)
Lucas, P., 'Common law marriage', *The Cambridge Law Journal*, 49 (1990), pp. 117-34
Machin, I., *The Rise of Democracy in Britain, 1830-1918* (Basingstoke, 2001)

Marr, J., *The History of Guernsey: The Bailiwick's Story* (1982; Guernsey, 2001 edn)
Marshall, M., *Criminal Law of the Bailiwick of Guernsey* (Guernsey, 1975)
Marshall, M., *Divorce and Separation Law in Guernsey, Alderney, and Sark* (Guernsey, 1980)
Marshall, M., *Family and Domestic Law in Guernsey* (Guernsey, 1983)
Martel, E., 'Philological report', *TSG*, 17 (1965), pp. 708–10
Mathew, W.M., *The Secret History of Guernsey Marmalade: James Keiller & Son Offshore, 1857–1879* (Guernsey, 1998)
Matthews, P., 'The impact of matrimonial property on inheritance law', *Jersey & Guernsey Law Review* (October 2010)
McHugh, P., *Prostitution and Victorian Social Reform* (London, 1980)
McKerrell, G., 'Prosecuting in Guernsey', *Jersey & Guernsey Law Review* (February 2012)
McLaren, A., 'Women's work and regulation of family size: the question of abortion in the nineteenth century', *History Workshop Journal*, 4 (1977), pp. 69–81
McLaren, A., 'Abortion in France: women and the regulation of family size, 1800–1914', *French Historical Studies*, 3 (1978), pp. 461–85
McLellan, J., 'The strange case of the Maladies Secrètes ordinance of 1912', *Jersey & Guernsey Law Review* (February 2013)
McMillan, J.F., *France and Women, 1789–1914* (London, 2000)
Mitchell, B.R., *European Historical Statistics, 1750–1975* (1975; London, 1981 edn)
Mitchell, B.R., *British Historical Statistics* (Cambridge, 1988)
Mumm, S., '"Not worse than other girls": the convent-based rehabilitation of fallen women in Victorian Britain', *Journal of Social History*, 29 (1996), pp. 527–40
Musset, J., *Le Régime des Biens entre Epoux en Droit Normand du XVIe Siècle à la Révolution Française* (Caen, 1997)
Ogier, D.M., *Reformation and Society in Guernsey* (Woodbridge, 1996)
Ogier, D.M., *The Government and Law of Guernsey* (Guernsey, 2005)
Ogier, D.M., 'New-born child murder in Reformation Guernsey', in G. Dawes (ed.), *Commise 1204: Studies in the History and Law of Continental and Insular Normandy* (Guernsey, 2005)
Ogier, M.E. (ed.), *Soroptimist Women International of Guernsey: Women in Guernsey at the Turn of the Millennium* (Guernsey, 1999)

ONS (series FM2, no. 16), *Marriage and Divorce Statistics: Historical Series on Marriage and Divorce in England and Wales, 1837-1983* (London, 1990)

Outhwaite, R.B., *Clandestine Marriage in England, 1500-1850* (London, 1995)

Ozanne, N.M., 'La Cour Ecclésiastique', *Review of the Guernsey Society*, 48 (1993), pp. 104-9

Perkin, J. *Women and Marriage in Nineteenth-Century England* (London, 1989)

Peters, C., 'Gender, sacrament and ritual: the making and meaning of marriage in late medieval and early modern England', *Past & Present*, 169 (2000), pp. 63-96

Platt, C., *A Concise History of Jersey: A New Perspective* (Jersey, 2009)

Poirey, S., 'The status of women in Norman law before the Revolution', *Guernsey Law Journal*, 27 (1999), pp. 136-43

Poirey, S., 'The role of lineage in matrimonial union in Normandy', in G. Dawes (ed.), *Commise 1204: Studies in the History and Law of Continental and Insular Normandy* (Guernsey, 2005)

Priaulx, T.F., 'Secular parish administration in Guernsey', *The Quarterly Review of the Guernsey Society*, 21-4 (1965-8), pp. 49-52

Probert, R., 'Control over marriage in England and Wales, 1753-1823: the Clandestine Marriages Act of 1753', *Law and History Review*, 27 (2009), pp. 413-50

Prochaska, F.K., *Women and Philanthropy in Nineteenth-Century England* (Oxford, 1980)

Pugh, M., *The Pankhursts* (2001; London, 2002 edn)

Ringer, F.K., *Education and Society in Modern Europe* (Bloomington, 1979)

Roach, J., *A History of Secondary Education in England, 1800-1870* (Harlow, 1986)

Roberts, E.M., *A Woman's Place: An Oral History of Working-Class Women, 1890-1940* (Oxford, 1984)

Robin, A.C., 'The population of the Bailiwick of Guernsey', *TSG*, 16 (1955), pp. 51-69

Rose, S.O., 'Widows and poverty in 19th-century Nottinghamshire', in J. Henderson and R. Wall (eds), *Poor Women and Children in the European Past* (London, 1994)

Rowbotham, J., '"Only when drunk": the stereotyping of violence in England, c.1850-1900', in S. D'Cruze (ed.), *Everyday Violence in Britain, 1850-1950: Gender and Class* (Harlow, 2000)

Schneider, Z.A., *The King's Bench: Bailiwick Magistrates and Local Governance in Normandy, 1670-1740* (Woodbridge, 2008)

Sebire, H., *The Archaeology and Early History of the Channel Islands* (Stroud, 2005)

Seccombe, W., 'Starting to stop: working-class fertility decline in Britain', *Past & Present*, 126 (1990), pp. 151-88

Sharp, E.W., 'The shipbuilders of Guernsey', *TSG*, 27 (1970), pp. 478-502

Sherwill, A., 'Sark and divorce', *The Quarterly Review of the Guernsey Society*, 18 (1962), pp. 23-5

Smith, F.B., *The People's Health, 1830-1910* (1979; London, 1990 edn)

Spring Rice, M., *Working-Class Wives* (1939; London, 1981 edn)

States of Guernsey, *Guernsey Annual Electronic Census Report, 2014* (Guernsey, 2015)

States of Guernsey, *Guernsey Annual Electronic Census Report, 2015* (Guernsey, 2016)

Steinbach, S., *Women in England, 1760-1914: A Social History* (London, 2004)

Stevens Cox, G., *St Peter Port, 1680-1830: The History of an International Entrepôt* (Woodbridge, 1999)

Stevenson, K., '"Ingenuities of the female mind": legal and public perceptions of sexual violence in Victorian England, 1850-1890', in S. D'Cruze (ed.), *Everyday Violence in Britain, 1850-1950: Gender and Class* (Harlow, 2000)

Stone, L., *The Road to Divorce: England, 1530-1987* (1990; Oxford, 1995 edn)

Syvret, M. and Stevens, J. (eds), *Balleine's History of Jersey* (1950; Andover, 1998 edn)

Taylor, S.E., 'Women's involvement in the States of Guernsey', in M.E. Ogier (ed.), *Soroptimist International of Guernsey: Women in Guernsey at the Turn of the Millennium* (Guernsey, 1999)

Thane, P., 'Women and the poor law in Victorian and Edwardian England', *History Workshop Journal*, 6 (1978), pp. 30-51

Thane, P., 'The social, economic and political status of women', in P. Johnson (ed.), *Twentieth-Century Britain: Economic, Social and Cultural Change* (Harlow, 1994)

Thane, P., *Happy Families? History and Family Policy* (London, 2010)
Thom, D., 'Better a teacher than a hairdresser?', in F. Hunt (ed.), *Lessons for Life: The Schooling of Girls and Women, 1850–1950* (Oxford, 1987)
Thomas, K., 'The double standard', *Journal of the History of Ideas*, 20 (1959), pp. 195-216
Thomas, M. and Dowrick, B., 'The future of légitime—vive la différence', *Jersey & Guernsey Law Review* (October 2013)
Tosh, J., *Manliness and Masculinities in Nineteenth-Century Britain: Essays on Gender, Family and Empire* (Harlow, 2005)
Tough, K. 'Health in the Occupation', in D.A. Jeffs (ed.), *One Hundred Years of Health: The Changing Health of Guernsey, 1899–1999* (Guernsey, 1999)
Trotter, J.M.Y, 'The cost of an execution', *The Quarterly Review of the Guernsey Society*, 15 (1959), pp. 73-5
Turnbull, A., 'Learning her womanly work: the elementary school curriculum, 1870–1914', in F. Hunt (ed.), *Lessons for Life: The Schooling of Girls and Women, 1850–1950* (Oxford, 1987)
Vickery, A., 'Golden Age to separate spheres? A review of the categories and chronology of English women's history', *The Historical Journal*, 36 (1993), pp. 383-414
Walby, S., *Theorising Patriarchy* (Oxford, 1990)
Walkowitz, J.R. and Walkowitz, D.J., '"We are not the beasts of the field": prostitution and the poor in Plymouth and Southampton under the Contagious Diseases Acts', *Feminist Studies*, 1 (1973), pp. 73-106
Walkowitz, J.R., *Prostitution and Victorian Society: Women, Class, and the State* (Cambridge, 1980)
Walkowitz, J.R., 'Male vice and feminist virtue: feminism and the politics of prostitution in nineteenth-century Britain', *History Workshop Journal*, 13 (1982), pp. 79-93
Walters, M., *Feminism: A Very Short Introduction* (Oxford, 2005)
Wardle, D., *English Popular Education, 1780-1975* (Cambridge, 1976)
Wheadon, E.A., 'The history of the tomato in Guernsey', *TSG*, 12 (1935), pp. 338-50
Wiener, M.J., 'Alice Arden to Bill Sikes: changing nightmares of intimate violence in England, 1558-1869', *Journal of British Studies*, 40 (2001), pp. 184-212

Wiesner-Hanks, M.E., *Gender in History: Global Perspectives* (2001; Oxford, 2011 edn)

Wilkinson, N., 'Photographers working in St Peter Port, 1843-1910', *Société Guernesiaise Family History Section Journal*, 10 (1997), pp. 18-19

Woods, R., *The Demography of Victorian England and Wales* (Cambridge, 2000)

Woollacott, A., '"Khaki Fever" and its control: gender, class, age and sexual morality on the British home front in the First World War', *Journal of Contemporary History*, 29 (1994), pp. 325-47

Zedner, L., 'Women, crime, and penal responses: a historical account', *Crime and Justice*, 14 (1991), pp. 307-62

Zweiniger-Bargielowska, I. (ed.), *Women in Twentieth-Century Britain* (Abingdon, 2001)

Unpublished Theses and Dissertations

Bennett, A., 'A history of the French newspapers and nineteenth-century English newspapers of Guernsey' (unpub. MA dissertation, Loughborough University, 1995)

Mulkerrin, D., 'The development of elementary education in the island of Guernsey 1893-1935', (unpub. MA dissertation, University of London, 1981)

Salazar Gourley, I.C., 'A survey of the history and development of education in the Bailiwick of Guernsey, Channel Islands, pre-Reformation–1976' (unpub. MA dissertation, University of British Columbia, 1976)

Index

Abortifacients (chemical), 155–8
Abortion, 154–60, 225, 227
Adultery, 83, 96, 98, 101, 102, 104, 106, 107, 108, 109
Advocates (female), 47, 227
Age of consent, 128, 225
Age of majority, 66 n.8, 92, 94 n.122
Agriculture, 13, 39–40
Alcohol, 115, 116, 119–20, 165
Alderney, 1, 77, 87 n.99
Anglicanism, 19
Anglican marriages, 72–8, 113
Approbation des Lois, 70, 71, 114, 121
Arnold, Sir William, 104 n.162
Asquith, Herbert, 191

Bailiff, role of, 6–7
Beale, Dorothea, 29, 218
Bigamy, 78, 103, 104
Birth rates, 52–3
Birth control *see under* contraception
Blackstone, Sir William, 72
Bodichon, Barbara, 218
Brelsford, Rosalyn, 47, 227
British, Continental and General Federation for the Abolition of the State Regulation of Vice, 169, 172 n.114, 174 nn.122 & 127, 177

Brock, Daniel De Lisle, 68
Brothels, 161, 164, 180–1
Businesswomen, 45–6
Buss, Frances, 29, 218
Butler, Josephine, 168–9, 174–5

Caird, Mona, 64
Calvinism, 19, 102
Canon law, 63–4, 72–3, 78, 95–6, 135
Carey, Edith, 197–8
Carey, Sir Peter Stafford, 7, 82, 114, 119, 121, 123, 124, 125, 128
Carey, Sir Thomas Godfrey, 175, 176, 177
Carey, Sir Victor, 202
Carey, Sir William, 191
Carey, Vera, 205, 228
Casey, Henry, 101 n.150, 107–8, 112
Central Midwives Board, 58
Chant, Laura Ormiston, 172, 173
Charity work, 46, 182, 209
Charivari, 115 n.18
Cherry, Jenny, 209, 211, 228
Child custody, 92–4, 98, 99, 100, 107, 211
Child guardianship, 78, 92, 93, 94, 211, 227
Child sexual abuse, 126–34

Concealment (of birth), 151, 154
Constables (parochial), 6, 111, 167, 170, 195, 227
Contagious Diseases Acts (England and Wales), 168–9, 192
Contraception, 53, 154–8
Cornet Street (St Peter Port), 161, 163, 164
Country Hospital, 24
Coutume, Norman, 69–72
Coverture, 72
Crime
    female, 142–6, 147–60, 167
    patterns, 141–5
    rates, 140–1
    sentences for, 146

De Havilland, John T.R., 104
District Nursing Associations, 59–60, 61 n.146
Divorce
    England and Wales, 103–4
    France, 102
    Guernsey, 104–9, 226
    Scotland, 103, 106
Doctors (female), 46, 224
Domestic abuse
    causes, 115
    prevalence, 114–15
    reporting and prosecution, 114–17
Domestic Science Centre, 33, 34
Douaire, 88, 91, 98
Drake, Aylmer, 105

Ecclesiastical Court, 64, 76 n.56, 95–6, 98
Education, 6, 27–36, 51, 188, 190, 218, 220
Elections (of States Deputies), 6, 190, 197–200, 202–3, 204–7

Elizabeth College, 27, 30, 32
Emergency Hospital, 60, 61
Emigration, 20–1
Endogamy, 67–9

Family Planning Clinic, 155
Farming *see under* agriculture
Fauch'rie d'âne see under *charivari*
Fawcett, Millicent, 192
Feminism, 2 n.9, 85, 100, 168–9, 211, 218, 220
Ferbrache, Emma, 207, 208–10, 228
Fletcher, Enid, 207, 228
France
    age of consent, 128 n.78
    divorce, 102
    inheritance, 88 n.103, 89 n.106
    married women's property, 87 n.99, 219
    parental rights, 94 n.124, 219
    status of women, 72, 219–20
Franchise
    British parliamentary elections, 191 n.21, 194–5, 200
    English local government elections, 187–8
    Guernsey Jurats' elections, 6 n.2, 187
    Guernsey parochial elections, 187, 189, 203, 224, 227
    Guernsey States Deputies' elections, 187, 190, 196, 202, 225, 226
Franc-veuvage, 88, 91, 98

Giffard, Sir Henry, 125
Girls' Public Day School Trust, 29–30
Girton College, 218
Graesser, Isabella, 207, 228

Greffe, 75
Gross indecency, 133, 134
Guernsey Chamber of Commerce, 189, 199, 225
Guernsey Ladies' Educational Association, 30
Guernsey law (sources of), 69–70
Guernsey League of Freedom, 212
Guernsey Reform Association, 190, 196
Guernsey Rescue and Preventive Society, 131–2, 181–5

Hale, Sir Matthew, 81, 83, 125
Hawkers, 119
Health Visitors, 59, 61
Herm, 1
Horticulture, 14–16
Housework, 37

Illegitimacy, 67, 147–50, 224, 226
Immigration, 18–20
Imperial Contribution, 212
Incest, 135–7, 225
Indecent assault, 130, 131, 133, 134
Infant Health Associations, 59
Infant mortality, 53–4, 61
Infanticide, 2, 147–54
Inheritance law, 71, 87–92, 224, 225
Intermediate Schools, 31, 32, 33, 50, 224
Isle of Man, 9, 190 n.14
Isle of Wight, 9

Jeremie, Frederick, 189
Jersey
    abortion law, 160 n.67
    age of consent, 129

civil marriage, 75 n.48
female franchise, 196 n.39, 197 n.46, 203
female States Deputies, 199 n.57
inheritance law, 88, 92 n.115
management of prostitution, 178 n.137
separation and divorce, 95–6, 97, 107 n.177
size and population, 1 n.1, 9, 19
venereal diseases law, 180
Jethou, 1
Juries, 7, 125, 126
Jurats (functions of), 6–7

Kenney, Annie, 193 n.26

Lady Ozanne Maternity Home, 59–60
Le Cheminant, Alfred, 171–2, 182–3
Le Messurier, Albert, 171, 172, 176, 178, 182
Lee, Rev. G.E., 173, 176
Legitimisation (of children born out of wedlock), 67
Lieutenant-Governor (functions of), 5, 7
Livres en Crime, 80 n.66, 112, 139, 150
Local government (in England and Wales), 187–8
Local Option, 199
Luff, Frederick, 196

MacCulloch, Sir Edgar, 7 n.4
Magistrate (stipendiary), 101 n.150, 112, 126, 147
Maladies Secrètes laws, 171–81

Marriage
    age of, 66, 78
    contracts, 85
    Guernsey law of, 72–8
    Guernsey rates of, 65–7
    in England and Wales, 72–4, 75, 76, 77, 78, 82 n.78
    in Scotland, 72 n.39, 82 n.78
    prohibited degrees of, 75–7
Married women's property, 83–7
Maternal mortality, 55–8, 62
Maternity benefit, 61, 227
Maternity Hospital, 60, 61
Martel, Nellie, 193 n.26
Medical Officer of Health, 46, 52, 53, 54, 56, 58, 61, 180, 181
Methodists, 113, 171, 172
Midwives, 55–8, 226
Militia, 5, 143
Mill, John Stuart, 81, 113, 126, 192

Nationality (effect of marriage on), 80, 178
Neonaticide *see under* infanticide
Nonconformity, 19–20
Norton, Caroline, 93

Occupation (German, of Guernsey), 60, 65, 91, 107, 150, 164, 180–1, 183
Occupations, female, 36–51, 223
Ozanne, Florence, 48, 183
Ozanne, Lady Frances, 60 n.139
Ozanne, Patricia, 198, 199, 205, 211

Pankhurst, Christabel, 193, 211
Pankhurst, Emmeline, 192
Parishes (Guernsey)
    administrative structures, 6
    electorate, 6, 23–4, 187, 189, 204, 213–14, 224, 227
    office-holding, 23–4, 189, 195, 224, 227
    poor law, 78–80, 148
    schools, 27–8, 31–3, 50, 188–9, 190
Partage, 89, 90
Patriarchy, 3, 71–2
Philanthropy *see under* charity work
Pipe, Myra, 59
Policing (of Guernsey), 111
Police Court (composition and functions), 6–7, 100–1, 111–12, 139
Population (of Guernsey), 9, 17–18
Préciput, 89, 90, 91
Privy Council, 8, 177
Probation Officers, 174
Procureur, HM (functions of), 7, 117, 124 n.58
Prostitution
    French, 164–5, 166–7, 170, 181
    hazards of, 165–6
    juvenile, 127, 129, 169
    local incidence of, 160–4
    local management of, 167–79
Pupil-teachers, 31–2

Quarrying *see under* stone trade

Randall, Marie, 195, 198–200, 201, 204–5, 207, 208–9, 211, 213 n.107, 225, 228
Rape, 81–2, 120–1, 122–6, 136
Rectors (Guernsey parochial), 7, 74, 104–5, 173, 176, 203

Restitution of conjugal rights, 82–3, 107, 109, 220
Robilliard, Kathleen, 205–7, 208–10, 228
Roman Catholicism, 19–20, 72, 75, 77, 102, 225
Ross, Marguerite, 205–7, 208–10, 228
Royal Court (composition and functions of), 6–7, 8, 9, 98 n.138, 100 n.147, 106, 111–12, 139–40, 187

Sark, 1, 77, 87 n.99, 106 n.173
Sarre, Walter, 212
Scholarships, 32, 34–5
Schools *see under* education
Scotland
   divorce, 103, 106
   marriage, 72 n.39, 82
   married women's property, 86 n.94
   restitution of conjugal rights, 82 n.78
Seafaring, 10–11, 20–2
Separation
   by Police Court, 100–2
   evolution of laws relating to, 95–102
   quant aux biens, 97–9
Servants (domestic), 20, 22, 44, 223
Sex ratios, 21–3, 65–6
Sexual violence
   against adults, 122–6
   against children, 126–37
   general, 120–37
   reporting and prosecution, 122, 131–2
Sexually transmitted diseases, 127, 167–8, 170, 178–81

Sherwill, Sir Ambrose, 86, 87, 91, 104, 105, 106, 120, 135, 198, 214
Shipbuilding, 10–11
Sinclair, Dr Mary, 46, 224
Smuggling, 10, 20
Social classes (distribution of), 23–5
Social Purity movement, 129, 172–7, 182
Sodomy, 133–5
St Peter Port
   female occupations, 44–6
   population, 9, 16–17
   prostitution, 160–8, 178–9, 181
   sex ratios, 21–2
   social composition, 23–4
Standard of living, 25, 53–4
Stillbirth rates, 54, 61
Stone trade, 11–13, 21, 22, 42, 43
Stopes, Marie, 155, 158
Suffrage campaign (UK), 192–3, 194, 200
Symons, Dr Angelo, 60, 181

Telephonists, 38 n.49, 39, 223
Terrien, Guillaume, 70
Tourism, 16
Town Hospital, 24, 27, 31 n.19, 50, 127, 148, 165, 166 n.85, 167, 178, 179, 180, 181, 210 n.98

Universities (female admission to), 35–6, 218
Unlawful carnal knowledge, 127–31

Venereal diseases *see under* sexually transmitted diseases

Wages (female), 49–51
Wesley, John, 113
Wheadon, Norah, 207, 208, 209, 210, 226, 227, 228
Widows, 49, 66–7, 79–80, 88, 92–3
Wife murder, 119–20
Wilson, Henry, 172 n.110, 175

World War I, 12, 19, 21 n.39, 22, 47, 52, 65, 91, 142 n.12, 145, 164, 194, 195, 196, 209
World War II, 16, 19, 34, 52, 60, 65, 91, 107, 150, 164, 167, 180–1, 183, 202–3
Worley, Nina, 205, 211, 212–14

www.ingramcontent.com/pod-product-compliance
Lightning Source LLC
Chambersburg PA
CBHW070538010526
44118CB00012B/1162